Single-Case Designs for Educational Research

Craig H. Kennedy
Vanderbilt University

Allyn and Bacon

Boston • New York • San Francisco
Mexico City • Montreal • Toronto • London • Madrid • Munich • Paris
Hong Kong • Singapore • Tokyo • Cape Town • Sydney

To Tiina Hyvönen, for reasons she knows best

Executive Editor: *Virginia Lanigan*
Series Editorial Assistant: *Scott Blaszak*
Executive Marketing Manager: *Amy Cronin Jordan*
Senior Production Editor: *Annette Pagliaro*
Editorial Production Service: *Trinity Publishers Services*
Composition Buyer: *Linda Cox*
Manufacturing Buyer: *Andrew Turso*
Cover Administrator: *Joel Gendron*
Electronic Composition: *Publishers' Design and Production Services*

For related titles and support materials, visit our online catalog at www.ablongman.com.

Between the time Website information is gathered and then published, it is not unusual for some sites to have closed. Also, the transcription of URLs can result in unintended typographical errors. The publisher would appreciate notification where these errors occur so that they may be corrected in subsequent editions.

Library of Congress Cataloging-in-Publication Data

Kennedy, Craig H.
  Single-case designs for educational research / Craig H. Kennedy.
    p. cm.
  Includes bibliographical references and index.
  ISBN 0-205-34023-7
    1. Education—Research—Methodology. 2. Single subject research. 3. Case method.
  4. Experimental design. I. Title.

  LB1028.K443 2005
  370'.7'2—dc22

                                                        2004048701

Printed in the United States of America
26   18

Contents

Preface

When I began studying behavior analysis in the early 1980s, several recent textbooks assisted in my developing understanding of single-case designs. As I progressed from undergraduate, to graduate student, to professor, I noted that more recent materials were not being developed that incorporated contemporary content and design issues relating to single-case research. I suspect a large part of the reason for this is the ethos among researchers that published journal articles are the best source for innovations in research methodology. As researchers tackle new and previously unanalyzed problems, they will adapt the research methods available to fit their newly developed experimental questions. In other words, successful researchers practice innovation, not imitation. This is a statement I strongly agree with and something I try to teach my students. However, as a university instructor fortunate enough to teach courses on single-case design methodology, I wanted a text that was technically rigorous and also contained contemporary information and examples. These are the conditions that led me to write this book.

This book is not written for my colleagues in academe. They are already well schooled in the procedures that comprise single-case designs, as their research clearly demonstrates. Rather, this book is written for students interested in learning how to use single-case designs for analysis. The book is not about codifying a set of rules that must be stringently followed. Such a perspective on experimentation is antithetical to the idea of research and scientific progress, although, I am afraid, it is the way many students learn about experimental design, irrespective of disciplinary boundaries. My goal in writing this book is to teach future researchers how to think about the use of single-case designs. Experimental designs should always follow from the experimental question. It is the experimental question that is of paramount importance in research, paralleled only by the data obtained from an experiment. Experimental designs, which are simply procedures for arranging analytical comparisons between conditions, are only tools that researchers use to answer their experimental questions.

This book, then, is intended as a graduate-level text, perhaps at the advanced level of study. One of the complexities of writing a methodology text on single-case designs is that this approach to research is inextricably linked to behavior analysis. The two have developed contemporaneously and have contributed to the success of each other. Single-case designs were originally developed as tools to analyze behavioral processes in the experimental analysis of behavior. It was not until the development of applied behavior analysis that people considered the use of single-case designs for more utilitarian purposes. This makes teaching students about the basic elements of single-case designs, such as measurement and multiple baseline designs, relatively easy, because there is no need for content knowledge relating to behavioral processes. However, when more advanced design concepts are encountered, they are often based on the analysis of behavioral processes. Therefore, to grasp more complex single-case design issues, a strong working knowledge of behavior analysis is necessary. This makes writing an accessible textbook on single-case designs a difficult balance. I have tried, and hopefully succeeded, in striking a balance between the two.

Two books, in particular, have shaped my own understanding of single-case designs and behavior analysis: Sidman's *Tactics of Scientific Research* (1960) and Johnston and Pennypacker's *Strategies and Tactics of Behavioral Research* (1993). The influence of these books on my understanding of behavior analysis and experimental design will be obvious to anyone who is familiar with them.

The book is structured into five parts. Part One establishes the background for using single-case designs by discussing why people conduct experiments and reviewing the intellectual history of single-case designs. Part Two discusses strategic issues in conducting single-case experiments, focusing on establishing functional relations, types of replication, and the development of experimental questions. Part Three presents issues key to collecting usable information—quantifying behavior, recording their occurrences, and establishing consistent data collection protocols. Specific design tactics are presented in Part Four. Some of these designs have appeared in previous textbooks; others are more recent innovations from the research literature not previously incorporated into a single-case methods book. Finally, Part Five explores issues related to understanding the data that emerge from conducting single-case research. As a collection, my goal is for these chapters to provide a foundation in the essential elements of single-case design that will allow the reader to learn more about this unique approach to experimentation.

A few qualifications are in order. First, I must apologize for an overreliance on my own research to illustrate certain ideas and concepts. This citation frequency in no way reflects the importance of my own work. Instead, it is a reflection of the fact that an investigator is most familiar with his or her own research. Therefore, this is the source material most readily accessible to me as an author. Also, Chapter 2 of this book presents an abbreviated history of single-case designs, behavior analysis, and education. Its contents likely reflect my own professional training in behavior analysis and education, and my personal interest in the history of these fields. Undoubtedly, I have made omission and commission errors because of my poorly developed historiography skills.

Whenever possible, I have attempted to highlight the research of younger investigators to emphasize the work of the next generation of leaders in single-case designs. I hope my senior colleagues will appreciate the wisdom of this approach and not take offense. The next generation, after all, is our future.

Virginia Lanigan, executive editor at Allyn and Bacon, was invaluable in bringing this text to publication. I would like to thank Stacy Butterfield, Erik Carter, Joan Grim, Melissa Kerr, and Kristen Mueller, who read parts of the text while taking my course on single-case designs. They provided me with outstanding critical feedback. This book benefited immensely from many conversations with my valued colleagues Travis Thompson and Mark Wolery. I would also like thank Jennifer McComas and Fred Spooner, who critiqued an earlier version of the text, as well as the reviewers: Fredda Brown, Queens College; Teresa Taber Doughty, Purdue University; Leasha M. Reese, University of West Florida; and Mark Wolery, Vanderbilt University. I also thank Melissa Rogers for helping me edit and prepare the text. Finally, I would like to thank my partner, Tiina Hyvönen, who puts up with my eccentricities and obsessions for reasons that are not entirely clear to me.

There are no rules of experimental design.
　　　　　—Murray Sidman, *Tactics of Scientific Research* (1960, p. 214)

Part **I**

Background

1

Conducting Experiments

Most gains made in educational practice have resulted from researchers conducting experiments. Whether those gains have been made by group comparison methods, ethnography, epidemiology, economic analysis, or single-case designs, the mechanism by which progress has occurred is experimentation. The use of experimental methods to better understand educational practices was championed by a diverse group of scholars in the early twentieth century, including John Dewey (1958), George Herbert Mead (see Baldwin, 1987), B. F. Skinner (1954), and John B. Watson (1924). Each of these individuals noted that for systematic progress to occur, research was needed to allow education to rise above the politics, personal biases, and fads that dominate educational policy making.

Although there is far to go in creating a universally effective and efficient educational system, the efforts of researchers have transformed educational practice in the late twentieth century. What are now considered common practices in schools have emerged from the educational research of previous decades. Examples include peer-mediated instruction, data-based decision making, curriculum-based assessment, systematic instruction, token economies, inclusive education, phonics-based reading strategies, and accessing the general education curriculum, among many, many others.

These gains have been made by conducting experiments to answer questions to which there are no readily apparent answers. By carefully crafting a question and then using a set of techniques to methodically study the phenomenon, a clearer idea of how different events interrelate can be revealed. In a sense, researchers ask specific questions such as "How do things work?" If I want to know how a new teaching technique might improve student learning, my best bet is to conduct an experiment to answer that question. I could simply answer "My way is obviously better" or "Because we have always done things this way and it is the best way," but I am more likely to improve student learning if I experiment.

What Is an Experiment?

An experiment is basically an approach to answering questions. By systematically studying a set of questions, answers emerge that help guide educators toward increasingly ef-

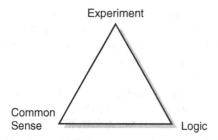

FIGURE 1.1 *Three general ways of discovering new knowledge: common sense, logic, and experimentation.*

fective practices. However, there are important differences between how a layperson goes about answering a question and how a researcher answers a question. Figure 1.1 shows three different ways of answering questions.

The approach most familiar to people is the use of common sense. I do not mean to use common sense in a derogatory way, but rather as a label for a set of strategies that are common to all of us. People arrive at assumptions about "how the world works" through everyday experience. For example, a child new to a school may notice that her classmates all raise their hands before answering the teacher's questions or asking for help. If students do not raise their hands, the teacher does not provide them with his attention. The new child may quickly learn that she needs to raise her hand to get the teacher's attention. If this occurs, she has used her everyday experiences to learn about how to behave in her new classroom and, perhaps, in other novel settings in the future. Not surprisingly, this approach generally works well for us in our daily lives.

However, there is a downside to answering questions using everyday experience. Although accumulated wisdom can often be effective in guiding our daily lives (your grandmother is, indeed, a source of important knowledge about how the world works), common sense also has its limitations. The primary limitation of common sense is that it is derived from correlated events and descriptions of situations. Simply because two events tend to co-occur and there is a pattern to their co-occurrence, does not mean that they are related. This places important constraints on how useful common sense is as a tool for our understanding the world. For example, a person might observe that each day the sun rises in the east, crosses the sky, and sets in the west. For the majority of recorded history, people used this observation to infer that the sun circles the earth. Such an observation is confirmed by daily experience and makes sense if only those experiences are the basis for drawing conclusions. Although we like to think that as a modern, educated society we no longer believe the sun circles the earth, a recent survey of Americans and Britons found that 27% and 35%, respectively, still believe that the sun circles the earth (Sagan, 1995).

Unfortunately, common sense stops at the level of correlation and does not pursue a more rigorous set of tests to verify or discount the nature of covariants. As the dictum taught in every introductory science class says, "Correlation does not imply causation." Lest the reader think this is not a problem in the field of education, it may be instructive to note that the primary way educational policies are decided in a school district is by the school board. A school board's task is to make decisions about what is taught, who is taught where, how students are taught, and other related issues, such as school discipline. How-ever, despite the importance of these decisions, it has been noted that less than 10% of school board members have any type of degree relating to education, and virtually none have training in research (e.g., Newman & Brown, 1993).

Fortunately, people have developed other ways of answering questions that apply more rigorous tests about events before arriving at conclusions. An alternative to everyday experience as a means of understanding nature emerged in Greek and Persian cultures (Kantor, 1963). This approach, which we will call "logical analysis," uses formal mathe-matical systems to test and arrive at conclusions. When conducting a logical analysis, a per-son needs to clearly define the question, use an established set of procedures to test possible answers to the question, and then arrive at a conclusion (Marr, 1986). For example, one could develop the following proposition: "All behavior occurs for a reason; reading is a form of behavior; therefore, the reasons why people read can be identified." A rule set could then be used to test the logical adequacy of the proposition and its conclusion: "The reasons why people read can be identified" (Cohen & Nagel, 1962). A number of individ-uals have attempted to show that such mathematical analyses are the basis of philosophical knowledge, sometimes referred to as "refined knowledge" (e.g., Whitehead & Russell, 1925).

However, there is a very important limitation to this approach. Although the system is clear and rigorous in what it does, the system is purely linguistic. That is, it never actu-ally makes contact with natural phenomena and demonstrates the existence of the logical outcome. Although it presents hypotheses to test, the tests themselves are only verbal ar-guments. This has led to concerns that logical analysis is an inwardly defined system that is not tested in the real world. Harking back to our solar system question, one could for-mally propose that the sun circles the earth and develop a mathematical model of how it works (see Kuhn, 1957). Such a system, referred to as Ptolemaic astronomy, was the sine qua non of understanding our solar system for centuries. However, such a logical argu-ment does not demonstrate the existence of the phenomenon, only that it could exist as a logical outcome of a verbal argument. Such limitations to logical analysis led to the de-velopment of experimentation as an alternative way of learning about how the world works.

What makes experimentation different from common sense or logic is that it requires individuals to systematically test their assumptions. Indeed, there are a set of characteris-tics that distinguish experimentation from other human endeavors that might not be imme-diately obvious to those not trained as researchers.

1. *A clear experimental question needs to be asked* (see Chapter 5). Such questions are often referred to as "hypotheses" (see Box 1.1). However, there are different types of hy-potheses, with some being more specific than others. For example, I might ask any of the following questions regarding a particular teaching technique:

1. Does the use of time delay as a prompting technique lead to children acquiring addi-tion and subtraction skills?
2. Does the use of time delay as a prompting technique result in faster acquisition of ad-dition or subtraction skills than trial-and-error feedback?

BOX 1.1 • *Different Types of Hypotheses*

An experimental question can be considered a type of hypothesis. However, in many areas of education, psychology, and sociology, hypotheses have a more formal meaning and role in experimentation. This role can be traced to the early twentieth century and the emergence of inferential statistics as a tool for agrarian research.

Tests using inferential statistics require the statement of a formal hypothesis (often referred to as a null hypothesis). In this sense, a hypothesis is not so much an experimental question as a statement about the anticipated results of the study. Once a formal hypothesis has been stated, the study can be conducted, the results statistically analyzed, and the statistical results used to either confirm the hypothesis or fail to reject the null hypothesis.

However, in behavior analysis and most biological sciences (e.g., biology, chemistry, or neuro-

science), such an arrangement is deemed an impediment (or, at least, unnecessary) to competently conduct research. Instead of creating formal hypotheses to confirm or reject, researchers focus on developing appropriate experimental questions and techniques to analyze them. The focus is not on the adequacy of an experimenter's prediction about the outcomes of his or her research (i.e., formal hypothesis testing), but on allowing the phenomenon to be revealed through careful experimentation.

Researchers in behavior analysis and the biological sciences may use inferential statistics as a tool from time to time, but the emphasis is on experimental technique and an appreciation that nature is far more complex than we can conceive; therefore, it is better to let nature answer our experimental questions than to test the adequacy of our own guesses.

3. Are parameters of the matching law, such as magnitude of reinforcement or latency of reinforcement, the reason that time delay is more effective than trial-and-error feedback in teaching basic math skills?

Hypothesis 1 is a general question about whether a particular teaching technique is effective. This is a very general type of hypothesis and one that proposes a potentially important experimental question. Hypothesis 2 is more specific and asks whether one type of teaching technique is better than another. Hypothesis 3 asks a very specific question regarding what behavioral process is responsible for the effectiveness of a particular teaching strategy. All of these are valid experimental questions that vary in specificity. Indeed, hypotheses can range from open-ended questions to very precise predictions about how things work. However, regardless of the level of specificity, all hypotheses specify an experimental question in an objective manner that can be tested (see Mager, 1962, for more on objective statements).

2. *A clear plan must be developed for measuring the events of interest.* That is, a researcher needs to identify what needs to be measured to adequately study the experimental question. For example, if I am studying the effects of a teaching technique on math skill acquisition, one thing I need to measure is math performance. In addition, based on the nature of my experimental question, I may also want to gather information on the types of errors that are made, the time that elapses between correct responses, performance on novel types of math problems, and/or the occurrence of off-task behaviors. Typically, the events of interest are formalized into an observational code and a set of procedures outlined for when and how the events of interest will be measured (see Part Three of this book for more on measurement).

Another aspect of research that differs from other ways of exploring nature focuses on conducting an experimental analysis. The world is full of events that are constantly changing. This flux of activity is part of how our everyday lives function. However, it makes the systematic study of causes very difficult. If things are continually changing, it is hard to ascertain what are simply correlated events and what are causal relations among events. Therefore, researchers use experimental designs to separate what is correlated from what is causal. To accomplish this, all events—also referred to as variables—are held constant except for one. This one variable—referred to as an independent variable (see Chapter 3)—is then allowed to operate, then withdrawn, then allowed to operate again, and so on. For example, if an investigator wants to study how teacher attention influences the problem behavior of a child, adult attention could be selectively presented when problem behavior occurs, then withdrawn for a period of time, and then re-presented. In addition, the researcher would need to hold all other potentially influential events constant (e.g., task type, task difficulty, and the presence of peers), while varying teacher attention, so that there are no correlated events co-occurring with changes in teacher attention. If problem behaviors (in this case the dependent variable) increase when attention is provided and decrease when attention is withdrawn, this pattern suggests that the behavior is related to teacher attention. By systematically presenting and withdrawing an independent variable while holding other variables constant and measuring changes in the dependent variable, experimental control can be demonstrated. By demonstrating experimental control through the use of research designs, an estimation of the degree to which a particular variable influences behavior can be established (see Part Four of this book for a discussion of types of experimental designs).

3. *The results must be analyzed.* Once the experiment is conducted, a series of exploratory analyses of the data are made to find out what types of patterns exist. These exploratory analyses seek to reveal how the independent variable influenced the dependent variable(s). Once the nature of the data patterns have been established, a researcher then seeks to summarize them for presentation to an audience. This is done so that the patterns that were found to occur as a result of the experiment can be clearly and concisely presented to other researchers. In essence, exploratory data analysis is a method for finding out "what the data have to say." These patterns are then summarized in tables and graphs so that information can be conveniently communicated to a larger audience (see Part Five of this book for a discussion of data analysis).

4. *The results of the experiment need to be publicly reported and subjected to peer review.* A hallmark of experimentation is that the process is very transparent, meaning that any other person interested in what the researcher has done can obtain information about what occurred, where it was done, how it was done, when it was done, what resulted from those efforts, and how the researcher interprets her findings. A general rule of thumb is that the experiment is described in sufficient detail so that another person can read the manuscript reporting the study, replicate the procedures, and see if he or she obtains the same results. A manuscript reporting an experiment is then submitted to a peer-reviewed journal in which experts evaluate the believability of the experiment and decide whether it was competently conducted and should be published. Finally, any experimental outcome is suspect until another group of researchers replicate the procedures and findings (see Chapter 4). This focus on public reporting, evaluation by experts, and replication by independent research groups makes the research process unlike most other human activities. There is no room in the process for vagueness, deceit, or false claims because everything is available for public scrutiny and rigorous evaluation. (See the *Publication Manual* of the American Psychological Association, 2001, for more information on the preparation and peer review of research papers.)

Experimental Progress

Just as the process of conducting experiments differs substantially from everyday activities, so does the course of experimental progress. The stereotype most people have of research would suggest that it is an efficient, logical process that makes linear progress toward a particular goal. For instance, a researcher decides to solve a particular problem, devises an appropriate experimental question, and then conducts an experiment that solves the puzzle. Such a process, if it has ever happened, is rare. This is because research is a very messy, inefficient, and nonlinear process.

One of the most interesting aspects of experimental progress is the unpredictability of the endeavor. Rarely do experimental questions result in precisely what was hypothesized to occur. That is why strict hypothesis testing (Box 1.1) is not very effective. For example, a researcher may set out to study curricular issues relating to student misbehavior. The experimental question might focus on whether task difficulty is related to increased levels of student noncompliance—the harder the work, the less compliant the student. However, during the course of establishing a baseline, the researcher might notice variability from one day to the next in student behavior, even though task difficulty is being held constant from day to day. On further investigation, the researcher might discover an unanticipated event covarying with noncompliance. For example, the student may come from a home where her parents cannot afford to provide breakfast, and on days when she arrives late for school, she misses the opportunity to have breakfast in the school cafeteria. This missing of a meal may be associated with noncompliance apart from, or in conjunction with, task difficulty. To adequately address this question, a good researcher would need to analyze not only task difficulty in relation to noncompliance, but also the role of missing breakfast in relation to these variables. Although this might seem as though it is unrelated to the original hypothesis, to adequately answer the question, a somewhat different experimental question would need to be studied.

This aspect of the research process has led to the observation that "any experiment worth its salt will raise more questions than it answers" (Sidman, 1960, p. 8). Sometimes those new questions can be predicted before the experiment is conducted; at other times, as in the breakfast example, those new questions will only be revealed once the experiment is in progress. This truism suggests that a wise researcher should stay vigilant during an experiment to a range of events that might influence behavior. B. F. Skinner (1983) once remarked that his most important scientific discoveries were due to serendipity and might have been missed had he not been willing to follow his data even though they did not fit his original hypothesis. For example, his discovery of the behavioral process we now call "superstitious behavior" (i.e., responding maintained by an adventitious reinforcement contingency) occurred because the apparatus he was using to condition behavior malfunctioned. The apparatus failure inadvertently produced a contingency that created response-independent reinforcement, thus demonstrating how superstitious behavior can be shaped and maintained.

Similarly, the course of a program of research rarely goes precisely in the direction a researcher anticipates. Consider the example of sleep deprivation and problem behavior. Several research groups in the 1990s identified correlations between sleep deprivation and increases in problem behavior (Fisher, Piazza, & Roane, 2002; Horner, Day, & Day, 1996; Kennedy & Itkonen, 1993; O'Reilly, 1995; Symons, Davis, & Thompson, 2000). This finding came about when researchers were attempting to account for day-to-day variability in problem behavior that could not be understood from events being manipulated during functional behavioral assessments. If environmental events were held constant, problem behavior still fluctuated from day to day. On further investigation, sleep deprivation emerged as an influential variable in its own right, although the researchers had not set out to study sleep.

In my own research, this line of inquiry took an unexpected turn. Findings across researchers suggested that negatively reinforced behavior was being affected by sleep deprivation, but it was unclear whether positively reinforced behaviors were similarly affected. Two issues needed to be analyzed to answer this question. First, a range of variables might have been co-occurring with sleep deprivation that were influencing behavior. Second, the specific types of reinforcers maintaining behavior needed to be explicitly controlled. These concerns required complete control of the environment to isolate single reinforcer functions, while holding other variables constant, and the direct manipulation of sleep. Such requirements dictated that an animal model be used to clarify questions regarding sleep deprivation. This led me and my colleagues to conduct a series of laboratory experiments with nonhuman subjects that revealed that sleep deprivation increased negatively reinforced behaviors (e.g., Kennedy, Meyer, Werts, & Cushing, 2000), but decreased or did not change positively reinforced behaviors (Kirby & Kennedy, in press). Thus, given the questions that emerged from our initial research findings, the direction of subsequent research was adjusted accordingly.

This example illustrates that research is a highly inductive endeavor. Only by conducting experiments can we get clear answers to our questions, but at the same time the answers are often a surprise. Experimentation in many respects is like exploration: there are no signposts to guide a researcher; instead, the researcher pushes forward into the unknown and creates a road map for those who follow. This observation highlights the cumulative nature of experimental findings. Most "discoveries" are the result of dozens of experiments, often conducted by several different research groups. The reason for this can be described in a metaphor. Think of each experiment that people conduct as an individual piece of a large jigsaw puzzle. Each piece needs to be fit into place, but no single piece defines what the final product is. In the long term, the critical outcome is not the fitting of a single piece into the puzzle, but the completion of the entire puzzle.

Similarly, individual research studies replicate and build on each other. One research group may conduct an experiment demonstrating that students with learning disabilities can learn new skills, such as phonological decoding, in general education settings. They may then conduct a second study to extend this finding by comparing the rate of learning in special versus general education settings and find that they are similar. Another research group may conduct a related study, asking a similar comparative question regarding the quantity and quality of social interactions in different settings, and may find that general education participation produces superior outcomes. Yet another research group may read all of these experimental findings and ask about the impact of academic and social development on students in general education settings who do not have disabilities. Other research groups may replicate these studies for students with moderate disabilities; another research group may focus on students with gifts and talents; and so on. The net result of these studies is a clearer picture of the strengths and limitations of educating students with and without disabilities in general education settings. No single study could answer all the relevant questions, but conducting a range of studies, each asking a slightly different question, both checks the results of previous studies and extends those studies in new directions. The cumulative result of this process is improved knowledge about educational practices. However, the development of such a knowledge base can take years and sometimes decades (see Chapter 4).

Despite its nonlinear nature, however, experimentation does result in progress. It may be difficult to predict from one experiment to the next the particular course a line of research will take. However, the way the research process is oriented seems to ensure that progress is made. By requiring researchers to make public their procedures, findings, and interpretations of experimental results, the process is open to others for critique, debate, and replication. The accumulated result of this process is an improved understanding of an educational problem. The result at any single point in time may be more effective educational procedures, a better understanding of the complexity of the problem, or the realization that a particular line of research is not productive. Whatever the outcome, the process results in knowledge advancing beyond what could be known from common sense or logical analysis.

Assumptions of Researchers

Researchers approach experimentation with a different set of assumptions than most people use in their personal or professional lives. Often these assumptions are not explicitly recognized but, instead, are learned through the research apprenticeship process referred to as graduate training and postdoctoral study. Although most researchers do not spend a great deal of time contemplating epistemological assumptions relating to scientific inquiry (instead, they are likely engaged in the act of conducting research), there is a consistent set of beliefs that researchers hold. These assumptions tend to be very robust and occur across a broad range of disciplines and approaches to research (Underwood, 1957).

One assumption held by researchers was discussed at length in the previous section. That is, everyday experience and even stringent logical analysis are not enough to understand the world. Instead, systematic inquiry is needed to parse out correlation from causation. By engaging in carefully described and arranged experiments that others can replicate, more is learned about how the world works than by other approaches to acquiring knowledge.

A second assumption relates to the lawfulness of the world. Typically referred to as determinism, this belief postulates that events have identifiable causes. Apples fall from trees toward the ground, gasoline ignites at a certain temperature, and behaviors occur in certain patterns as a function of their consequences. If behavior X occurs in a particular pattern, there must be a set of events related to behavior X that cause it to occur in such a pattern. For example, if a child cries every time her father drops her off at preschool, there must be something about the antecedent and consequent events that surround that episode that cause the child to cry. For nonresearchers, determinism is easier to accept and, perhaps, understand for the physical sciences than for educational or psychological phenomena. Nevertheless, all events have a cause, and identifying those causes is the foundation of experimentation, whether a particular researcher articulates this assumption or not.

Closely related to the notion of determinism is the assumption of material causes. Hundreds of years ago, when asked why water turns from a liquid to a gas, most educated people would have invoked a metaphysical explanation—for example, that the essential spirits in the water had become excited and left for heaven. Or, the reason a person acted the way he did was because a homunculus in his head directed him to act that way. This type of explanation (still alive and well in our contemporary society) invokes causes that do not physically exist (MacCorquodale & Meehl, 1948). To say the least, metaphysical causes are difficult to experimentally investigate.

By focusing on material causes, researchers are forced to deal with physical events as causal entities. Things that are being studied need to be operationally specified and accurately measured. In addition, to find the source of the occurrence of those events, some other event must be identified and tracked in relation to that which is the event of interest. If the occurrence of scolding by a parent tends to follow the yelling of a child and the nonoccurrence of scolding is related to the nonoccurrence of yelling, then scolding might be related to yelling. Additional manipulations of scolding as a consequence for yelling may suggest that the two events are so closely related, and in a particular pattern of occurrence, that we would say that yelling is caused by scolding. No appeal to forces that exist in some other place or time or physical dimension are needed to explain the behavior (Skinner, 1950).

Earlier in this chapter an aspect of experimentation was noted that is different from most other ways of knowing—namely, replication. Chapter 4 covers different types of replication in detail; here, the point is that independent replication is one of the foundations of research. Any published report of research should explain why a study was conducted, exactly what was done, what the results were, and how those data might be interpreted. This allows other researchers attempt to independently replicate the experiment to see if similar results can be obtained. In general, there is a consensus among researchers that any finding is suspect until it has been replicated. The infamous case of "cold fusion" is an example of this issue (see Taubes, 1993). Briefly, a pair of physicists claimed to be able to initiate nuclear fission under low temperatures, something that was fundamentally inconsistent with what was known about this phenomenon through thousands and thousands of studies. Research groups from around the world attempted to replicate this finding, but even after many years and many experiments, no other research group could replicate the findings. (Indeed, the original researchers could not replicate their own findings!) Because no one could replicate the original results, researchers have come to regard the finding as an error in experimentation (i.e., poor experimental methods and/or inaccurate interpretation of results). The ability of others to replicate new findings is a critical component of the research process.

A belief in the cumulative nature of research findings, then, is an important assumption among researchers. As was previously discussed, each study is like an individual piece of a jigsaw puzzle, which is not complete until a range of experiments have been completed.

This process (1) serves to check on the veracity of individual research findings, (2) is self-correcting in that errors will be found and alternative findings/interpretations publicly presented, and (3) results in an increased understanding of the phenomenon being investigated. In applied areas, such as educational research, there is also an implicit assumption that this whole process results in better educational practices. The end result is that students, teachers, and community members benefit from the work that we refer to as experimentation.

Along with a more complete understanding of a phenomenon, there is also an expectation that at some point a more parsimonious understanding of it will result. By parsimonious, what is meant is that a set of findings can be summarized in as simple a manner as does justice to the phenomenon. For example, when the initial finding showing that time delay as a technique for transferring stimulus control (Touchette, 1971) could be extended to educational contexts (Halle, Marshall, & Spradlin, 1979), nobody knew exactly what would result. However, after two decades of research by multiple research groups, a great deal is known about when, where, how, and to what degree time delay is an effective teaching strategy. Not only are the general parameters of time delay well understood, but the techniques can be summarized as a handful of procedures for practitioners to use (Wolery, Ault, & Doyle, 1992). In this case, parsimony resulted from a more complete knowledge of how the behavioral processes worked and how they could be organized. What results is not only a greater understanding of what comprises a certain area of research, but also an efficient way of organizing those findings.

Conclusion

Research as an approach for answering educational questions emerged in the twentieth century. Since then, experimentation has provided tremendous insight into processes that improve educational practices and outcomes for a wide variety of students. However, research itself is a difficult concept for most people to grasp, in part because the typical citizen has little knowledge of, and no direct experience with, the process. As a matter of course, we propose questions and find answers to them in our everyday lives, and to the extent that things unfold as we anticipate, we are satisfied with the results. There is no obvious need to pursue issues further, as long as things work. Despite the general success of common sense in our day-to-day experience, it often falls short when confronted with complex questions.

It is because of this limitation of common sense that people have developed a set of techniques for answering complex or nonintuitive problems, which is referred to as experimentation. The research process is rigorous, not easily understood, and effortful. However, when done properly it is an invaluable tool. Experimentation is not a "thing" to be reified and kept at a distance, but a tool set for asking questions about the world. At its most utilitarian, it is something to be used to solve people's problems.

The remainder of this book explores one approach to experimentation, referred to as single-case designs. These designs embody the quintessential properties of experimental methods and are ideally suited for a range of questions relevant to educational contexts. They are an exciting set of tools that allow people to ask questions that can be answered using individual students, classrooms, or schools, with no need for "control" or "contrast" groups as comparisons. These designs have a rich history in educational research as well as an exciting future for exploring currently unsolved questions relating to education.

2

History of Single-Case Designs

Approximately thirty-five years ago, Donald M. Baer and his colleagues made this statement regarding the status of the field of behavior analysis, from which single-case designs are derived:

> The analysis of individual behavior is a problem in scientific demonstration, reasonably well understood (Skinner, 1953, sec. 1), comprehensively described (Sidman, 1960), and quite thoroughly practiced (*Journal of the Experimental Analysis of Behavior,* 1958–). That analysis has been pursued in many settings over many years. Despite variable precision, elegance, and power, it has resulted in general descriptive statements of mechanisms that can produce many of the forms that individual behavior may take. (Baer, Wolf, & Risley, 1968, p. 91)

Since this time, research using single-case designs has provided tremendous insights into processes that improve educational practices and outcomes for a wide variety of students. For decades, this approach to experimental design has yielded easier-to-implement and more effective interventions, a deeper understanding of behavioral processes, more accurate and usable measurement systems, and greater benefits for students, families, and schools.

Single-case designs are used to demonstrate experimental control within a single participant. That, in a nutshell, is the definition of single-case designs. However, we need to unpack that deceptively simple definition to better understand what constitutes these designs. Single-case designs demonstrate experimental control using one person as both the control and experimental participant. For this reason, these designs are also referred to as $n = 1$ designs. Unlike case histories, single-case designs demonstrate a rigorous degree of experimental control. Case histories are based on correlations among events, but single-case designs specifically hold all conditions constant except for the independent variable, which is systematically introduced and withdrawn to study its effects on behavior (see Chapter 3). In addition, single-case designs are not a single type of experimental design, but an overarching approach to experimentation that has multiple variations, all of which meet the defining characteristics of this approach to research (see Part Four).

Along with the characteristics just mentioned, there are some underlying assumptions in the use of single-case designs that should be explicitly noted. These assumptions constitute what is referred to as the epistemological basis of single-case designs, which is largely based on the field of behavior analysis (see Chiesa, 1994). First, this approach to research is idiographic. This means that research is used to approach its subject matter by understanding how individuals behave, not by describing mathematical averages of groups of individuals (Sidman, 1952). Stated differently, these designs are used to discover why a person does what he does and then test whether other people behave the same way under similar conditions or, if not, why. Proof is developed one participant at a time, under a high degree of experimental rigor. This can be contrasted with group comparison research, which looks for general tendencies among large numbers of participants and differences among group averages (see Underwood, 1957).

Another assumption has to do with the nature of the variables being studied. The only requirement that single-case designs impose on the variables used to study behavior is that they be physical events. This means that the events must have material existence. Another way of saying this is that everything measured as an effect or done as an intervention must be operationalized. To operationalize a variable, it needs to be described in concrete terms that can be agreed on as occurring, or not occurring, by anyone who understands the operational definition (see Chapter 7). This assumption means that some terms we use in everyday discourse are amenable to being operationalized, even though we use them as if they have causal status. Examples of these hypothetical constructs include inferences about intentions ("I think she meant to do that"), mental states ("She may have had a lapse in memory"), or emotions ("He acted that way because he was angry").

However, the need to operationalize experimental variables does not preclude the study of brain-behavior interactions. As long as internal activities, also referred to as private events, can be operationalized and directly measured (i.e., they can be shown to exist), then they are permissible components of an experimental analysis of behavior, as can be seen in Box 2.1 (Moore, 1984). Again, it is not the location of a variable but the ability to measure it, rather than infer it, that is at issue (see MacCorquodale & Meehl, 1948).

A third assumption is that an inductive approach to understanding human behavior is the most productive strategy. The overarching goal of conducting research is to explain

BOX 2.1 • *Can the Brain Be Part of the Analysis of Behavior?*

The answer to this question is an emphatic yes. However, if this question was posed thirty years ago, the answer would have been an equally emphatic no. A great deal has changed in neuroscience in recent decades that allows direct measurement of events occurring in the brain. Examples of such data include events such as oxygen metabolism (measured via functional magnetic resonance imaging [*f*MRI]), binding of neurotransmitters to certain brain nuclei (measured via computed tomography [CT] scans), and neuronal firing patterns (measured via electrophysiological recording of event-related potentials [ERP]). Because these are measurable events, not inferences or assumptions, they are variables that can, and are, being used to analyze behavior. As neuroscience is advancing, increasing opportunities are occurring to expand the variables studied in single-case designs (Kennedy, Caruso, & Thompson, 2001).

something. Researchers who use single-case designs approach their subject matter with a great deal of respect for its complexity. Rather than developing an a priori theory of why people behave as they do and then conducting experiments to test the accuracy of the theory, single-case designs are used to explore the nature of behavior and develop theories from the data that are collected. This former approach is widely used in traditional psychology and is referred to as "theory-driven research," "top-down theorizing," or "deductive research." This can be contrasted with a behavior-analytic approach, which is often referred to as "grounded theory," "bottom-up theorizing," or "inductive research."

The general approach that single-case designs are used for is to directly study how human behavior functions and use that information to develop more robust explanations (which can be referred to as theories). An example of this difference can be illustrated with research on choice making. In economics, rational choice theory has been used to explain consumer spending (von Neumann & Morgenstern, 1947). Rational choice theory states that consumers optimize their spending among available options (i.e., they spend rationally based on their expectations of value). This theory was developed independent of research data, and its adequacy was initially based on logical arguments. When research was conducted, it was conducted to test the accuracy of the theory, not to ask open-ended questions about how consumers actually spend. This is an example of top-down theorizing.

A bottom-up approach can be illustrated by the work on concurrent operant schedules of reinforcement. Concurrent operants compare response allocation in situations where two different options are available for reinforcement. Or, put another way, this research focuses on experimentally analyzing choice situations. In concurrent reinforcement schedules, one experimental variable is altered at a time, its effect on behavior noted, and then the other variable is analyzed, and so on. After many experiments were conducted, a general set of patterns became clear that described how choice making occurs. In this case, a quantitative formula was proposed, referred to as the matching law, that explained how organisms as simple as birds or organizations as complex as corporations made choices (Davison & McCarthy, 1987). For better or worse, we do not make choices rationally, but instead our behavior tends to be biased toward options with higher payoffs. In this instance, the bottom-up approach produced a far more adequate explanation for this type of complex behavior (Herrnstein, 1990).

Using single-case designs, knowledge is developed incrementally, experiment by experiment. This is a very conservative approach to arriving at explanations, but in the long term has proven to be the most productive strategy because of the high degree of direct contact that researchers maintain with their subject matter (Keller, 2002). As the astronomer Sidney van den Bergh noted about the relation between theory and experimentation, "Our job is to listen to what nature is telling us and not impose our own esthetics." Only naive researchers think they are more clever than nature.

All of these characteristics and assumptions associated with single-case designs are directly linkable to the historical antecedents of this approach. There are three historical precursors to what we refer to as single-case designs: biology, medicine, and psychology. Each of these disciplines, which are linked by the common theme of trying to understand animate life, developed research strategies that focused on idiographic, objective, and inductive approaches to explaining their particular subject area.

Historical Antecedents to Single-Case Designs

The concept of a new field, separate from physics or chemistry, focusing on understanding how living organisms develop and mature was not proposed until the early nineteenth century. The first proposal for a discipline that we now know as biology came from Jean-Baptist Lamarck's *Philosophical Zoology* (1809/1984). In this treatise, Lamarck called for a new scientific field to study how plants and animals come into existence, reproduce, and evolve. At this point in time, the term *philosophical* had a very different meaning from what we mean by the word in the twenty-first century. Stemming from the Age of Enlightenment, philosophers were individuals who intensively studied a problem using systematic techniques that eventually evolved into what we call the scientific method (see Bacon, 1620/2000). Hallmarks of this new approach to acquiring knowledge were making objective observations, manipulating one variable at a time, holding other variables constant, carefully recording findings, and replicating results. This approach to gaining knowledge about the world is referred to today as empiricism.

The best known scholar in biology during the mid–nineteenth century was Charles Darwin. Both Darwin (1859) and Alfred R. Wallace (1875) developed the concept that individual organisms within a species vary slightly from one another and generation to generation and that environmental conditions can select some individuals to be more likely to reproduce, making the variations they exhibit more likely to occur in future generations. We now refer to these concepts as evolutionary biology (see Gould, 2002). Both Darwin and Wallace arrived at their conclusions simultaneously and by using similar experimental methods. That is, they studied individual cases (e.g., a particular bird species), looked for variations in individuals within the same species and across species, recorded their observations, and used these data to draw conclusions about how nature is structured and functions (Catania, 1973).

The research of individuals such as Darwin and Wallace was largely descriptive in that they could not directly manipulate evolutionary processes, they could only describe patterns in evolutionary processes. During the last half of the nineteenth century, a more experimental approach was adopted, particularly in embryology (now referred to more generally as developmental biology). The goal of this area was to understand how organisms develop from a fertilized egg to a mature organism (Keller, 2002). Importantly, developmental biologists could directly manipulate a variable of interest (e.g., the amount of yolk within an egg) and observe its effects on the developing embryo. This allowed biologists to gather direct experimental evidence about how discrete events influence biological development and paved the way for the field of genomics that emerged a century later (Collins, Green, Guttmacher, & Guyer, 2003).

In a related and contemporaneous field of study, medicine also developed approaches for conducting research in the nineteenth century. Medicine has a long history of using case histories to inform physicians about new innovations in treating patients. For example, Ephraim McDowell was a surgeon practicing medicine in the early nineteenth century. At this time, internal surgery was largely an abstract concept yet to be successfully demonstrated. If you had a tumor in your abdomen, for example, you would die a slow and painful death as the tumor grew and suppressed the functioning of various organs. McDowell

(1817) developed a surgical technique for successfully removing ovarian cysts (a common type of tumor), which he repeated with other patients and then published so that other surgeons could replicate his technique with their patients. This was one of the first published works of a replicable technique for conducting successful internal surgery.

A significant limitation of case histories, as previously noted, is that they are based on an unfolding sequence of events that are not experimentally controlled, only systematically observed. In addition, case histories rely on naturally occurring events, which limits what can be studied as well as when. For example, a physician might be treating a patient and, along with the prescribed treatment, the patient might also start a series of self-prescribed treatments without telling the doctor.

Combining the need for an experimental approach to medical issues and developments in experimental biology, Claude Bernard (1865/1927) introduced the idea of experimental medicine. A key component of Bernard's experimental medicine was the use of animal models to study questions relating to human physiology (Thompson, 1984). Animal models are experiments that use an analogous situation in a nonhuman species to analyze the effects and mechanisms influencing the phenomenon of interest in humans. For example, Bernard studied such phenomena as diabetes and blood oxygenation in animals to reveal how the pancreas and hemoglobin function in relation to disease processes in humans. This type of direct experimental approach using animal models has been the foundation for many of the medical innovations during the twentieth century (Cooter & Pickston, 2000). Again, this type of experimentation was based on idiographic, objective, and inductive research procedures. (As an aside, the reader is also referred to the work of Charles S. Sherrington [1906/1989] for the use of animal models directly relating to neuroscience and behavior [Sherrington, 1975].)

A final area that has influenced single-case designs, and the one most familiar to readers of this book, is experimental psychology. Not surprisingly, the first researchers in experimental psychology at the beginning of the twentieth century emerged from medicine and biology. Two of the most prominent early researchers studying psychological topics were Ivan M. Sechenov and Ivan I. Pavlov. Sechenov (1965), often referred to as the "father of Russian physiology," was an international pioneer in neurophysiology. He had been trained in Europe in biology and medicine, and used these skills to study human behavior via neural processes. His work was largely driven by the idea that all human behavior was a series of reflexes mediated by the nervous system. The experimental methods he used were based on his biological and medical training and reflected many of the characteristics previously discussed, including the use of animal models, idiographic techniques, and the inductive accumulation of experimental evidence. Like Pavlov, whom we will discuss next, Sechenov's focus was not on creating new experimental designs; instead, he applied what he had learned in biology and medicine to a new topic—psychology (Kazdin, 1978).

Pavlov (1960) discovered the learning processes we now refer to as respondent conditioning. Pavlov was a physiologist studying digestive processes in mammals. Indeed, he won the Nobel Prize in physiology of digestion in 1904 for this work. However, his discovery of respondent conditioning was serendipitous. While studying salivary duct secretion using an animal model, Pavlov noticed that saliva would begin flowing prior to the introduction of food to the animal's mouth. Typically, salivation is a reflexive event elicited by the presence of food in the mouth. However, Pavlov's subjects had learned to associate certain noises and people with the food and began salivating when they heard familiar noises or saw familiar people. This meant that a physiological reflex could be conditioned

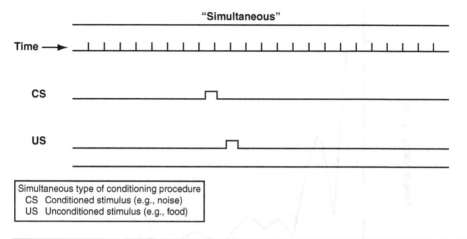

FIGURE 2.1   *Schematic of respondent conditioning (first developed by Ivan I. Pavlov).* "Simultaneous" refers to the type of conditioning procedure. US stands for unconditioned stimulus (e.g., food), and CS for conditioned stimulus (e.g., noise). By pairing the US with the CS, the CS comes to elicit the response previously occasioned by the US.

Source: From F. S. Keller and W. N. Schoenfeld, *Principles of Psychology,* 1950 (fig. 3, p. 22). New York: Appleton-Century-Crofts. Copyright 1995 by the B. F. Skinner Foundation. Reproduced by permission.

to be psychologically associated with arbitrary stimuli. This process—respondent conditioning—is also referred to as stimulus-response psychology (see Figure 2.1).

At the same time that Pavlov was conducting his work on respondent conditions, an American named Edward L. Thorndike (1898) was conducting his dissertation on another form of learning, which Thorndike labeled the "law of effect." Thorndike used an animal model, much like a biologist, to analyze how learning occurred. His primary apparatus was a box that required some arbitrary response (e.g., pushing a lever) for the animal to escape and gain access to food. Access to the food was the driving force for the animal to learn a novel behavior. An example of the learning curves Thorndike obtained using this method is presented in Figure 2.2 (page 18). The graph shows that over successive trials, the novel behavior was emitted faster and faster. This was the first time that the process of learning had been measured and analyzed in a systematic fashion. Thorndike used a variety of responses, including chaining behaviors into a sequence, and replicated his procedures from one animal to the next, even using different species to establish the generality of his learning curves. Interestingly, Thorndike, while a professor at Columbia University, established one of the first programs in educational psychology, providing a bridge between experimental psychology and education (Joncich, 1968).

Another influential figure in bringing a biologically based perspective to psychology was John B. Watson (1924). Watson is not so much known for his research as for his advocacy of an approach to psychology that was radically different from other psychologists of his time. Early in the twentieth century, most psychologists focused on people's subjective experiences of events (e.g., description of the sensations experienced when seeing a particular color), often using group comparison designs to contrast different experimental

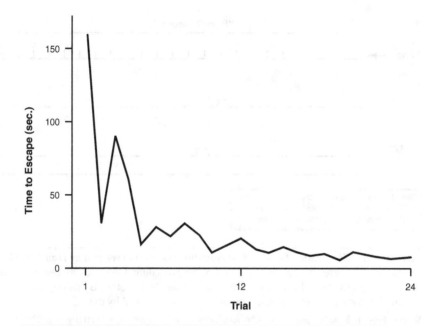

FIGURE 2.2 *A learning curve demonstrating Thorndike's law of effect.* The number of seconds required to escape from the puzzle box and obtain food is listed along the *y*-axis. The number of successive trials is presented along the *x*-axis.

Source: Thorndike (1898).

conditions (Boring, 1950). Watson's perspective was that only events that were observable by others (i.e., that could be objectively defined and observed) should be the subject matter of experimental psychology. This approach was quickly referred to as behaviorism. The focus of behaviorism was to make psychology as objective and precise as biology and other natural sciences that did not rely on subjective reports. This perspective influenced an entire generation of young scholars who were looking to make psychology more scientific (Todd & Morris, 1994).

Most notable among this next generation of behaviorists was B. F. Skinner. Skinner completed his doctorate at Harvard University approximately thirty-five years after Thorndike had studied there. While conducting his dissertation, which would eventually be published as the *The Behavior of Organisms* (1938), Skinner developed an approach to psychology that was heavily influenced by experimental biology (Boakes, 1984; Todd & Morris, 1995).

In keeping with experimental biology, Skinner used less "complex" animals to model the behavior of people. This approach used the continuity assumption, derived from evolutionary biology, which is based on physiological, anatomical, and behavioral characteristics being conserved across species, with subsequent species elaborating (and incorporating) features from which they have evolved (Hake, 1982). Hence, behavioral processes that are present in rats or pigeons are expected to be conserved in primates such as human beings. Skinner also used highly simplified environments. The goal was to hold constant all possible variables except the variable of experimental interest. By doing this, environmental processes influencing behavior can be individually identified and the functional relations they enter into with behavior can be analyzed (see Chapter 3).

Along with these features, Skinner's approach also modeled biological practices in that it was idiographic, operational, and inductive. Skinner's experimental approach was to use a rat or pigeon as the organism, select an arbitrary response that could be quickly emitted and repeated (e.g., a lever press), choose a biologically powerful reinforcing stimulus (e.g., food), and slightly deprive the animal of that stimulus. This arrangement allowed for a single response to be measured continuously in time to study the effects of reinforcement on patterns of behavior. One such pattern is presented in Figure 2.3. This graph presents a cumulative record of behavior. Along the *x*-axis (horizontal line) is time. Along the *y*-axis (vertical line), each occurrence of behavior is recorded by a slight rise in the line. In this way, the rate of responding in real time can be recorded and visually analyzed (see Chapter 15). This general approach to studying behavior has become known as the experimental analysis of behavior, and a journal devoted to this approach to research was established in 1958 (*Journal of the Experimental Analysis of Behavior,* 1958–present).

Emergence of Behavior Analysis

Skinner's primary findings were that the contingency between a response and reinforcer determines the probability of that response and that intermittent schedules of reinforcement produce very distinct patterns of responding (Skinner, 1938; Ferster & Skinner, 1957). For example, the contingent delivery of a reinforcer for a lever press on a fixed-interval schedule (i.e., reinforcement is only available for a response after a fixed amount of time has passed) produces a scalloped pattern of behavior increasing in probability as the end of the time interval nears (see Figure 2.3). This approach is referred to as operant conditioning or response-stimulus psychology.

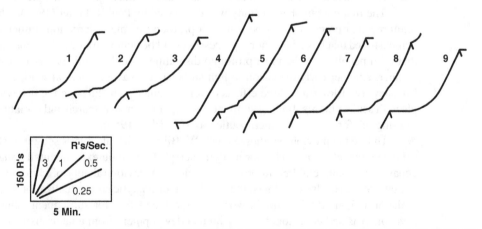

FIGURE 2.3 *Performance on a fixed-interval (FI) reinforcement schedule.* The cumulative record shows successive responses as upward movement of the line along the *y*-axis, or ordinate. Time is represented along the *x*-axis, or abscissa.

Source: From C. B. Ferster and B. F. Skinner, *Schedules of Reinforcement,* 1957 (fig. 156, p. 162). New York: Appleton-Century-Crofts. Copyright 1995 by the B. F. Skinner Foundation. Reproduced by permission.

Skinner also conducted early experiments on topics such as superstition, anxiety, language, and systematic instruction (see Skinner, 1983). However, there are two other reasons that Skinner is considered the most famous psychologist of the twentieth century (Bjork, 1993). First, he extrapolated his laboratory findings with rats and pigeons to the everyday lives of people (Skinner, 1953). This allowed him tremendous insight into the causes of human behavior and caused a great deal of resistance from laypersons and experts alike (reminiscent of the stormy reception that evolutionary biology received a century earlier).

Second, he produced an entire generation of researchers who went on to prominent scientific careers and who produced, themselves, subsequent generations of behavior analysts. Most of these individuals were trained by Skinner or his associates in the 1940s and 1950s at Harvard, Columbia, or Indiana Universities (Dinsmoor, 1990). A too-brief mention of the most noteworthy of these individuals is given here. William K. Estes studied anxiety and learning (Healy, Kosslyn, & Shiffrin, 1992). Peter B. Dews developed what became known as behavioral pharmacology (Dews, 1987). Joseph V. Brady integrated biomedical and behavior-analytic research (Hodos & Ator, 1994). Charles B. Ferster conducted the initial experiments on schedules of reinforcement and time-out (Skinner, 1981). Murray Sidman worked on avoidance responding (Sidman, 1989). Richard J. Herrnstein developed the first analyses of choice making and the quantitative analysis of behavior (Baum, 2002). Many of these individuals are pictured in Figure 2.4, which was taken during the third conference on the Experimental Analysis of Behavior in 1949.

The previously mentioned research was all conducted with nonhumans in the laboratory to establish the existence of basic behavioral processes, such as positive reinforcement, negative reinforcement, concurrent operants, multiple schedules, behavioral contrast, and behavioral momentum, among others (see Catania, 1998). A next generation of research, initiated in the late 1950s and continuing through the 1960s, emerged from this work and extended the basic behavioral processes to the behavior of humans. Not surprisingly, these early studies on human operant behavior were conducted in laboratory settings, just like the previous research.

The first human operant study was conducted by Paul R. Fuller (1949), who studied reinforcement processes in a person with profound mental retardation. Fuller's findings demonstrated that basic behavioral processes could be demonstrated in humans and showed that even people with the most profound disabilities could learn if taught in a systematic manner. Another early extension to human behavior was the doctoral work of Ogden R. Lindsley. Lindsley studied the effects of reinforcement schedules on the behavior of people with schizophrenia, finding similar effects to nonhuman research and initiating the idea of using reinforcement as a therapeutic tool (Lindsley, 1956).

Unlike the previous studies, Sidney W. Bijou in the late 1950s sought to study typical development from a behavior-analytic perspective. Bijou experimentally analyzed the behavior of young children in order to develop a behavioral theory of child development (Bijou, 1995). He also developed the first behavior-analytic conceptualization of mental retardation (Bijou, 1963). Bijou's work laid the foundation for subsequent generations of psychologists and educators to study human development from a naturalistic, experimental perspective (Baer & LeBlanc, 1977).

In 1958, the first application of behavioral principles from the laboratory occurred (Allyon & Michael, 1959). The Allyon and Michael study differed from previous experiments on human operant behavior in that it did not focus on establishing the generality of

FIGURE 2.4 *Group photograph of people attending the third conference on the Experimental Analysis of Behavior (1949). Left to right, first row:* Mike Kaplan, Donald Perlman, Nat Schoenfeld, Ruth (Morris) Bolman, Fred Keller, Fred Skinner, Phil Bersh. *Second row:* Harold Coppock, Ralph Hefferline, Helmut Adler, Fred Frick, Elaine (Hammer) Graham, Joe Notterman, Bill Jenkins. *Third row:* Ben Wyckofk, Joel Greenspoon, Bill Daniels, Van Lloyd, Dorothy Yates, unknown, Norm Guttman. *Fourth row:* Lloyd Homme, Joe Antonitis, Sam Cambell, Jim Dinsmoor, Charlie Ferster, George Collier. *Fifth row:* unknown, Burt Wolin, Doug Ellson, Fred Lit, Clancy Graham, Bill Verplanck, Bill Estes. *Sixth row:* Mac Parsons, Dave Anderson, Don Page, Murray Sidman, Phil Ratoosh, George Roth. *Seventh row:* Don Cook, Rod Funston.

Source: From J. A. Dinsmoor, "Academic Roots: Columbia University, 1943–1951," *Journal of the Experimental Analysis of Behavior,* 1990, *54,* 129–150. Copyright 1990 by the Society for the Experimental Analysis of Behavior. Reproduced by permission.

behavioral processes from nonhumans to humans but instead focused on using those behavioral principles to solve a social problem. What Allyon and Michael did was to use the concept of reinforcement contingencies to improve the living conditions of people with schizophrenia in an institutional setting. By arranging various contingencies for the delivery of salient events, Allyon and Michael were able to improve the behavior not only of patients, but also of staff (whom the patients depended on). In many respects, this was the first study in applied behavior analysis to be conducted, although it would be another decade before that term was introduced.

Charles B. Ferster was the first individual to take laboratory findings from behavior analysis and use them to improve the behavior of children with autism. Ferster and DeMyer (1961) conducted a series of analyses on how to shape and maintain behavior in children with autism. By using reinforcement contingencies, they were able to establish complex behaviors in children who were thought incapable of such performances. Their findings showed that even children with very complex disabilities could be taught through the use of systematic instruction.

A few years later, Wolf, Risley, and Mees (1964) published a study that showed how to alter the behavior of a child with autism in a therapeutic manner. Wolf et al. worked with a child with autism who engaged in self-injury and refused to wear eye glasses. These authors worked with his staff and parents to implement a differential reinforcement program that included time-out from positive reinforcement. The result was a dramatic decrease in self-injury and increased wearing of eye glasses. In addition, there were generalized improvements in this boy's behavior across settings and tasks.

This work in autism was replicated and extended by Ivar O. Lovaas and his students. Lovaas, although he was not the first individual to work with children with autism, was the first to initiate a prolonged program of research with this population. Lovaas was able to identify environmental causes for self-injury (Lovaas, Freitag, Gold, & Kassorla, 1965) and restrictions in the ability of children with autism to attend to various stimuli (Lovaas, Schreibman, Koegel, & Rehm, 1971), among other findings. In addition, many of the current leaders in the field of autism collaborated with Lovaas in the 1960s and 1970s, including Edward G. Carr, Marjorie Charlop, Robert L. Koegel, and Laura Schreibman.

The advances of the early 1960s in applying the experimental analysis of behavior to social problems rapidly spread to a range of topic areas. Donald M. Baer (1962) studied behavioral processes relating to typical and atypical child development. James A. Sherman (1965) used reinforcement techniques to establish imitation and spoken language in adults with schizophrenia who were thought to be mute. Israel Goldiamond (1965) initiated the first studies of operant conditioning to reduce stuttering and increase fluent speech. Harlan Lane (1963) studied the development of language in people who were deaf. Murray Sidman began to study the receptive and expressive language of people with aphasia (Leicaster, Sidman, Stoddard, & Mohr, 1971). Arthur W. Staats studied the development of reading abilities (Staats, Staats, & Schutz, 1962). Nathan H. Azrin and colleagues began a series of studies on how to make institutional settings more humane and livable for residents (Holz, Azrin, & Allyon, 1963).

At this time, behavior analysts were beginning their first forays into educational settings. Two early efforts are particularly noteworthy. B. F. Skinner (1961) developed the teaching machine. Skinner devised an electromechanical device that would present written questions to children, allow them to respond, and provide them feedback about the accuracy of their answers. This work was a forerunner of computer and Web-based teaching strategies. In addition, Fred S. Keller (1968) developed the personalized system of instruction (PSI). Using PSI, students are taught curriculum content through a self-paced program that uses shaping of more and more complex question-answer pairings until the student meets a proficiency criterion. This approach has been widely adopted, particularly by institutions of higher education.

With all of this work occurring in the application of behavioral principles, the Society for the Experimental Analysis of Behavior (SEAB), publisher of *JEAB,* elected to create a new journal, the *Journal of Applied Behavior Analysis.* SEAB's goal was to establish a journal to publish applications of the experimental analysis of behavior to issues of social concern. Montrose M. Wolf was elected as the first editor of *JABA* and the initial board of editors was comprised of many of the researchers previously mentioned (see Figure 2.5).

Editor:
Montrose M. Wolf, University of Kansas

Associate Editor:
Donald M. Baer, University of Kansas

Executive Editor:
Victor G. Laties, University of Rochester

Board of Editors:
W. Stewart Agras, University of Vermont
T. Ayllon, Georgia State College
Nathan H. Azrin, Anna State Hospital
Albert Bandura, Stanford University
Wesley C. Becker, University of Illinois, Urbana
Jay S. Birnbrauer, University of North Carolina
C. B. Ferster, Georgetown University
Israel Goldiamond, University of Chicago
James G. Holland, University of Pittsburgh
B. L. Hopkins, Southern Illinois University
Fred S. Keller, Western Michigan University
Peter J. Lang, University of Wisconsin
Harlod Leitenberg, University of Vermont
Ogden R. Lindsley, University of Kansas
O. Ivar Lovaas, University of California, Los Angeles
Jack L. Michael, Western Michigan University
Gerald R. Patterson, University of Oregon
Todd R. Risley, University of Kansas
James A. Sherman, University of Kansas
Murray Sidman, Massachusetts General Hospital
Gerald M. Siegel, University of Minnesota
B. F. Skinner, Harvard University
Howard N. Sloane, University of Utah
Joseph E. Spradlin, Parsons Research Center
Arthur W. Staats, University of Hawaii

FIGURE 2.5 ***The founding editorial board for the* Journal of Applied Behavior Analysis.**

A particularly influential paper by Baer, Wolf, and Risley (1968) was published in the first volume of *JABA* that helped codify the dimensions of the new field of applied behavior analysis. Baer et al. outlined seven dimensions that characterized applied behavior analysis.

- The focus of this area is the *application of behavioral principles* to areas that are judged to be in need of improvement.
- The focus of change is on a person's *behavior* and requires objective and precise measurement.
- In order to demonstrate change in a person's behavior, single-case designs need to be used to *analytically evaluate* the effects of an intervention.
- The interventions that are used are specified in operational terms to clearly specify what is being done, so a *replicable technology* of behavior change can be created.
- The effects of interventions on behavior need to be understood in regard to known behavioral processes to link these effects to a coherent *conceptual system.*
- The focus of analyses is on producing *effective outcomes* that show clear benefits to the recipients of the interventions.
- Interventions need to have *generalized effects* across relevant settings and behaviors.

Many of these dimensions are explicitly derived from the antecedents of applied behavior analysis in terms of scientific practices, such as being behavioral, analytical, and conceptual. The others are clearly tied to the applied nature of this endeavor. With a new journal and a clear view of what applied behavior analysis was, researchers from a range of disciplines began gravitating toward this new approach to solving social problems.

Linking Educational Research and Behavior Analysis

One area that quickly adopted applied behavior analysis was educational research, particularly for students who were the most challenging to teach. Beginning in the 1950s and hitting a peak in the 1960s, universities throughout the United States started opening departments of special education to prepare teachers to effectively educate children and youth who were not adequately being served in the existing educational systems (Trent, 1994). As a new approach to education, special education was being developed from scratch. The primary criterion for adopting a particular practice was not whether traditional educators thought that it was the appropriate approach to take, but whether the approach worked (Langemann, 2002).

One of the first special educators to adopt applied behavior analysis was Norris G. Haring (Wolery, in press). Haring's general approach was relatively straightforward: special educators will be more effective teachers if they adopt a systematic approach to instruction (Haring & Phillips, 1972). In the mid 1960s this was a strategic decision that required a belief that the evidence supporting behavior analysis could be applied to educational issues such as special education.

In regard to the establishment of special education departments at universities, four departments stand out for having quickly adopted applied behavior analysis as an approach to educational issues. These departments were located at the University of Washington, University of Kansas, University of Oregon, and Peabody College (now part of Vanderbilt University). Interestingly, Haring was the founding chair of the first two departments. These departments, and others, quickly began producing new researchers who were linking behavior analysis and education to develop new and effective classroom practices.

In fact, the first paper to appear in the initial issue of *JABA* was by R. Vance Hall, who studied the effects contingent teacher attention had on the academic engagement of students in general education classrooms (Hall, Lund, & Jackson, 1968). At the same time, Hill M. Walker demonstrated a very similar effect for students with behavioral disorders (Walker & Buckley, 1968). These were the first demonstrations that classroom teachers could be more effective if they directed their attention to students behaving appropriately rather than waiting until they misbehaved.

At the same time, Thomas C. Lovitt began developing systematic instruction techniques for improving the learning of students with learning disabilities (Lovitt & Curtis, 1969). This research combined systematic prompting and feedback to improve the academic performances of students. Working on similar issues of stimulus control, but with people with severe disabilities, Joseph E. Spradlin was simultaneously conducting applied and basic research on learning processes (Spradlin, Cotter, & Baxley, 1973). This work led to an improved understanding of symbolic behavior and how to more effectively teach a group for students who, at the time, were considered unteachable.

Odgen R. Lindsley continued to extend basic operant findings to ever more applied issues (Lindsley, 1991). Working separately, Lindsley and Owen R. White (Alper & White,

1971) developed techniques for teachers to base their instructional decision making on objective data regarding student performance rather than on their personal perceptions. Just like researchers in a laboratory, if teachers used objective information rather than their personal perceptions, it was demonstrated that they could be more effective at accomplishing their jobs. From this work, data-based decision making has become a hallmark of effective teaching practices.

Beth Sulzer-Azaroff and G. Roy Mayer produced a series of studies, together and separately, that demonstrated effective approaches for managing student behavior at a schoolwide level (Sulzer & Mayer, 1972). Their work focused on the careful application of behavioral processes derived from laboratory research. The work of these researchers had a strong influence on how school psychologists and educational administrators approach school discipline issues.

Also during this early period of applying behavioral principles to educational topics, Doug Guess, Wayne Sailor, and Donald M. Baer studied language development in people with severe disabilities (Guess, Sailor, Rutherford, & Baer, 1968). This work demonstrated that complex language forms could be taught to students who were typically characterized by the lack of language. The success of this work was instrumental in focusing attention on providing meaningful educational opportunities for students with severe disabilities.

Phillip S. Strain and Richard E. Shores initiated the idea of teaching social skills to students with disabilities (Strain, Shores, & Kerr, 1976; Strain & Tim, 1974). These researchers used prompting and reinforcement techniques, much like those noted previously, to establish new social behaviors in students' repertoires. Their demonstrations were the first studies showing that appropriate social behaviors could be directly taught and used to gain entrée into a new set of social reinforcers that children might not otherwise contact.

Each of the individuals that have been mentioned in this section had highly productive careers, both as behavior analysts and educators. Each person produced several generations of students too numerous to mention in such an abbreviated history. As a result, most colleges of education in the United States now have behavior analysts among their faculty, something that did not exist thirty years ago. In fact, there is an international organization that was created in the 1970s, the Association for Behavior Analysis, for researchers and practitioners interested in studying behavior using behavior-analytic approaches.

Conclusion

The foundations for single-case designs emerged in fields that many educators are not familiar with, such as biology, medicine, and psychology. These are the disciplines that took on the challenge of studying animate life in the 1800s. Researchers in these fields learned through a century of experience that the most productive means of studying their subject matter was to use techniques that focused on intensive analyses of individual cases, moving from there to establish their generality among larger populations. As noted previously, this is a conservative approach to knowledge production. However, if the alternative is false leads and misguided theorizing, research strategies such as single-case designs should not be viewed as conservative in the long term. Rather, these approaches have been repeatedly demonstrated to be productive strategies for learning about how human behavior works.

In applying these techniques to educational issues, researchers have made a great deal of progress in a relatively short period of time. Much has been learned about behavioral processes, such as reinforcement and attention, that underlie how we learn. Not only has this information yielded consistent and reliable results in the laboratory, the application of these behavioral processes has repeatedly been shown to change behaviors of relevance to educators. These techniques are effective enough that they have become standard practices in the training of most educators, even if some people might not be aware of their origins.

There is clear evidence of the relevance and importance of single-case research to contemporary educational issues. Professional certification has been established for behavior analysts interested in applying these concepts to areas such as education (see the Behavior Analyst Certification Board). Increasingly, school districts are requiring that professionals working with students with behavior problems become certified in this area. National organizations such as the American Psychological Association and the National Association of School Psychologist have recognized behavior analysis and single-case designs as established and valid approaches. Recent federal laws, such as the Individuals with Disabilities Education Act (IDEA), have required behavioral strategies, like functional behavioral assessment, to be used by schools.

Although the field of behavior analysis is only half a century old, it has made extraordinary progress in moving from the laboratory to the classroom. As will be illustrated in the remainder of this book, through examples of the use of single-case designs, there is a broad range of educational methods that have been discovered and refined using these techniques. The use of single-case designs has a fascinating history, a vibrant contemporary culture, and a bright future.

Part **II**

Strategic Issues

3

Functional Relations

When someone conducts a study, one goal is to establish experimental control. You can think of experimental control as demonstrating that an intervention reliably produces a particular change in behavior. For example, if I am testing a new intervention to reduce talking out during math instruction, I would need to accomplish several things to demonstrate experimental control. First, I would want to show that the student's behavior changes following intervention, when compared to preintervention. Second, I would want to show that if I remove the intervention, that her behavior changed back to its preintervention pattern. Finally, if I reintroduce the intervention, I would expect to observe a change in the student's behavior similar to the first time I introduced the intervention. If these changes in behavior only occur when I introduce or remove the intervention, then I am establishing experimental control.

Figure 3.1 shows an example of the process just described (Azrin, Jones, & Flye, 1968). The behavior of interest was the percentage of words stuttered during spontaneous speech in a social interaction (i.e., the percentage of disfluencies). The initial condition was a typical conversation occurring with a speech therapist. After recording speech for several minutes to identify a pattern of disfluencies (i.e., approximately 30%), the experimenters introduced an intervention. The change introduced by the experimenters was a tactile stimulus, disguised as a wrist watch, that produced a timed pulse that the participant could use to pace his speaking. The start of the intervention coincided with a decrease in disfluencies to less than 5% of utterances, with this change being sustained as long as the intervention was in place. The intervention was then removed, and disfluencies increased to approximately 25% of utterances. After establishing an initial pattern of behavior, introducing an intervention, removing the intervention, and observing the behavior to consistently vary in relation to the intervention, the experimenters had demonstrated experimental control.

Independent and Dependent Variables

When using single-case designs, establishing experimental control means demonstrating a functional relation. A functional relation can be defined as establishing a consistent effect on a dependent variable by systematically manipulating an independent variable. Depen-

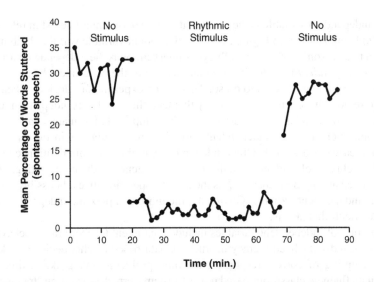

FIGURE 3.1 *Process of establishing experimental control.* The percentage of intervals in which disfluencies (i.e., stutters) occurred during a social interaction (*y*-axis). The behavior was recorded in real time and summarized on a minute-by-minute basis (*x*-axis). The initial condition, labeled as No Stimulus, was a routine conversation. The intervention, labeled as Rhythmic Stimulus, was introduced and then removed.

Source: From N. Azrin, R. J. Jones, and B. Flye, "A Synchronization Effect and Its Application to Stuttering by a Portable Apparatus," *Journal of Applied Behavior Analysis,* 1968, *1,* fig. 7, p. 292. Copyright 1968 by the Society for the Experimental Analysis of Behavior. Reproduced by permission.

dent variables are typically estimates of the behaviors you are analyzing. For example, in Figure 3.1 the dependent variable was the mean percentage of words stuttered. Often, the term *dependent variable* is synonymous with the measurement system being used to record behavior (see Part Three). The reason it is referred to as a dependent variable is that if a functional relation is established, the level of the behavior being measured is dependent on the presence or absence of the independent variable. There is no limit, other than tractability, regarding the number of dependent variables you can use in a study.

The following are examples of dependent variables used in recent educational research: number of words read per minute, percentage of observations that a person was happy, duration of self-injurious behaviors, percentage of correctly executed football tackles, percentage of sight words accurately read, occurrence of precurrent behaviors for problem solving, percentage of questions correctly answered on a French-language exam, latency to following requests, proportion of social interactions with appropriate social amenities, inter-response times between bites taken during snack time, and so on. These examples are far from exhaustive, being used only to highlight the concept of a dependent variable. Any variable that is of experimental interest and meets the requirements outlined in Part Three of this book is an acceptable dependent variable.

An independent variable is the event that is of experimental interest in relation to the behavior(s) being studied. In Figure 3.1, the independent variable was the rhythmic stimulus applied to a person's wrist. Typically, your intervention is the independent variable. Use of the term *independent variable* is based on this part of the experiment being free to vary when the experimenter chooses to do so. That is, the experimenter decides when to apply it, when to remove it, or when to alter it; by this fact, the variable is independent of the experimental situation. Independent variables can be comprised of as many elements as are of experimental interest. Some independent variables are singular, as in the use of teacher praise to increase on-task work. Other independent variables contain multiple components, such as the inclusion of students with disabilities into general education settings. A critical issue, discussed at length in Chapter 7, is the need to operationalize all possibly relevant aspects of an independent variable. Obviously, the more complex the independent variable, the more difficult this task is.

Examples of independent variables include contingent teacher praise, behavior intervention plans, individualized literacy instruction, data-based teacher decision making, systematic prompting of correct responses, teaching problem-solving skills, time trials to increase math fluency, classroom-based reward systems, errorless learning strategies, and so on. Independent variables are often used to improve an educational situation. At other times, independent variables are used as tools to understand why certain behaviors occur or do not occur (see Chapter 5).

To recapitulate: a functional relation is the demonstration of experimental control over the dependent variable by the independent variable. It is a convincing demonstration that your intervention is what changed someone's behavior. This observation raises an interesting issue. What about other events that might have changed the person's behavior that were not measured? For example, a child could have started, stopped, or changed a particular psychotropic medication; a student's family may have become indigent; an adolescent may experience turmoil in a romantic relationship; or a third-grader's parents might start after-school reading instruction. Each of these events can have a profound effect on a student's behavior at school. However, as a researcher, you may not be aware of these events.

An example of how variables outside the experimenter's control can affect behavior is presented in Figure 3.2 (top panel). The data represent the problem behavior of an adolescent, Adam, with severe disabilities, including self-injury and aggression (Kennedy & Meyer, 1996). The behavior was negatively reinforced by escape from instructional demands. In one condition, the demands were terminated for a specific duration each time the student engaged in problem behavior (dark circles). In a second condition, the student engaged in a preferred task (open circles). Each condition was conducted once per day. Low levels of problem behavior were observed in the preferred task condition, but highly variable responding was observed in the demand condition. It appears as though the problem behavior is negatively reinforced by escape from task demands, but the effect changes from time to time. In this particular study, the authors were interested in the influence of sleep deprivation on behavior and therefore were documenting the amount of sleep the student received each night. When sleep deprivation is noted by asterisks in Figure 3.2 (bottom panel), it becomes clear that the variability in behavior is associated with nights of poor sleep. Such data illustrate how a variable outside of the experimental situation can influence a student's performance in the experimental situation.

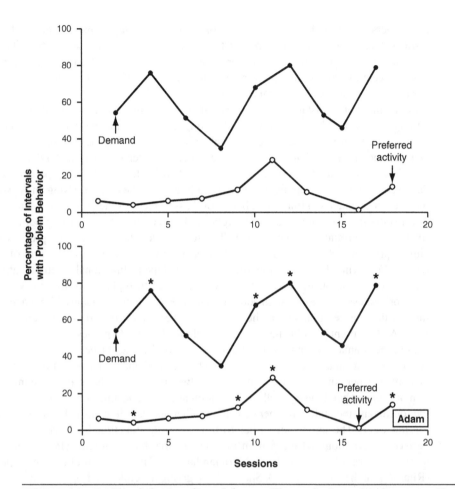

FIGURE 3.2 *Problem behavior of an adolescent.* The *y*-axis shows the percentage of intervals with problem behavior, and the *x*-axis shows individual sessions. The data set displayed in the top panel shows information on problem behavior collected during an experimental session. The data set displayed on the bottom panel shows information on problem behavior collected during the experimental session and the student's sleep patterns at night. (Asterisks indicate nights when he was sleep deprived.)

Source: Adapted from C. H. Kennedy and K. A. Meyer, "Sleep Deprivation, Allergy Symptoms, and Negatively Reinforced Problem Behavior," *Journal of Applied Behavior Analysis,* 1996, *29,* tab. 1, p. 135. Copyright 1996 by the Society for the Experimental Analysis of Behavior. Reproduced by permission.

Extraneous Variables

Events that can influence behavior, but are not included as independent or dependent variables in a study, are referred to as extraneous variables. The sleep deprivation noted in Figure 3.2 is an example of an extraneous variable. To demonstrate a functional relation, researchers need to hold extraneous variables constant during an experiment. In laboratory settings, this is readily accomplished and is a primary reason why researchers find these settings so amenable to careful experimental analyses. However, educational research, by its nature, occurs primarily in real-world settings. Because of this, the control of extraneous variables becomes very important and very difficult. To the extent possible, a researcher should either hold constant extraneous variables or measure them to study their possible relation to behavior; otherwise these variables might confound the interpretation of the results.

The concern with extraneous variables is that they may be the source of behavior change, not the events that you, as the researcher, are referring to as the "independent variable." Take, for example, a seven-year-old child with attention deficit hyperactivity disorder (ADHD) who is disrupting his class by calling out to the teacher. Using an A-B-C chart, the teacher conducted a functional behavioral assessment of the child's problem behavior. The results showed a near-perfect correlation between the child's calling out and the delivery of a reprimand by the teacher. The teacher concluded from this process that the child's problem behavior is maintained by positive reinforcement in the form of adult attention. Following this conclusion, the teacher developed a functional communication training procedure (see Carr & Durand, 1985) designed to replace calling out with a more appropriate response resulting in adult attention (e.g., raising his hand). The teacher implemented the intervention, and on the first day the behavior dropped to near-zero levels.

At this point should the teacher conclude that the hypothesis-driven intervention caused the dramatic change in behavior? Let's say the teacher has heard the dictum that "every experimental observation should be checked and checked again." Following this advice, the teacher continues collecting data for two more days. The result is a continued pattern of frequent hand raising, followed by adult attention and almost no calling out. Then, on the fourth day, the child's mother calls the teacher and asks how his behavior has been during the week. The teacher describes to the parent the functional behavioral assessment-derived intervention and the pattern of behavior that has occurred. After listening to the teacher, the parent says that the pediatrician has prescribed a test trial for methylphenidate (Ritalin®) for the child's ADHD. She has been giving the child the drug every day that week.

Such a series of events suggests that any conclusion drawn about the effectiveness of the behavioral intervention or medication would be premature. First, both the behavioral and psychotropic drug interventions began at the same time, so both correlate with the change in behavior. It could be that one of the interventions is the source of the behavior change, that their combination is needed for the effect to occur, or that some other event produced the change. Second, although the drug and behavioral interventions were both introduced and their effects on behavior measured for several days, we have no idea if the withdrawal of one or both of the potential independent variables would coincide with a return to the baseline pattern of responding. Finally, we do not know if, following a return to baseline, whether the reintroduction of one or both interventions would change behavior.

In effect, the teacher needs to repeat these findings to better understand the source of change in the child's behavior. Again, it could be that the behavioral intervention changed behavior, the medication changed behavior, their combination was needed to change behavior, or some other event caused the behavior to change. Without repeating baseline and intervention, we will not know the source of the behavior change. Indeed, both interventions will need to be independently introduced and withdrawn if we want to learn about their separate and combined effects on behavior.

All of this involves replication. The teacher and parent could decide to hold medication constant and withdraw the behavioral intervention, or vice versa, and then reinstate both interventions. If this was done, it would be a test of the effects of the behavioral intervention. Let's say that when the communication-based strategy is withdrawn, behavior returns to preintervention levels. Can we conclude that the behavioral intervention is effective and the drug ineffective? "Maybe" would be the most prudent answer.

When extraneous variables influence behavior, they become threats to internal validity. Internal validity is a concept drawn from group comparison designs and refers to the degree to which a researcher can be confident that an independent variable is what changed behavior, not the extraneous variables (Campbell & Stanley, 1967). Using single-case designs, internal validity is demonstrated by establishing a functional relation between independent and dependent variables.

Following the nomenclature introduced by Campbell and Stanley (1967), threats to internal validity can be of eight types:

1. *History effects* are events that occur outside of the experimental situation but can potentially influence the behavior under study. Examples include events such as sleep deprivation, health problems, or out-of-school math tutoring. In addition, history effects in educational research also encompass events such as substitute teachers, unanticipated fire alarms, and students being called out of class.

2. *Maturation effects* are a second type of threat to internal validity. Children mature over time, and these developmental processes present a problem to researchers. Referred to as "maturation effects," normal developmental processes can influence the behavior under study, particularly in experiments that occur over a long period of time. For example, when studying the effects of an intervention on language development, if the experimental effect from the independent variable is slow, it may be unclear how much of the effect is from normal maturation rather than the intervention.

3. *Testing effects* are threats to experimental control resulting from changes in behavior that occur when exposed to a testing situation. The idea is that exposure to questions regarding the curriculum being taught to a student might, in fact, teach them something about the testing context (e.g., how to answer questions more accurately), or the testing situation may teach something about the material to be learned. In such instances, behavior can change simply as a result of testing, apart from any intervention being analyzed.

4. *Instrumentation effects* take two general forms. First, malfunctions in software and/or hardware being used to record behavior might occur. For example, a software glitch or a stuck key on a keyboard during a computer-based assessment can alter the data that are obtained and produce unwanted changes in recorded behavior. Second, behavior being recorded by observers can result in inaccurate representations of responding. One example of this is poorly trained observers who inaccurately record the behaviors of interest. Another concern is that observers will gradually alter how they define and record behavior over the course of a study, a phenomenon known as observer drift. Each of these types of instrumentation effects will be discussed at length in Chapter 7.

5. *Regression to the mean* is another threat to internal validity. This is a statistical sampling phenomenon in which highly unlikely outcomes ("outliers") occurring within a normal distribution tend not to reoccur when resampled (see Gould, 1981). In behavior analysis, there is no such thing as an outlier behavior. All behavior occurs for a reason, and outliers are simply a manifestation of a behavioral process that has yet to be analyzed and understood. This makes the concept of statistical regression not very useful for a research approach based on repeated measures (see next section).

6. Participant selection bias relates to the equivalence of people being assigned to different treatment groups. This threat, like regression to the mean, is derived from a group comparison approach to research derived from traditional psychological research (see Chapter 2) and does not easily map onto a single-case design logic with individuals.

7. Selective attrition of participants refers to individuals dropping out, or being removed from, a study for some systematic reason that is unrecognized by the researcher. Although this is historically a concern in group comparison designs, it also can affect single-case designs. For $n = 1$ designs, selective attrition is a concern, because people with certain characteristics may not be able to complete an experiment. For example, the intervention may be too complex, it may not be socially acceptable, it may run counter to some cultural practices, or it may produce unwanted side effects. This is not so much a concern for the internal validity of a single-case design, but can be an important issue for systematic replication (i.e., establishing the generality or external validity of findings; see Chapter 4).

8. Interactions among selective attrition and other threats are the final concern in regard to internal validity. In such cases, a threat such as history effects or testing effects systematically influences why participants do not complete a study. In single-case designs, because of their inductive nature, this type of threat is really an elaboration of the previously mentioned concern. This is because interactions between variables causing selective attrition are essentially a refinement in the potential experimental question: Why did some participants not complete the study but others did?

Identifying when extraneous variables are threats to internal validity is a critical aspect of the research process. A seasoned researcher will know when and where to look for extraneous variables and how to control for their influences on behavior. Perhaps the most effective guide to identifying extraneous variables comes from the data themselves. Anytime that there is variability in your data that you cannot account for by known events, that variability represents the influence of unknown (extraneous) variables on behavior. In this sense, variability in data for single-case designs is not a nuisance to be ignored but an indication of other sources of control over the behavior being analyzed. For this reason, variability in the data often represents an opportunity to learn more about the types of events that can influence behavior.

There are obviously a large number of extraneous variables present in natural environments, particularly educational settings, and many of them cannot be directly controlled as they can in the laboratory. However, there are systematic techniques for studying behavior that can allow for important questions to be answered via single-case research in educational settings. And, as reviewed in Chapter 2, these designs have a long history of being used successfully. Because all the events just described are possible threats to the establishment of a functional relation, researchers use various types of experimental designs to try and control for their possible influences on behavior (see Part Four).

Baselines

The starting point for most experimental analyses of behavior is the establishment of a baseline. "Baseline conditions serve as the background or context for viewing the effects of a second type of condition" (Johnston & Pennypacker, 1993, p. 225). An experiment has to start somewhere, and a baseline, as we will see, is a logical starting point.

The notion of a baseline may seem simple, but it is actually a complex concept. How a researcher constitutes a baseline has important implications for what conclusions can be drawn from an experiment. A poorly designed baseline may render an experiment uninterpretable or severely constrain the interpretation of findings. To appreciate why this is, we will need to discuss what constitutes a baseline and how it is used in single-case designs.

There are several elements that comprise a baseline. One aspect of a baseline are the procedures used. Procedures refer to specific aspects of the environment and how it is structured and functions. The physical setting, including the size of the room, arrangement of furniture, and general characteristics of the staff, is one component. For example, does the study take place in a small room with only a services staff person present, or does the study take place in a gymnasium with dozens of other students and several adults present? Another component relates to who interacts with the student of interest, including other students, educators, paraprofessionals, research staff, and so on. For example, are students working in teams of three or four people monitored by paraprofessionals, or are students working alone with an educator engaging in didactic instruction? In addition to who interacts with the focal student, another issue is what the student does when interacting. What are adults doing in the classroom? How do they react to specific behaviors? How do the student's peers react to behaviors of interest? Are there explicit or implicit reinforcement contingencies in place for certain behaviors?

There are at least three additional aspects of educational baseline procedures that need to be explicitly described. First, what is the curriculum, if any, that students are contacting? Is there a structured curriculum with predefined units and tests? Second, what instructional procedures are in place? What type of instruction is provided to students? How is the instruction paced? How often does a teacher request information from students? How does the educator provide feedback regarding student performance? Third, what types of materials are provided in the context of interest? Are the students using laptop computers, paper-and-pencil worksheets, or manipulable objects?

The preceding paragraphs have attempted to describe the basic elements of baselines in educational settings. However, each experiment is somewhat unique and there are, undoubtedly, many other features that may be relevant to a particular study. In general, the more thorough the description of baseline procedures, the better able future readers will be able to interpret any changes in behavior produced by the independent variable (as well as the pattern of behavior established in baseline).

An example of a good baseline description is provided by Dugan et al. (1995). These researchers were studying the effects of cooperative learning groups on the performance of two students with autism in a general education classroom. Their description of baseline procedures included the following:

Participants were 2 students with autism and 16 fourth-grade regular classroom peers in an inner-city elementary school. . . . The teacher rated the 16 peers for their knowledge and typical performance in social studies activities; 5 students were rated high, 8 average, and 3 low. All instruction took place in the regular classroom with the teacher monitoring the sessions and a special education paraprofessional assisting with monitoring and administering pretests and posttests. One or two experimenters were present and provided occasional directions but primarily served as monitors to ensure program fidelity and as data collectors. A 2-week initial baseline was conducted during 40-min. teacher lecture on social studies material given four times per week. This traditional teacher-led format was one that the teacher was currently using for social studies as well as for other content areas. Sixteen students and the 2 students with autism were seated in assigned groups of 3 or 4 in the classroom. The presentation covered topics arranged as units in the text *States and Regions,* including the Northeast and the Southeast. The teacher's lecture and discussion format included introducing key words and facts, posing questions to individuals, and using maps. The students were expected to use texts and take notes. (Dugan et al., 1995, pp. 177–178)

Baselines are used to establish initial patterns of behavior. That is, how often do behaviors occur, how long do they last, how much time passes between their occurrences, and how do they co-occur with other behaviors of interest? One characteristic of single-case designs is the use of repeated measures to document patterns of behavior. Repeated measures refers to a research method in which multiple samples of behavior are collected over time. Unlike group comparison research, which often measures behavior at a single time point (e.g., a pretest), single-case designs repeatedly measure the behaviors of interest during baseline and intervention.

Depending on the situation, observations may occur throughout a school day, once per day, several times per week, once a week, or once a month. How frequently behaviors are sampled is related to the situation being studied. In general, the more frequently behavior is sampled, the more representative the resulting pattern of behavior. However, the amount of time and resources also increases as the frequency of behavioral sampling increases. As with most issues of experimental design, the researchers conducting the study need to use their best judgment about what is a representative level of sampling. If behavior is variable during the week, then multiple samples during the week would be necessary to capture that pattern. If behaviors are consistent, then less sampling may be appropriate.

By using repeated measures, researchers can establish how often a behavior occurs and how much that behavior varies from observation to observation. Figure 3.3 shows two examples of baselines displaying different patterns of behavior. Cushing and Kennedy (1997) studied the effects of peer support programs on the task engagement of students without disabilities who served in these programs. The baseline was the student without disabilities working individually while the general educator lectured. Students' task engagement was measured for the same class period each day of the week. For the purposes of this discussion, only the initial baselines will be discussed. Cindy showed a highly variable initial baseline, with task engagement ranging from 0 to 76% ($M = 38\%$). Kealoha, on the other hand, had a mean task engagement of 44%, with moderate variability (range, 25 to 53%).

In the baselines for Cindy and Kealoha, a predictable pattern of behavior was established prior to intervention. For Kealoha, the pattern of behavior was one of consistency, whereas for Cindy, the predictable pattern was one of high variability (see Chapter 15). A general rule of thumb in single-case research is that the more variable the data pattern, the

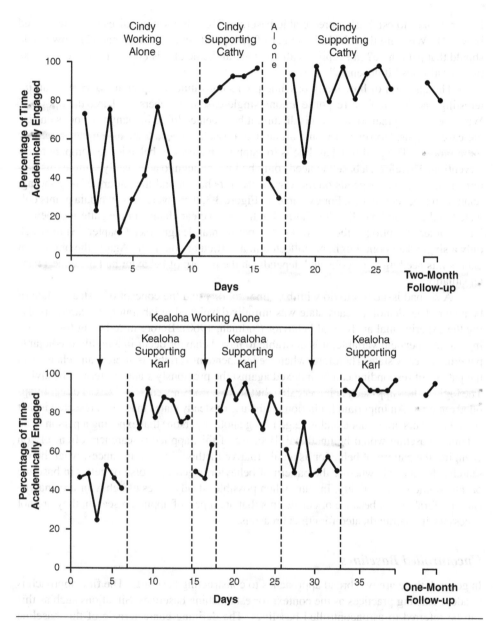

FIGURE 3.3 *Effects of peer support programs on students without disabilities.* The percentage of intervals in which students were academically engaged is shown along the *y*-axis. Data were collected once per day, five days per week (*x*-axis). The top panel shows the analysis of Cindy's behavior, and the bottom panel shows the data for Kealoha's behavior. Baseline consisted of the student working alone. Intervention was Cindy or Kealoha serving as a peer support for Cathy and Karl (students with severe disabilities), respectively.

Source: From L. S. Cushing and C. H. Kennedy, "Academic Effects of Providing Peer Support in General Education Classrooms on Students without Disabilities," *Journal of Applied Behavior Analysis,* 1997, *30,* figs. 1 and 2, p. 145. Copyright 1997 by the Society for the Experimental Analysis of Behavior. Reproduced by permission.

longer it takes to establish a predictable baseline. This observation raises two interrelated issues: (1) What are the minimal number of data points in a baseline? and (2) How stable should that pattern be? In keeping with the general theme of this book, the answer to these two questions is "It depends."

The question of how many baseline points constitute a minimum baseline is an interesting one. The default response among single-case researchers is "Three data points." Whatever the original source of this dictum, it has been codified in many textbooks on single-case designs. However, I would argue that a baseline needs to be as long as necessary but no longer. The goal of a baseline is to establish patterns of behavior to compare to intervention. Therefore, a baseline needs only be long enough to adequately sample this pattern. This judgment depends on the variability of behavior and the pattern of responding, relative to other conditions. For example, in Figure 3.3, there were only two data points collected in the second baseline for Cindy, but there is a clear change in the pattern of behavior. Another exception is the use of brief experimental designs (see Chapter 13) in which only a single data point might be collected in a particular condition. Again, the number of data points needing to be collected depends on the pattern of behavior and the experimental situation.

A second issue has to do with baseline stability and the concept of a steady state of behavior. The idea of a steady state was initially developed in laboratory research involving the experimental analysis of behavior (Sidman, 1960). Before introducing (or removing) an independent variable, it is desirable to have behavior occur in a highly predictable pattern, or steady state. Therefore, when the independent variable is altered, any changes in the pattern of responding can be indexed against the previously stable pattern of behavior. The logic of this approach is impeccable, but its requirements cannot always be met in applied contexts. An important limitation on the use of steady states in applied research is that some behaviors are so undesirable (e.g., biting another person) that exposing a person to an extended baseline would be unethical. Because of this, applied researchers often rely on changing the pattern of behavior as an alternative method. In such instances, what the researcher looks for is whether the pattern of behavior is getting worse or better in baseline or intervention, respectively. In sum, when possible, steady states of behavior are analytically preferable, but because of constraints that are a part of applied research, they are not necessary if contraindicated for ethical reasons.

Uncontrolled Baselines

In general, there are two broad approaches to constructing baselines. The first approach is to adopt existing practices as the context for establishing baselines. Situations such as this can be referred to as uncontrolled baselines. The defining characteristic of this baseline strategy is that nothing is changed from existing practices. For example, if studying the acting out of a student with behavior disorders in a self-contained classroom, researchers could simply enter the classroom and begin observing and recording behavior. Or, the social interactions of a student with severe disabilities might be recorded during a playground situation in which no systematic intervention is in place. Typically, once an uncontrolled baseline is established, an intervention package is then implemented and improvements in the behaviors are noted.

Uncontrolled baselines are a concern for at least two reasons. Often, behaviors are occurring at zero, or near-zero levels, or they are occurring at very high levels. These floor and ceiling effects, respectively, are a concern because they limit the degree to which the occurrence of behavior can vary. That is, a highly restricted range of occurrence is all that is available as a baseline comparison. Optimally, behaviors vary around the midpoint of the measurement scale, allowing for both increases and decreases in behavior following introduction of an independent variable. In addition, uncontrolled baselines often establish highly artificial situations in the sense that there is no realistic expectation that behaviors might improve during baseline. For example, if a researcher exposes a child who cannot read to sight words without feedback as a baseline condition, the only surprise would be if the child actually began to read. Uncontrolled baselines are reasonable for demonstrating the effectiveness of a new type of intervention, but they contribute little additional information to a systematic body of research (see Chapter 5).

This observation is related to another concern about uncontrolled baselines. Because the researcher is adopting currently existing, and often deficient, educational practices, there are often multiple changes that are introduced when the independent variable is applied to the baseline. Take, for example, the acting-out behavior of a student with behavior disorders. An intervention might change social reinforcement contingencies (e.g., teacher praise), affect tangible reinforcement contingencies (e.g., a token economy), alter the curriculum (e.g., use of lesson plans and units), introduce a new teacher (e.g., a highly skilled graduate student), or restructure classroom seating arrangements (e.g., all desks facing away from the windows). Although each component in this multicomponent intervention might be effective, it is hard to know which was effective and why; thus, little is learned about effective teaching practices.

With these concerns noted, there are instances when use of an uncontrolled baseline is justifiable. As previously mentioned, if a line of research is at an early stage of development, the demonstration that a novel intervention can be effective is certainly warranted. This is a logical starting point for beginning the analysis of a new intervention. However, as soon as the new intervention has been demonstrated to be effective in particular contexts, these findings set the occasion for research on understanding why the intervention changes behavior.

Controlled Baselines

A second approach to constructing baselines is to hold all conditions constant, except for the variable that is the focus of comparison between baseline and intervention. Such an arrangement is called a controlled baseline, because specific conditions are created to constitute the baseline condition and are adopted in reference to the independent variable. For example, Piazza et al. (1998) established two separate baselines for a teenager with autism who engaged in pica (i.e., chewing on inedible objects like keys or rocks). The rationale for constructing two separate baselines was the need to compare different reasons why the teenager emitted pica. In a previous analysis, the pica had been shown to occur to gain access to keys or rocks (i.e., nonsocial reinforcement) and to gain social attention (i.e., positive reinforcement in the form of adult attention). The first baseline provided access to objects that could be safely ingested, while the second baseline provided social attention (but not the object) when she tried to ingest the object (see Figure 3.4). The baselines were then contrasted with noncontingent access to the stimuli (i.e., noncontingent tangible [NCT] and noncontingent attention [NCA]), and pica decreased. Additional manipulations were then

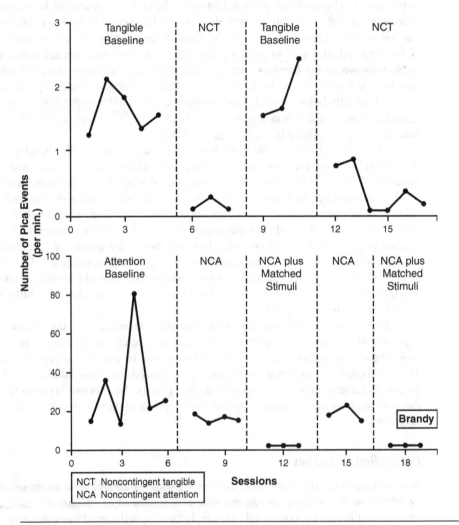

FIGURE 3.4   *Establishing controlled baseline for a teenager with autism.* Number of pica events per minute during an analogue functional analysis are represented on the *y*-axis. Information was collected across ten-minute sessions (*x*-axis). Baselines were arranged to maintain the pica on specific reinforcers previously identified to maintain the behavior. Interventions consisted of various experimental manipulations of the events established in baseline.

Source: From C. C. Piazza, W. W. Fisher, G. P. Hanley, L. A. LeBlanc, A. S. Worsdell, S. E. Lindauer, and K. M. Keeney, "Treatment of Pica through Multiple Analyses of Its Reinforcing Functions," *Journal of Applied Behavior Analysis,* 1998, *313,* fig. 7, p. 183. Copyright 1998 by the Society for the Experimental Analysis of Behavior. Reproduced by permission.

conducted to establish functional relations. The primary point for this discussion is that the baseline conditions were designed for an analytical comparison with the independent variable.

A second illustration of a controlled baseline can be drawn from Kennedy, Meyer, Knowles, and Shukla (2000). These authors used a multiple baseline across operant functions to study stereotypy (see Chapter 11). Each baseline was concurrently established to maintain stereotypy on a different reinforcer derived from a previous assessment: (1) positive reinforcement by adult attention, (2) negative reinforcement by escaping demands, and (3) nonsocial reinforcement when alone (see Figure 3.5, page 42). A functional communication training intervention (Carr & Durand, 1985) specific to each behavioral function in baseline was systematically introduced to analyze whether each reinforcer function would transfer to a novel behavior. Such controlled baselines held constant reinforcer functions throughout the study, allowing for an analysis of whether behavioral functions could transfer across topographies of responding (e.g., from stereotypy to sign language).

Controlled baselines provide a number of advantages over uncontrolled baselines. In particular, controlled baselines allow a researcher to move from demonstrations of intervention effectiveness to asking more refined experimental questions. This issue is discussed at length in Chapter 5, but will be briefly reviewed here for purposes of explication. Controlled baselines can be used to compare one type of treatment with another treatment to contrast which aspect of the two interventions is responsible for producing specific outcomes. For example, use of constant-time delay could be compared with constant-time delay plus social praise. Controlled baselines can also be used to conduct parametric analyses, which contrast different amounts or degrees of an independent variable to establish these effects on behavior. Such a strategy could be used to study the effects of differing amounts of reading instruction on reading proficiency and fluency. A third type of analysis enabled by controlled baselines is component analyses. This approach to experimentation can establish a particular intervention as a baseline and then remove an individual component of the independent variable to analyze its effect on behavior.

Historically, although they have been in use since the 1960s, controlled baselines have been the least used in educational research employing single-case designs. A primary drawback to controlled designs is that the setting in which the research is being conducted has to be reconfigured to establish a systematically designed baseline. Anyone familiar with educational environments knows the complexities involved in such an arrangement. However, the analytical benefits of establishing controlled baselines are worth the effort, because they allow for more refined experimental analyses. Such analyses allow for the establishment of functional relations that tell us a great deal more about why behavior changed than simply demonstrating that the intervention can be effective.

Demonstrating Functional Relations

Establishing a clear pattern of behavior during baseline sets the occasion for introducing the independent variable and studying its effect on behavior. If the pattern of behavior changes following introduction of the independent variable, there is reason to suspect that the intervention may have influenced responding. However, at this point it would be premature to

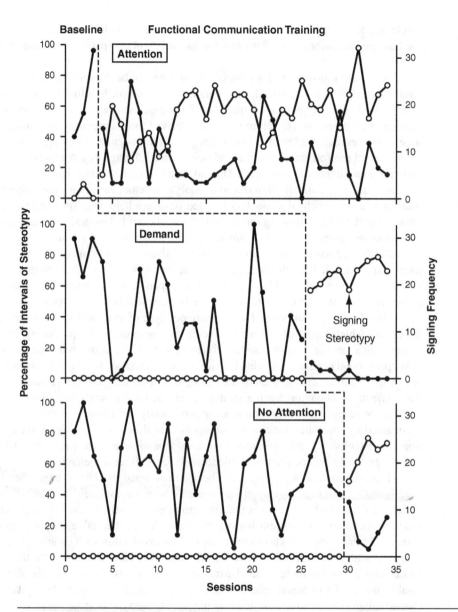

FIGURE 3.5 *Multiple baselines to study stereotypy of behavior.* The percentage of intervals of stereotypy is arrayed along the left side of the *y*-axis, and the frequency of signing is displayed along the right side of the *y*-axis. Consecutive five-minute sessions conducted once per day are arrayed in the *x*-axis. Stereotypy was maintained on various reinforcers identified in a previous analogue functional analysis. Functional communication training was used to transfer reinforcer functions to novel behaviors (i.e., signing).

Source: From C. H. Kennedy, K. A. Meyer, T. Knowles, and S. Shukla, "Analyzing the Multiple Functions of Stereotypical Behavior for Students with Autism: Implications for Assessment and Treatment," *Journal of Applied Behavior Analysis,* 2000, *33,* fig. 2, p. 565. Copyright 2000 by the Society for the Experimental Analysis of Behavior. Reproduced by permission.

BOX 3.1 • *Using Precise Language When Engaging in Research*

A common public stereotype is of the researcher who is painfully precise in her use of language. Every word she uses is carefully selected for its specific meaning, and only the minimum number of words needed to express an idea are used. Superfluous words or vagueness is avoided at all costs because it only leads to confusion, which is contrary to the goal of conducting research. Unlike most stereotypes, this one is actually quite accurate. The reason is simple. Research is a very precise endeavor, but one in which the researcher is often studying a phenomenon that is not well understood. Therefore, as a researcher is breaking new ground, it is best to be as careful as possible in describing what is being done and what results from these activities. The researcher cannot be sure exactly what she is discovering or how it will be understood five or ten years later.

In order to avoid as much confusion as possible, researchers use as few words as possible and carefully define what they mean. The only way to learn to do this is to monitor everything you say or write about your research and analyze it for conciseness and clarity. It also helps to solicit critical appraisals from others, although it is not always a pleasant experience. These are good practices to adopt, because researchers constantly monitor and discuss the meaning and appropriateness of terms. In other words, even if you do not critique your own technical language, other researchers will critique your use of language.

A good example of linguistic precision is use of the terms *functional relation* and *functional*

relationship. These terms are often used as if they were interchangeable. One of the first uses of the term *functional relation* was by Murray Sidman (1960) in his classic book on single-case designs, *Tactics of Scientific Research.* A functional relation, as previously noted, is the demonstration of control over the dependent variable by systematic manipulation of the independent variable. However, over time, language use has drifted, and some researchers now use the term *functional relationship* in a manner that is inaccurate.

The issue is this. The dictionary definition (Webster's *Ninth New Collegiate Dictionary*) of *relationship* is (1) the state of being related or interrelated (entered into a marriage relationship); (2) the relation connecting or binding two participants in a relationship, as (a) kinship, (b) a specific instance or type of kinship; (3) (a) a state of affairs existing between those having relations or dealings (had a good relationship with his family), (b) a romantic or passionate attachment.

In essence, the term *functional relationship* assumes a social and interpersonal meaning that goes beyond the demonstration of experimental control among independent and dependent variables. In contrast, the term *functional relation* describes an abstract connection between two variables, with no additional connotations or inferences. In sum, a marriage can be a functional relationship, but the experimental control you demonstrate in your research is a functional relation.

conclude that a functional relation has been demonstrated. At least one additional experimental manipulation is required to establish a functional relation (see Box 3.1).

As you can see from reading Box 3.2 (page 44), the situation just described can be referred to as an A-B arrangement of conditions. This A-B arrangement is a necessary, but not sufficient, set of conditions for establishing a functional relation as described earlier in this chapter. Although there may be a correlated change in the level of the dependent variable from A to B conditions, a range of extraneous variables could have coincided with the onset of the independent variable. Because of this, researchers need to conduct at least one additional experimental manipulation, a return to the baseline condition (i.e., A-B-A).

BOX 3.2 • *The ABCs of Single-Case Designs*

At this juncture, its time to introduce some technical nomenclature used in single-case research. In this type of research, baselines are often designated as the A condition. If a researcher in spoken or written communication refers either to the A condition or baseline, these terms are being used synonymously. Similarly, the initial intervention being analyzed is referred to as the B condition. Interventions, independent variables, and B conditions are typically synonymous. When discussing different types of single-case design tactics, the arrangement of conditions will be referred to using this alphabetic shorthand. For example, using an A-B-A design, the researcher would use baseline, inter-vention, and baseline as her sequence of conditions. Using an A-B-A-B design would imply that the following sequence of conditions occurred: baseline, intervention, baseline, and intervention. If additional interventions are introduced, those independent variables are designated using the next letter in the alphabet (e.g., C). An experimental design that tests two separate independent variables against a baseline condition might be designated as A-B-A-C-A-B-A-C. If two separate intervention conditions are combined, a plus (+) sign is typically added to note their combination (e.g., B+C condition). A hypothetical sequence might be this: A-B-A-C-A-B+C-A-B.

The planned return to baseline allows a second test of whether the independent variable actually influenced the dependent variable, rather than an extraneous variable influencing behavior change. This experimental manipulation is a form of replication. If changes in the dependent variable are largely due to the independent variable and not extraneous variables, the presentation and subsequent withdrawal of the independent variable should strongly influence the pattern of behavior (see Box 3.3).

Figure 3.6 shows four different patterns of data from A-B-A analyses. Some of the data in Figure 3.6 show functional relations, others do not. Panel 1 of the figure shows a

BOX 3.3 • *Planned Experimental Manipulations*

It was previously noted that interventions are referred to as independent variables because the experimenter directly controls the implementation and withdrawal of these variables. Implicit in this observation is that the implementation and withdrawal of independent variables is a planned event. That is, the experimenter decides to start intervention because baseline stability has been achieved or because data trends are in the opposite direction to anticipated intervention effects. This purposive process is also followed when removing or altering the independent variable. This can be contrasted with the unplanned, accidental, or serendipitous application or removal of an intervention. In such unplanned instances, the possibility that an extraneous variable may be associated with the changes cannot be ruled out, causing a potential confound in the study. If an extraneous event caused or was coincident with the change in the status of the independent variable, then it is possible that those extra-experimental events may also be responsible for some, or all, of the changes observed in behavior. For this reason, single-case researchers often specify the criteria for condition changes, or present the rationale for a condition change, prior to making a planned experimental manipulation. This aspect of single-case designs helps distinguish it from case histories and other uncontrolled approaches.

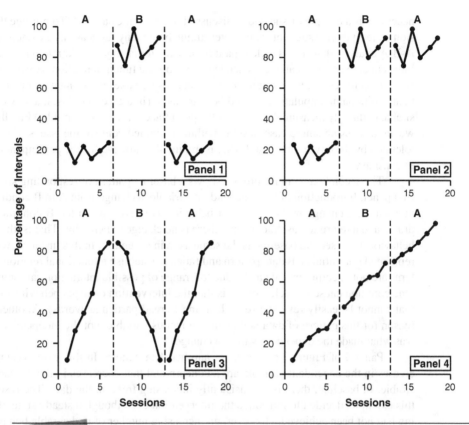

FIGURE 3.6 *Hypothetical data showing different patterns of behavior across an A-B-A experimental design.* The dependent variables are arrayed across the ordinates, while the time course of the studies is arrayed across the abscissa. Each panel is labeled 1, 2, 3, and 4 to correspond with the discussion in the text.

pattern just the opposite of what was shown in Figure 3.1, but as with the previous figure, there is a functional relation that has been established. In the first baseline condition (A), a low level of behavior was recorded, with little variability and no increasing or decreasing trend. When the intervention was introduced (B), an immediate increase in the level of behavior was observed, with little variability and no trend. At this point, we have shown a clear change from A to B, but it is possible that an extraneous variable may have coincided with the introduction of the B condition. To test for this possibility, the researcher plans to withdraw the intervention (B) once a stable pattern of behavior is established. When the intervention was withdrawn and the experiment returns to baseline (A), behavior returns to a pattern consistent with the original baseline. At this point, we have met the minimal requirements for establishing a functional relation.

Would additional manipulations with correspondingly consistent changes in behavior be even more convincing? Absolutely. However, how many experimental manipulations are necessary is a complex issue and is discussed in detail in Chapter 4. To presage that discussion, at least three issues enter into determining how many replications are enough. First, an A-B-A analysis that shows a clear pattern of behavior change in relation to the status of the independent variable is all that is needed to establish a function relation. However, if the researcher believes that there might be an extraneous variable covarying with the intervention, then additional manipulations would be warranted. (In a case like this, it also would be desirable to directly measure the status of the potential confounding variable.) Finally, because we are discussing single-case designs within an applied context, the issues of what can be tolerated by the environment and what is minimally intrusive for the participant are critical to consider.

The second panel in Figure 3.6 shows a baseline pattern of responding similar to the first panel. Introduction of the independent variable, a change from A to B conditions, produces a clear change in the pattern of behavior. However, when the B condition is withdrawn and a return to baseline occurs, there is no change in behavior. That is, the pattern of behavior in the second baseline is the same as in intervention. In this instance, we have not replicated our initial A-B data pattern and failed to establish a functional relation. Such patterns are not uncommon and can be due to a range of possible interactions among variables. One common cause of such a result is that the intervention changes behavior in a manner that cannot be easily reversed (e.g., learning to read particular words). Another common reason for this pattern of data is that an extraneous variable, not the independent variable, was what made the dependent variable change.

Panel 3 of Figure 3.6 shows yet another data pattern. In this case, assume that increases in the dependent variable are a concern and that decreases in this variable are desirable. In baseline, there is a consistently increasing trend in the data. The researcher, in this example, decided to introduce the intervention even though a steady state of responding had not been achieved. However, an increasing number of undesirable behaviors were being emitted, and in applied situations this can suffice if the intervention can change that pattern. In panel 3 of Figure 3.6, introduction of the B condition not only changed the pattern of behavior from baseline but completely reversed it. When the study was changed back to the A condition, the behavior immediately began to increase, session after session. Although there is complete overlap in the data across the A-B-A conditions, a functional relation was established because of the consistent changes in the pattern of the data.

Panel 4 of Figure 3.6 displays a final data set for consideration. Unlike the previous example, assume that increases in the dependent variable are highly desirable. In this hypothetical study, there was an increasing trend in behavior throughout baseline. When the intervention was applied, behavior continued to increase, and when the intervention was withdrawn, behavior continued to increase. The result of this study, for our hypothetical participant, is wonderful. However, no functional relation was established, and no experimental control was demonstrated. Because of the continuously increasing trend in the data, there was never any change in the pattern of responding from one condition to the next. In more pedestrian terms, we have no idea why things got better.

A useful way of thinking about independent variable manipulations is in terms of additions and subtractions of discrete events to the baseline condition. When an intervention is introduced, something is added to the situation (e.g., error correction in sight word reading) or removed (e.g., noncontingent teacher attention). Often, in educational research, several events are added and/or removed. Operationalizing the baseline condition and intervention will assist in explicitly identifying what aspects of the experimental situation are being altered. Such an understanding typically leads to an improved understanding of the nature of the experimental question and the effects on behavior that result from the analysis.

Conclusion

In educational settings (or laboratory settings for that matter), you will rarely see such clear findings as those in Figure 3.6. Instead, there is typically more variability, cyclical trends, and less dramatic changes across conditions. How to interpret such results takes years of training and practice. We will be dealing with these issues throughout the remainder of the book as we learn more about measuring behavior and using experimental designs, each of which, in and of itself, can influence interpretation of the data. It is important to understand that the initial goal of an experimental analysis is to establish a functional relation. However, pursuing that goal is complex, and it is best to be skeptical of findings that are consistent with the anticipated results. Human nature being as it is, we often critically scrutinize negative findings but quickly accept positive findings. Part of learning to be an effective researcher is to remember that you are seeking to understand how nature works, not telling nature how it works. This means that errors can occur at any time in a research study, and thus being objective and vigilant is required. It's a humbling experience to be a researcher, but well worth the effort in many respects (Hineline, 1991; Neuringer, 1991; Nevin, 1991).

The goal of research is to explain the world we live in. Part of the process necessary for arriving at explanations is identifying the causes of the phenomenon being studied. The establishment of functional relations is an important step toward such an outcome. When a study is conducted and believably demonstrates that the independent variable influenced the dependent variable, something has been learned. As more and more functional relations are established, a body of evidence accumulates that begins to provide researchers with clues about how some behavioral processes influence behavior. These multiple findings are then interpreted by researchers and used to assemble an explanation for why humans act the way they do (Kennedy, in press). In the next chapter, we will begin discussing how research proceeds from individual functional relations to the assemblage of larger bodies of evidence using two distinct, but related, experimental strategies—direct replication and systematic replication.

4

Direct and Systematic Replication

For researchers, the term *replication* means "performance of an experiment or procedure more than once" (Webster's *Ninth New Collegiate Dictionary,* 1985). Explicit in this definition is that some type of experimental manipulation is conducted once and then repeated once again. As we will see in this chapter, replication has many facets and derivations, but all aspects of replication are based on this seemingly simple concept. In fact, replication pervades the research enterprise. Almost every facet of research activity involves repeating an experimental activity. This has led some people to observe that replication is the foundation of science. Without replication, experimentation could not exist.

If I arrange to introduce an independent variable to a steady-state dependent variable performance and the level of the dependent variable changes, I might conclude that my experimental manipulation was the cause of the change in behavior. However, although I would like to conclude that my prowess as an experimenter was the source of behavior change, I would be very naive to assume so. I would be much wiser to replicate the independent variable manipulation with the same person to see if I get a similar effect a second time, maybe even a third fourth time. Even if I get the same effect again, it would be advisable to conduct this experiment again with another person to see if I get a similar effect, perhaps even with a third or fourth person.

The reason for being so careful before making a judgment about an experimental finding is that a multitude of events could have co-occurred with the independent variable, and any one of those events could be the cause of the behavior change. Such issues beg the question, "How many replications are sufficient to establish a functional relation?" The answer is that there is no fixed amount (see Box 4.1).

The degree to which a finding needs to be replicated depends on the experimental context, nature of the independent variable, characteristics of the population to be studied, status of the literature on the particular topic, and experience of the researcher, among many other factors. In essence, researchers have to rely on their own judgment regarding what degree of replication is acceptable. In addition, the findings need to be sufficiently replicated to convince others that a functional relation has been established.

Although there is no simple answer to how many times to replicate an experimental result to establish it as a believable finding, there is definitely a minimum number of times

BOX 4.1 • *How Many Replications Are Enough?*

When asked how many times a finding needs to be replicated, whether within an individual analysis or across participants, most applied behavior analysts would answer, "Two." That is, the initial demonstration and twice more (for a total of three demonstrations). Ask the same question of behavior analysts trained in laboratory settings, and you are likely to get the answer "One." That is, the initial demonstration and once more (for a total of two demonstrations). The basic researcher's response is based on economy, logic, and efficiency. A replication, by definition, is an initial demonstration that is repeated once. In some cases, it might be wise to attempt more replications, but it is not necessary. Why have applied behavior analysts arrived at a different and somewhat idiosyncratic answer to the question of replication? Are two replications that much better than one? What about three replications, or four?

There are probably as many answers (and rationales) to this question as there are single-case researchers. Conventions such as these develop over time and often become reified and not critically questioned. The critical issue under discussion is not which number is best but how to think about the issue of replication. As has been repeated several times in this chapter, there is no easy answer to how many replications are enough. In some cases, one replication will be the only justifiable amount. In other cases, two, three, four, or more replications may be the only justifiable experimental approach. Which of these is the case for any particular experiment is dictated by the experience and knowledge of the researcher and the nature of the experimental data. What needs to be remembered, though, is that research is a public endeavor and all aspects of an experiment need to be justified to a critical audience. How much is enough, but not too much, is a complex decision.

a finding needs to be repeated to qualify as a replication. Numerous research journals (e.g., *Journal of the Experimental Analysis of Behavior* and *Science*) have explicitly stated what qualifies as a minimally acceptable unit for replication—namely, a finding needs to be demonstrated once and then once again. From a logical perspective, this is the essence of replication; such replication provides the basis for being able to claim the existence of a functional relation. Whether this amount of relationship convinces the researcher that the finding is accurate is left to that individual's experience with the subject matter.

Ideally, researchers would have the luxury of repeating an experimental finding over and over again to their heart's content. However, several factors argue against an almost limitless approach to replication. First, repeatedly exposing a study participant to experimental manipulations may not be in the best interest of the individual. It is possible that repeatedly presenting and withdrawing an independent variable may have deleterious effects on behavior, although it is possible that positive benefits may also result. Second, the participant's environment may not allow for repeated manipulations. Third, repeating the experiment numerous times with other individuals may keep the researcher from discovering new functional relations that would be of further benefit. Finally, research resources (e.g., research participants, materials, classroom time, and so on) are typically limited and mitigate against excessive repetition of an experimental finding.

It is probably best when wrestling with the issue of replication to apply Occam's razor, or the rule of parsimony, as a decision-making guide. That is, a researcher needs to decide when enough is enough and when more is not necessary. Obviously, this is a moving target, depending on a range of experimental factors. One does not want to rush to judgment that an important new finding has been made and then not be able to replicate the phenomenon or have others fail to replicate it. However, excessive replication is wasteful and potentially harmful. Each replication undertaken needs to be evaluated using the criteria mentioned earlier so that a believable finding results, but excessive replication is avoided.

The previous discussion illustrates why replication is so important. By using replication as a focal point for experimental activities, researchers establish a self-correcting system. If researchers conduct an experiment with one participant, observe a positive finding, and then seek to show the effect again with the same individual, they are checking their results. If a replication is obtained, they can have more confidence in the robustness of their findings. If they fail to find an effect the second time, the initial finding may have been due to some behavioral process other than the independent variable. Similarly, if researchers are able to replicate their findings with a particular student but cannot obtain a similar effect with other students, concerns are raised. This process allows those involved in the research enterprise to check their own results before publicly presenting them. In addition, the findings of one research team can be checked by other researchers. If the original findings are confirmed, the field has greater confidence in the integrity of the functional relation. If the original findings are not confirmed, a red flag is raised that will require further explanation of the discrepant findings.

As the astute reader will have surmised at this point, there is no single type of replication, but rather multiple types of replication. The sections that follow will distinguish between direct replication and systematic replication, as well as various subtypes and issues specific to each approach to replication.

Direct Replication

A fundamental requirement for conducting an experiment is direct replication. Without this type of replication, there can be no experiment. Direct replication refers to the repetition of an experimental manipulation either within or between participants. For example, changing from baseline to the introduction of an independent variable allows a researcher to evaluate the effects of the intervention on the dependent variables of interest. If the experimenter then returns to baseline and reintroduces the independent variable, this would be an attempt at direct replication. It is an attempt because the researcher is testing to see if the same effect can be produced again. If again there is a similar effect on the dependent measures as a result of reintroducing the independent variable, then the original finding has been replicated. This example illustrates the use of direct replication within a participant, also referred to as intraparticipant replication.

Figure 4.1 shows an example of this approach to estimating the effect of an experimental manipulation on behaviors of interest in an effort to establish a functional relation. The figure shows the amount of time that a student (given the pseudonym Allie) emitted behaviors that were deemed indicators of happiness (Logan et al., 1998). Arrayed along the horizontal axis are the specific days on which data were collected. Along the vertical axis is the percentage of intervals of smiles. In this experiment, two types of independent variables were studied: (1) social interactions with students without disabilities and (2) social interactions with students with disabilities. On April 14, the dependent measure was stud-

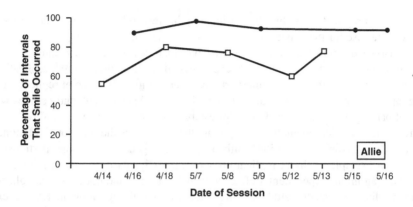

FIGURE 4.1 *Intraparticipant replication.* Comparison was made of the percentage of intervals with smiling by a student with multiple disabilities (Allie). Arrayed along the horizontal axis are the specific days on which data were collected. Along the vertical axis is the percentage of intervals of smiles. Circles represent interactions with students without disabilities. Squares represent interactions among classmates with multiple disabilities.

Source: From K. R. Logan, H. A. Jacobs, D. L. Gast, A. S. Murray, K. Daino, and C. Skala, "The Impact of Typical Peers on the Perceived Happiness of Students with Profound Multiple Disabilities," *Journal of the Association for Persons with Severe Handicaps,* 1998, *23,* fig. 1, p. 315. Copyright 1998 by TASH. Reproduced by permission.

ied in relation to social interactions among students with disabilities, with smiles occurring in approximately 55% of the intervals. On April 16, Logan and colleagues arranged for social interactions with peers without disabilities, resulting in smiling occurring in approximately 90% of the intervals.

If the researchers had stopped the study at this point, they would have shown a large difference between the two experimental conditions. However, at this point, that experimental effect would be unreplicated. As was discussed in Chapter 3, to establish a functional relation between independent and dependent variables, a consistent and believable pattern needs to be established. Because of this, Logan and colleagues repeated their experimental comparison. On April 18, peers with disabilities were interacted with, and during the next observation, peers without disabilities were interacted with. The result was a direct replication of the effects shown earlier, although the levels of behavior varied somewhat. At this point, the original finding was directly replicated within the participant (i.e., Allie). However, in this instance, the researchers opted to repeat several more times the comparison between independent variables. It is possible that they were concerned about the upward trend in the data on April 18 and were not convinced that this was a pattern that would continue if repeated. In addition, they were working with interventions that could easily be replicated with little concern for harm occurring to anyone.

Overall, the original findings from April 14 and 16 were replicated four times. In each of these replications, Allie smiled more when she was interacting with peers without disabilities. This would appear, then, to be a convincing demonstration that Allie was happier among peers without disabilities than among other special education students. By using direct replication within the participant, this research group was able to make a very believable case for the existence of a functional relation.

However, to further convince themselves that they had a robust finding, Logan et al. opted to engage in a second form of experimental confirmation—direct replication across participants, also referred to as interparticipant replication. This type of replication involves the repetition of an experimental finding with a second participant, and perhaps with additional participants. This procedure helps establish whether an experimental finding extends across one individual to another. Or, put another way, does the functional relation, demonstrated through direct replication within a participant, generalize to other participants?

An example of direct replication across participants is shown in Figure 4.2. After showing an initial experimental effect with Allie, Logan and colleagues sought to extend their finding to a second student. This student (given the pseudonym Kay) attended the

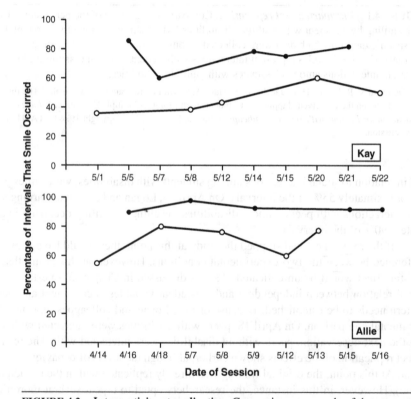

FIGURE 4.2   *Interparticipant replication.* Comparison was made of the percentage of intervals with smiling by two students with multiple disabilities (Kay and Allie). Arrayed along the horizontal axis are the specific days on which data were collected. Along the vertical axis is the percentage of intervals of smiles. Closed circles represent interactions with students without disabilities. Open circles represent interactions among classmates with multiple disabilities.

Source: From K. R. Logan, H. A. Jacobs, D. L. Gast, A. S. Murray, K. Daino, and C. Skala, "The Impact of Typical Peers on the Perceived Happiness of Students with Profound Multiple Disabilities," *Journal of the Association for Persons with Severe Handicaps,* 1998, *23,* fig. 1, p. 315. Copyright 1998 by TASH. Reproduced by permission.

same school as Allie and had similar characteristics. The same independent and dependent variables used with Allie were used with Kay. These included the same physical settings, peers, activities, time of day, and adults supervising the interactions. In essence, every aspect of the experimental preparation that could be reasonably controlled for was held constant across research participants. Such an arrangement allows for a relatively straightforward test of whether what was found for Allie would also occur for Kay.

A similar experimental design was used to test the two independent variables for the two participants (see Chapter 10). The results for Kay show a pattern very similar to what was found for Allie. Kay consistently smiled more when she interacted with peers without disabilities than with her peers with disabilities. This finding suggests that the phenomenon originally found for Allie's behavior was not entirely idiosyncratic. Instead, it was also found to extend to a second student, Kay. At this point, the finding has been replicated within a participant and across participants. All the basic requirements of experimental replication have been met.

These findings, therefore, beg the question, "Is this degree of replication enough? There is not a "yes" or "no" answer to this question. It depends on the range of issues discussed in this chapter. Two quotes from Sidman (1960) might be particularly apropos at this point in relation to the foregoing discussion. "The value placed on specific replicative techniques results not from a priori logical consideration but from a background of scientific accomplishment. The experience and judgment of the individual scientist are always involved in the evaluation of data" (p. 71). "Eventually, the experimenter will reach a point at which he decides that further replication would be less profitable than a new experiment" (p. 87).

Systematic Replication

This section explores what considerations go into extending initial research findings through a process referred to as systematic replication. This approach to replication differs substantially from direct replication. As we have seen in direct replication, the exact same experimental preparation (i.e., independent variable, dependent variables, experimental procedures, participant population, and so on) is repeated within or between research participants. In systematic replication, some aspect of the experimental preparation is changed and its effect on behavior analyzed. For example, in the Logan et al. study, the findings could be tested for a student population with a different type of disability than the one that Allie and Kay had (e.g., ADHD). Or, the Logan et al. study could be systematically replicated with a different age range of students. Or a different set of dependent measures could be developed that more adequately reflects the behaviors of interest (i.e., positive effect). The potential number of permutations on the original experiment is only limited by the experimenter's imagination and the complexity of the phenomenon being studied.

Systematic replication takes two general forms. First, variations in experimental preparations can be introduced within a particular experiment. Researchers might make a slight variation in the task required of the participants or the behaviors that are measured. A second type of systematic replication occurs across experiments. That is, some aspect of the experimental procedure is varied from one analysis to the next, and the similarities and differences in behavioral patterns are studied.

Intraexperiment Replication

Figure 4.3 shows an example of systematic replication within an experiment. The figure reports data from a study of adults with disabilities who had a job performing office duties (e.g., stuffing envelopes or folding letters). Because the workers had very substantial disabilities, they required a high level of support from a job coach. Typically, job coaches were assigned individually to a particular person (analogous to playing a "man-to-man" defense in basketball). The researchers—Parsons et al. (1999)—thought there might be an alternative approach that might be more effective and efficient (i.e., efficacious). The experimental question was whether a more dispersed supervisory approach (analogous to a "zone" defense) would work as well (i.e., one job coach switches back and forth between coworkers in an office area). Two dependent variables were of interest: work productivity and work assistance. (This discussion arbitrarily focuses on the latter, since both variables reflect the same systematic replication issues.)

Parsons et al. established baselines for specific tasks and workers using a traditional one-to-one support arrangement (see Chapter 11). From a systematic replication perspective, what is particularly interesting about this experiment is that Parsons and colleagues varied both tasks and workers to assess the robustness of their new intervention. They could have studied one worker across multiple tasks. This would have allowed them to draw conclusions about the generality of their findings across specific types of jobs (but not workers). Or, they could have focused on multiple workers and a single task type. This would have allowed them to draw conclusions about the generality of their findings across workers, but not work tasks.

Instead of varying one aspect of the experimental procedure, Parsons et al. varied two so that they could draw conclusions about the generality of the intervention across workers and job tasks. They did this by having three employees (Emma, Frank, and Wayne) work on three different jobs: tabbing, stuffing, and folding. Emma worked on tabbing; Frank, on stuffing and tabbing; Wayne, on folding. The results of the experiment showed that the job coach intervention was effective across these various permutations. The authors' design allows readers to judge the robustness of the independent variable across two parameters of the experimental preparation (i.e., job types and workers), thus extending their findings across variables within a single experiment. (It should be noted, however, that conclusions regarding job types are limited because two of the tasks were not directly replicated within the experiment.)

The study by Parsons and colleagues provides an example of how systematic replication can be used within an experiment to allow researchers to claim a more robust set of functional relations from a single study. An alternative approach is to extend functional relations by systematically replicating across experiments. Because there are logistical constraints on how many systematic replications can be designed into a single experiment, systematic replication across experiments is the primary means by which single-case researchers establish the generality of their findings.

Generality refers to the degree to which the findings of one experiment can be extrapolated to other circumstances (Birnbrauer, 1981). Put another way, it is the extent to which a functional relation extends to other behavior-environment relations that vary along some dimension. Those dimensions can include variables such as the grade level of a student, curriculum type, time of day, or degree of teacher training, among many others. Or,

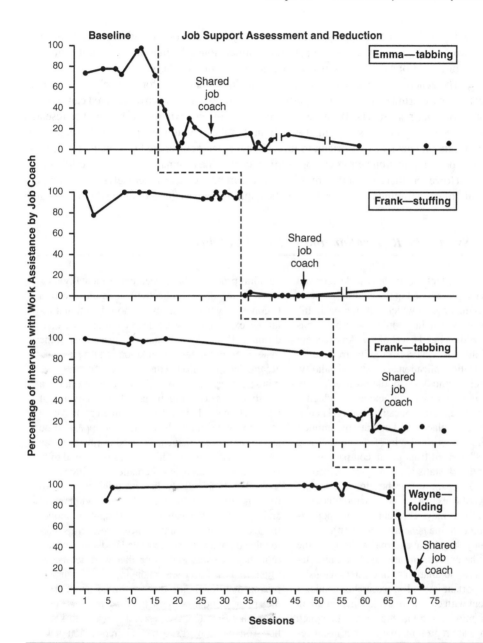

FIGURE 4.3 *Systemic replication within an experiment.* Percentage of observation intervals with work assistance provided by job coaches to adults with disabilities in an office work setting are represented on the *y*-axis, with sessions on the *x*-axis. Three different adults (Emma, Frank, and Wayne) were working on three different tasks (tabbing files, stuffing envelopes, and folding brochures).

Source: From M. B. Parsons, D. H. Reid, C. W. Green, and L. B. Browning, "Reducing Individualized Job Coach Assistance Provided to Persons with Multiple Severe Disabilities in Work Settings," *Journal of the Association for Persons with Severe Handicaps,* 1999, *24,* fig. 1, p. 296. Copyright 1999 by TASH. Reproduced by permission.

those dimensions can be expressly behavior analytic and could include variations in magnitude of reinforcement, changes in stimulus dimensions, fluctuations in rate of reinforcement, or alterations in motivating operations, among many others.

The generality of a functional relation is an important focus for researchers. After conducting an experiment, one should rightfully wonder if what has been discovered can be replicated by other researchers. Because the replication of one experiment by another research group necessarily entails some small variation(s) in the experimental preparation (e.g., a different school, teachers, or curriculum level) it is typically considered systematic replication. This type of replication helps develop confidence that the original findings are veridical.

However, there is another reason that researchers concern themselves with the generality of their findings (see Box 4.2). In the natural sciences, the extent to which a research

BOX 4.2 • *Systematic Replication and External Validity*

Because the antecedents of single-case designs and behavior analysis are based in the natural sciences, there are certain ways in which this approach differs from mainstream educational research that has its basis in sociology and psychology. An excellent example of this difference are the interrelated issues of systematic replication and external validity. Most research methods textbooks in psychology define *external validity* as the extent to which a finding from one experiment can be extrapolated to other participants, places, and conditions. Implicit in this definition is the logic of "samples" and "populations" derived from group comparison designs and related statistical analyses. In group comparison designs, a researcher draws a sample (e.g., undergraduates in a research methods course) with the goal that they represent a larger population (e.g., adults in the general population).

A study has high external validity if the findings of the experiment are highly representative of the larger population of interest. Obviously, this is an important issue. If a researcher conducts an experiment with eleven-year-olds in a suburban midwestern middle school, the extent to which those findings are representative of other instances is an important question. However, for behavior analysts, there is a more important question: What makes those eleven-year-old suburban midwestern middle schoolers act the way they do? To answer such a question requires an intense focus on internal validity and the behavioral processes that cause people to behave the way they do. Once those be-

havioral processes have been experimentally analyzed (using direct replication), then the question becomes in what instances do those functional relations exist, and to what degree under other conditions? For behavior analytic researchers, the generality of a functional relation requires experimental demonstration in the context of altering certain variables. This allows a researcher to establish the robustness of a functional relation. Given that all functional relations have parameters at which they no longer hold, there does not appear to be any other process that can be used to find out how nature actually works. This process is referred to in single-case research as systematic replication.

External validity has its origins in hypothetico-deductive reasoning and statistical inference, and systematic replication has its origins in inductive reasoning and natural science. These terms refer to related processes but are rooted in distinct epistemologies. It is not surprising that these terms are often used as if they are synonymous, nor is it surprising that people are often confused about what they refer to and how to use the concepts. It is probably fair to say that if a researcher wants to know how something works, systematic replication is the appropriate strategy. However, if a researcher wants to know the extent to which a finding is representative of what would be found in a larger population, then external validity is the appropriate focus. For researchers using single-case methodologies, the latter question makes little sense until the former question has been answered.

finding extends to other instances is not simply something to be confirmed to show that the original finding is generalizable to other samples of participants. Instead, additional studies (i.e., systematic replications) vary some aspect of the experimental preparation to determine the boundary conditions of the functional relation. This aspect of establishing the generality of functional relations via systematic replication uses experimental analyses to determine under what conditions a particular functional relation exists and when it begins to change or no longer exists. So, for behavior analysts, the more important aspect of a research finding is not if the results can be reproduced (that is only a starting point), but how the functional relations change as some aspect of the independent variable is altered.

For example, take an experiment showing that six-year-olds who are poor readers can improve their reading performances by receiving fifteen minutes per day of peer-mediated instruction (i.e., adult-supervised instruction by a classmate). An obvious question for additional research that could be asked is, "How would parametric variations in the amount of peer-mediated instruction influence reading performance?" A systematic replication of the original finding might compare 30 minutes of peer-mediated instruction with 15 minutes and 7.5 minutes of the same intervention. Hypothetical outcomes from such an analysis are arrayed in Figure 4.4. The data from this hypothetical analysis show reading performances improved by 20% with 7.5 minutes of exposure to the independent variable, 50% by exposure to 15 minutes of instruction, and 55% following 30 minutes of instruction. These data not only confirm that peer-mediated instruction improves reading performance over baseline, but also establish an interaction between the amount of instruction and gains in student performance. Such a finding better characterizes the relation between independent and dependent variables in a manner that an initial study focusing on demonstrating the effects of one level of the independent variable could not.

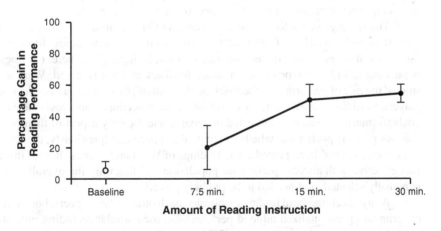

FIGURE 4.4 *Hypothetical parametric analysis.* The object of study was the effect of peer-mediated instruction on children's reading performances. The amount of instruction is arrayed along the *x*-axis, along with the baseline procedure. The *y*-axis displays the percentage of improvement in reading from testing the previous week. Data points are the mean performance for the children. (Bars represent one standard deviation.)

Interexperiment Replication

This type of inductive approach to replication builds the research literature on a particular topic by replicating the effects of previous experiments and extending them in new directions. In addition to broadening the range of effects a particular behavioral process may encompass, systematic replication also allows for establishing the limits of a procedure. For example, in Chapter 1, we discussed applied and basic research on the effects of sleep deprivation. Initial findings replicated the effects of sleep deprivation on negatively reinforced responding for humans and nonhumans. Such a finding established the interspecies generality of the phenomenon through systematic replication. However, when tests of sleep deprivation were conducted with positively reinforced behavior, very different results emerged: little, if any, effect was observed on behavior when participants were exposed to sleep deprivation. This inductive approach to replication was able to identify where the effects of sleep deprivation did and did not occur. Demonstrating this type of generality is the purpose of systematic replication.

Another example comes from the physical education literature. Three studies are provided here to highlight the process of systematic replication. In 1974, McKenzie and Rushall provided an initial demonstration of how competitive swimming performances could be improved by publicly posting the number of laps adults swam each day. Critchfield and Vargas (1991) replicated the earlier finding with collegiate swimmers (extending the earlier findings to a new participant population). In addition, they made an important comparison to separate the effects of swim instructor feedback and public posting of swimming performance. The earlier experiment had combined these two procedures as part of the independent variable. When Critchfield and Vargas disembedded these two procedures, they found that instructor feedback did not influence swimming but that public posting improved swimming performances. These results replicated the previous results of McKenzie and Rushall and refined those findings by showing that only a single element of their original component intervention was necessary to improve swimming.

The findings of McKenzie and Rushall and Critchfield and Vargas were replicated and extended by Ward and Carnes (2002). The Ward and Carnes study differed in several aspects from the previous studies, but only two will be highlighted here: (1) a new athletic population and (2) the type of performance feedback athletes received. Ward and Carnes studied the role of performance feedback on the athletic performances of collegiate football players. In addition, they studied a variant of earlier procedures: athletes selected their own goals (formerly, coaches had selected the goals), and the only aspect of their performance that was publicly posted was whether their goal had been met (previously, the absolute level of performance had been posted). The findings of Ward and Carnes showed this approach was effective with another participant population and that only the overall outcome of a personally selected goal needed to be publicly posted.

As a collection, these findings replicated each other in key aspects. For example, each experiment operationalized athletic performance, used similar recording procedures, and publicly posted athletic performances. In each instance, this combination of procedures was demonstrated to be effective in changing behavior. However, these experiments also varied in at least two key dimensions. First, each study extended the findings of the previous experiment to a new group of participants. Across the three studies, there is evidence that these procedures improved the performances of football players and different types of competitive swimmers (i.e., adult versus collegiate). Each new study also refined previous experiments by further isolating what were the effective components of the original independent variable. Critchfield and Vargas showed that public posting was critical for improving behavior, but incidental feedback by coaches was ineffective. Ward and Carnes further refined the intervention by showing that athletes could set their own goals and the only information that needed to be posted was whether the goal was met.

In this sports psychology example, systematic replication was used both to extend the generality of findings across participant populations and clarify the functional dimensions of the independent variable. In each experiment, the research groups built on previous findings that incorporated replication of previous results and extensions of the existing literature. This example highlights the dual function of systematic replication: (1) replicating previous experimental results and (2) elaborating and/or refining previous findings. No single experiment in such a process can answer all the relevant questions regarding an educational or psychological phenomenon. However, through the process of systematic replication, a research literature emerges that can adequately characterize the phenomenon of interest.

So, how does a researcher know when and how to systematically replicate previous experimental findings? As with direct replication, there are no absolute rules. There are a number of factors that enter into decisions regarding what form a systematic replication can take (see also Johnston & Pennypacker, 1994; Sidman, 1960). Factors that can influence the decision of when to replicate another experiment include the following:

1. *Novelty of the finding.* If a finding is new and unreplicated, having another research group repeat the experiment provides an important check on the integrity of the original findings. For example, if an investigator reports a new technique for teaching phonemic awareness to four- and five-year-olds, other researchers may want to see if it works for students in other schools.

2. *Context of experimental findings.* An extremely well-developed literature may require fewer additional replications than a relatively new area of research. For example, the use of curriculum-based measurement (Deno, Fuchs, Marston, & Shin, 2001; Fuchs & Fuchs, 1996) has received considerable research attention over several decades. Because of the large body of literature on this procedure, the need for additional replication is less compelling than an area of research in which the first experimental report has recently appeared.

3. *Familiarity with the experimental preparation.* This can entail either incorporating new techniques into a researcher's activities (e.g., a new computerized measurement system) or the need to repeat previous findings when working in new settings (e.g., in a new school system or with a different student population). In the former example, the replication might be undertaken so that the new system can be checked against the previously established system to compare the consistency or efficacy of the two data collection strategies. In the latter example, repeating a previously established functional relation allows the researcher to verify that a new experimental preparation can yield similar results.

4. *Existence of alternative explanations for a finding.* If a new, or even well-established, experimental finding exists and a research group suspects that there are alternative explanations, replication may be warranted. In this instance, the new experiment may use a new dependent variable or a more sensitive or reliable measurement system or may include an additional control condition that helps clarify the effect of the independent variable.

Additional Participant Populations

Systematic replication can also be used to establish the generality of research findings across participant populations. Not surprisingly, educational researchers tend to focus their experimental efforts on specific student populations, such as individuals with gifts and talents and/or those from low socioeconomic backgrounds. Establishing a functional relation among experimental variables with one population of students often raises questions about how robust the finding is. Part of answering this question is to test the generality of the finding across a range of learner characteristics.

Typically, when researchers engage in systematic replication they are seeking to extend or refine an independent variable that has previously been shown to enter into a functional relation with some behavior(s) of interest. Chapter 5 goes into detail regarding specific types of experimental questions, but some general issues are noted here. By its nature, systematic replication varies some aspect of the experimental preparation and can include variations in an intervention(s). In some instances, it may be of interest to remove some component of the independent variable and see how behavior changes or does not change. In other cases, some aspect of the intervention may be increased or decreased, as in our previous example using peer-mediated instruction (see Figure 4.4). Another possible approach to systematic replication is to compare one technique with another. Finding answers to each of these questions provides potentially important information about the functional properties of an independent variable and helps establish a better understanding of the behavioral processes involved.

Sometimes researchers seek to better understand a phenomenon by improving the way in which it is measured. In some instances, a researcher may develop a more efficient measurement system and want to establish its usability and accuracy. In other instances, additional measures of behavior may be incorporated to extend the scope of the analysis. In other cases, researchers may develop new measurement techniques that are more sensitive to the events of interest. In each of these examples, systematic replication can be used to better capture the behavioral events of interest by analyzing how various behaviors are measured.

A final area where systematic replication can occur is in the repeating of research findings using different approaches to establishing experimental control. During the past decade, educational researchers have increasingly used a wide variety of approaches to conducting research. Given that each approach to research has strengths and limitations, checking experimental findings that used group comparisons, surveys, or ethnographic techniques helps researchers better understand the nature of the original findings. In particular, the use of single-case designs to replicate findings that used different methodologies allows for a more careful check on the behavioral processes that might be influencing behavior.

Failures to Replicate

What happens if an experimental effect is not replicated via direct or systematic replication? For example, what could be concluded if in the Logan et al. (1998) experiment an effect was achieved with Allie but no difference or an opposite effect was achieved with Kay?

Or, in the Parsons et al. (1999) experiment, what conclusion could be drawn if experimental effects had not been replicated with Frank's working on envelope stuffing? Such findings are not unusual, and when they occur the researcher must accurately determine the reason for their occurrence.

In general, negative findings resulting from attempts to replicate have three patterns: (1) finding no effect, (2) finding an opposite effect, or (3) finding a partial or mixed effect. Any of these outcomes can occur as a result of attempts at direct or systematic replication. Failure to replicate an experimental effect is relatively self-explanatory: no change in behavior occurs when the experiment is replicated. Finding an opposite effect involves the independent variable inducing an effect that is the inverse of the original experimental outcome. Partial or mixed results occur when there is variability in the effect of the intervention.

Outright failures to replicate seem to be relatively rare, or at least they are rarely reported in peer-reviewed journals. This is probably because failures to replicate usually raise more questions about the replicative attempt than the original experiment itself. Typically, failures to replicate are interpreted as suggesting that some aspect of the new experimental preparation was not appropriately followed when attempting the replication. It is not uncommon when attempting to replicate another investigator's work that some small, but crucial, aspect of the previous experiment is omitted or altered in the replication attempt. For this reason, when experienced researchers encounter a failed replication, their initial bias is to check to see if some procedural detail was omitted or inaccurately conducted in the replication. However, if researchers can make a compelling case that they have faithfully followed the original experimental protocol and repeatedly failed to obtain an experimental result, significant concerns are raised about the integrity of the original finding.

Similar issues are raised when researchers replicate another person's experimental preparation and obtain results opposite of the original investigation. The first round of questions raised by such an outcome focuses on how carefully the original experimental protocol was followed in the attempt to replicate. If the original experimental methods are being faithfully replicated, then opposite findings suggest that there is some type of interaction effect occurring that was previously unidentified (see Hains & Baer, 1989). That is, the experimental replication has identified some type of interaction among behavioral processes that the original experiment did not. Such results can occur because one or more of the behavioral processes was not present in the original research, the measures used were not sensitive to the phenomenon, or some aspect of the procedures did not permit the effect to occur. Unlike outright failures, replications that find different experimental outcomes are usually viewed as possible discoveries of new behavioral processes or novel interactions among behavioral processes.

The interpretation of mixed outcomes from a replication largely follows the same logic as the finding of opposite results. That is, if the experimental methods were accurately followed (and the burden of proof of this is always on the researcher conducting the replication), then a new process or a more complex interaction between or among variables may have been identified. Again, such an experimental result is usually greeted by the research community—if not always the original investigator—as an exciting source of new discoveries.

Failures to replicate or incomplete replications are some of the most complex and difficult issues a researcher can face. A large part of this complexity stems from the interpretation of negative findings. What exactly can be concluded when somebody fails to find an experimental effect? The number of possible sources of influence on such an experimental outcome and the resulting speculations are only limited by a person's ingenuity in concocting possible explanations. Because there are often many plausible alternative explanations in these cases, such experimental outcomes are best interpreted with a great deal of caution and the results considered tentative until further replications are conducted. When failures to replicate occur or alternative results are obtained, the best course of action is to conduct further experimental analyses of behavior to identify the sources of behavioral variability. By following such a course of action, researchers place themselves in a position of potentially demonstrating new functional relations rather than simply reporting contradictory findings that might have multiple interpretations.

Conclusion

Replication is a complex topic that is at the core of the endeavor called research. Its complexity arises from the nature of the act itself. Every facet of an experiment can potentially be directly and/or systematically replicated. These facets include variables that are currently poorly understood or have yet to be discovered. In addition, because there are no absolute rules regarding when to replicate, what form a replication should take, or when to move on to a new analysis, researchers are forced to use their own judgment. Replication requires researchers to make informed judgments that have no guarantee of being successful, but those decisions are guaranteed to be critically analyzed by the investigators' peers.

Although replication is a difficult issue to grapple with, it is also the process through which research literatures emerge and thematic lines of research develop. By carefully crafting experimental questions, finding answers to those questions, and then moving on to the next set of experimental questions, empirical findings accumulate. Through this process, we gain a better understanding of what comprises a particular educational issue, how it is structured and functions, and ways to improve it. Both direct and systematic replication play a fundamental role in this process.

5

Experimental Questions

When researchers decide to conduct an experiment, they usually start with some type of experimental question—that is, some general statement about what type of question will be asked when conducting an experiment. For example, the researcher may be interested in a new method for teaching young children with autism to produce more complex language. A general experimental question might ask whether a naturalistic language-instruction technique, such as milieu therapy (Garfinkle & Kaiser, in press), increases the length and complexity of a child's utterances. The basic question in this instance takes the form of "Is the teaching technique effective?"

Formulating an experimental question is important for a number of reasons. First, it requires the researcher to clarify the goal of the experiment. Research often starts with an innovative idea and a great deal of enthusiasm. However, in the rush to analyze the new idea, researchers may not adequately define what they are about to do. This is important, because a range of issues need to be dealt with when moving from an exciting idea to a successful experiment. Issues that need to be addressed include:

1. Has another research team conducted a similar investigation?
2. What were the procedural details of related experiments that might provide important information about what to include or avoid in conducting a related study?
3. Is the new idea tractable—that is, could the experiment actually be conducted in a reasonable amount of time?

Asking questions such as these before an experiment is begun substantively increases the probability of conducting a successful, interpretable, and important study.

Prematurely starting an experiment can also result in problems implementing the study and developing procedures that will allow for the demonstration of a functional relation. Most experienced researchers have learned the hard way that rushing to conduct a new experiment often leads to a flawed investigation and uninterpretable findings. Following up on an innovative idea with a carefully crafted experimental question can help avoid such errors. The reason for this is that explicitly stating an experimental question forces the researcher to think through various procedural issues that might not have been initially considered.

Developing an experimental question also forces researchers to be able to clearly communicate their idea to other people. This, again, requires researchers to think clearly about the nature of the experiment. What precisely is the experiment about? What will be measured? Exactly what is it about the independent variable that will result in behavior change? Will the measures adequately capture the effects of the intervention on behavior? Will the experimental design adequately control for plausible confounds? Not only does developing an experimental question require further evaluation of an idea by the researcher, but it allows others to critique the proposed experiment, which often results in an improved experimental plan.

Experimental questions can vary in their specificity but should contain a certain set of elements that are necessary to properly characterize what will be done. These elements include: (1) the student population, (2) the nature of the independent variable, and (3) the dependent variable(s) to be measured. The student population refers to the relevant characteristics of the people who are the focus of the experiment. For instance, in the earlier example, the student population could be characterized as children with autism. Depending on the nature of the experimental question, additional details might be necessary, such as standardized estimates of expressive and receptive language or the extent of each student's autistic characteristics. The specification of independent and dependent variables should be self-explanatory. As with the population under investigation, the degree of specificity used to characterize the intervention and behaviors being studied follows from the nature of the experimental question. For example, an initial experiment to investigate the behavioral effects of a new instructional procedure might be much more general than an experiment in a well-characterized area of research that is exploring the behavioral processes that cause a particular intervention to be effective.

Putting all of this information together with the example mentioned in the first paragraph, the experimental question might be "What effect will milieu language therapy have on the requesting of children with autism?" Such a statement makes clear to an informed reader what will be done in the experiment, what types of behavior will be measured, and who the focal participants are. Formulating such explicit experimental statements also allows researchers to clarify what they intend to do and to take their experimental interests from an exciting idea to a tractable experimental question.

In addition to the elements just discussed, researchers may also specify the effect the independent variable will have on behavior. However, such a statement is not necessary to formulate a clear experimental question. It does, on the other hand, add a predictive element to the formulation of the question. For example, researchers could change their experimental question to include a prediction about the effect of the intervention on behavior: "Will milieu language therapy increase the requesting of children with autism?" When researchers add the predicted outcome to an experimental question, they are specifying a hypothesized outcome for the experiment.

As was discussed at length in Chapter 1, hypotheses take various forms, with some being more useful than others. Many researchers believe that specifying a precise effect on behavior is necessary for an adequately formulated experimental question, while others would say that such predictions are unnecessary and might even be counterproductive. The basis for the former opinion is the belief that researchers should know what effect their interventions will have on behavior before conducting the experiment. Supporting arguments for the latter opinion often note that by specifying a predicted outcome, researchers may be unnecessarily committed to one particular experimental outcome and thus might not be as aware of other possible outcomes. Again, different research groups adopt different practices regarding experimental questions. There is probably no right or wrong answer on this issue. As always, the final arbiter is the effectiveness of one experimental practice over another in leading to meaningful findings.

Another aspect of experimental questions is the nature of the question itself. That is, at a more abstract level, what type of question is being asked? Researchers do not always think about their questions in this way because they are focused on the day-to-day issues of effectively conducting direct and systematic replications. However, if you reflect on this issue, you will notice that there are a fairly small number of categories by which experimental questions can be characterized, with each having its own merits and uses. The remainder of this chapter discusses the four basic types of experimental questions: (1) demonstration, (2) comparison, (3) parametric, and (4) component. These four types of experimental questions provide a complete characterization of the types of experiments that researchers conduct in single-case research.

Demonstrative Analysis

The first type of experimental question focuses on demonstrating the existence of a particular functional relation. In its most basic form, this type of question asks, "Will the independent variable alter the dependent variable?" For example, does an error correction procedure that repeats the math problems a student gets wrong improve his math skills? Or, will modeling of fluent speech decrease the disfluencies of a child who stutters? In general, demonstration questions seek to answer how a particular intervention affects various behaviors of interest (see Table 5.1). Hence, as noted in Box 5.1 (page 66), it is the experimental question most frequently addressed in educational research.

TABLE 5.1 *Types of Experimental Questions*

Demonstration

Will the independent variable alter the dependent variable?

Will an error correction procedure that repeats math problems a student answers wrongly improve his math skills?

Will modeling fluent speech decrease a child's disfluencies?

Will written cues, videotaped feedback, and the use of children's stories improve a child's social interaction skills?

Comparison

Will independent variable 1 or independent variable 2 alter the dependent variable to a greater degree?

Will sign language alone or sign language plus spoken language differentially affect a child's expressive and/or receptive communication?

Will an intervention derived from functional behavioral assessment improve the problem behaviors of a student more than an arbitrarily selected intervention?

Will error correction improve the students' spelling when compared to a traditional spelling strategy?

(continued)

TABLE 5.1   *(Continued)*

Parametric

What effect will incremental increases in the level of the independent variable have on the dependent variable?

What changes in reading fluency will result from 7.5 minutes, 15 minutes, or 30 minutes of peer-mediated instruction?

What effect will VI 6-second, VI 12-second, VI 30-second, and VI 60-second schedules of reinforcement have on the math performances of students with ADHD?

What effect will 5 seconds or 15 seconds versus 45 seconds of escape from instruction have on the rate of negatively reinforced problem behavior?

Component

Will removal of one element from a multicomponent intervention change the level of the dependent variable?

Will removal of the "rule statements" component from the "good behavior game" change the frequency of students' problem behaviors?

Will adding an response-extinction component to functional communication training reduce the self-injury of a child?

Will removal of public posting from a goal-settings-plus-public-posting intervention alter the tackling accuracy of collegiate football players?

Figure 5.1 presents an illustrative example. Thiemann and Goldstein (2001) studied the effect of a multicomponent intervention on the social behavior of children with autism. The independent variable used by the authors included written cues of when and how to socially interact, videotaped feedback of the child's social interaction, and the use of children's stories to teach appropriate social skills. The behavioral measures included social skills such as securing the attention of another child, initiating a comment about the play

BOX 5.1 • *The Problem with Being Effective*

One of the hallmarks of behavior analysis is its effectiveness (see Baer, Wolf, & Risley, 1968). Multiple examples exist of the substantive progress that has been made by researchers working in this tradition over the last several decades. However, there is an important concern with being so effective. Because so much progress is being made in demonstrating the effectiveness of new techniques, less experimental attention is focused on why the techniques are effective. Hayes, Rincover, and Solnick (1980) referred to this as the "technical drift" of applied behavior analysis. The concern is that new techniques are being described and their effects on behavior documented, but researchers do not understand the behavioral processes that cause these techniques to be effective (i.e., why they work). The concern is that behavior analysis may be developing a "bag of tricks" that cannot be related back to basic learning processes. Discovering why interventions are effective and why they are not effective may allow researchers to develop a science of learning that will be more effective than a simple catalog of techniques. This is particularly the case for instances where complex interactions among behavioral processes will need to be identified and analyzed. It is likely that many of our current failures to change behavior may be due to these unknown complex behavioral processes. It may seem paradoxical, but in the short term, being successful in changing behavior may result in limited effectiveness in the long term.

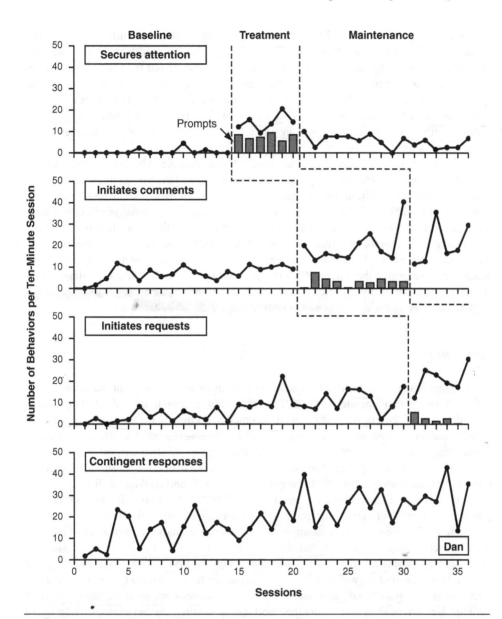

FIGURE 5.1 *Example of demonstration question.* Researchers measured the number of times a child with autism used appropriate social skills to interact with a playmate without disabilities. The behaviors included Secures Attention, Initiates Comments, Initiates Requests, and Contingent Responses. Closed circles represent the number of times each behavior occurred during a ten-minute session. The shaded bars represent the number of prompts provided by a teacher.

Source: From K. S. Thiemann and H. Goldstein, "Social Stories, Written Text Cues, and Video Feedback: Effects on Social Communication of Children with Autism," *Journal of Applied Behavior Analysis,* 2001, *34,* fig. 2, p. 436. Copyright 2001 by the Society for the Experimental Analysis of Behavior. Reproduced by permission.

activity, inviting the other child to play, and responding to the other child's requests. The former three dependent variables each increased only when the multicomponent intervention was introduced by the research team, indicating a functional relation between intervention and social behavior. The only response that increased without intervention was responding to the other child's requests. As a result of this analysis, Thiemann and Goldstein concluded that "following implementation of the visually mediated treatment, the children with social impairments demonstrated improved and more consistent rates of targeted social behaviors compared to baseline performance" (p. 442).

Such experimental questions are used to demonstrate whether an intervention changes behavior in some way. Such questions are the foundation of an empirically based educational literature. These types of questions allow researchers to study how a particular independent variable will change a learner's performance. The cumulative effect of asking such questions is the ability of researchers to respond to practitioners', families', and administrators' requests for information about various educational practices by showing them which interventions work and which do not. This type of experimental question also allows researchers to describe the type of effect that an intervention can be expected to have on responding. In addition, this type of experimental question sets the stage for more complex analyses of how and why interventions change behavior (see below).

Comparative Analysis

Another approach to experimental questions is comparing independent variables. Typically, two or more independent variables are studied in relation to a fixed set of dependent variables. That is, two or more distinct environmental arrangements are studied in relation to the same set of behaviors. For example, researchers might study the effects of two different interventions on the communicative development of children who are deaf. One intervention might be comprised of learning to communicate using American Sign Language (ASL). A second intervention might be comprised of ASL and spoken English (i.e., "total communication"). The experimental question might be "Do the two different interventions produce differential effects on receptive and/or expressive communication?"

Figure 5.2 shows another example of a comparative analysis. In a study of spelling performance, Vargas, Grskovic, Belfiore, and Halbert-Ayala (1997) compared two approaches for teaching English to Hispanic students whose first language was Spanish. The first strategy had students write each word three times while viewing a correct example (referred to as the "traditional" approach). The second strategy required students to correct their spelling errors after comparing their performance with a correct example (referred to as the "error correction" approach). The dependent variable was the number of words spelled correctly. In addition, for one student correct letter sequences were also measured (Jose). The two approaches were alternated across days with a list of words. This comparison strategy was replicated across three word lists. As can be seen in the figure, the error correction procedure was more effective for Sixto and Consuelo and generally more effective for Jose when letter sequences were analyzed. Such a finding led Vargas et al. (1997) to recommend that teachers use an error correction procedure for students who speak English as a second language when teaching them to spell English words.

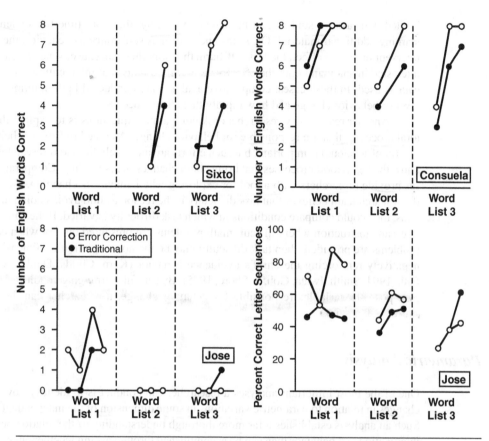

FIGURE 5.2 *Example of comparative analysis.* Number of words correctly spelled by three students were measured. Closed circles represent reading sessions that used a traditional approach to sight word reading; open circles represent reading sessions that used an error correction procedure to teach sight word reading.

Source: From A. U. Vargas, J. A. Grskovic, P. J. Belfiore, and J. Halbert-Ayala, "Improving Migrant Students' Spelling of English and Spanish Words with Error Correction," *Journal of Behavioral Education,* 1997, 7, fig. 1a, p. 19. Copyright 1997 by Human Sciences Press, Inc. Reproduced by permission.

Researchers use comparative analyses for a number of reasons. One reason is to study the effectiveness of different educational interventions. A practical reason for comparing independent variables is to find out which intervention is more effective in changing behavior. How effective an intervention is refers to the absolute changes in behavior that result from being exposed to the independent variable. That is, after repeated exposures to the intervention, how much behavior change has occurred? For example, Baer, Wolf, and Risley (1968) noted that an intervention that raised a child's grades from Ds to As is more desirable than a strategy that changed the same child's grades from Ds to Cs.

Researchers are also interested in the efficiency of interventions. An important concern in educational contexts is the amount of time or effort required to teach students specific elements of the curriculum. Because educational resources, including time, are limited, the faster a student can be taught something, the more time the student has for learning additional material. Or, in instances such as self-injurious behavior, the faster an intervention has an effect, the less self-harm the individual can cause. When researchers are interested in analyzing both the effectiveness and efficiency of interventions, the term *efficacy* is used. In these cases, comparative analyses are conducted both in terms of overall level of behavior change and how rapidly that change occurs.

Another reason why researchers ask comparative questions is to explore the behavioral processes that are responsible for behavior change. As noted in Box 5.1, being effective (or efficacious) is important, but such efforts are ultimately limited if researchers do not know the behavioral processes that bring about changes in responding. Comparative analyses provide researchers with a tool for exploring why behavior is changing. For example, if a research team believes that task difficulty is the reason a child avoids doing math problems, they could compare conditions in which task difficulty is varied. If the child attempts to escape instruction when difficult math problems are presented but not when easy math problems are provided, then task difficulty may be the noxious stimulus dimension that is negatively reinforcing the child's avoidance behavior (Kern, Childs, Dunlap, Clarke, & Falk, 1994; Smith, Iwata, Goh, & Shore, 1995). By carefully arranging conditions that compare possible variables responsible for behavior change, a researcher can discover the causes of behavior.

Parametric Analysis

One of the most important analyses a researcher can conduct is to identify how behavior changes in relation to parametric variations in some dimension of the independent variable. Such an analysis establishes a far more thorough understanding of the relation between an intervention and behavior than can be accomplished through asking whether an intervention is effective or not. For instance, consider the example of peer-mediated instruction provided in Chapter 4 (Figure 4.4). The investigators originally focused on demonstrating that 15 minutes of peer-mediated instruction could improve reading performance by 50% above the baseline practices used in the classroom. This finding is important but does not provide any information about the interrelation between the intervention and behavior change. It is an all-or-nothing finding. However, when the researchers parametrically varied the amount of time spent in peer-mediated instruction, a more complete picture emerged. The functional relation that was established showed that 7.5 minutes of instruction produced a 20% gain in performance (but with increased variability in those gains) and 30 minutes produced only a 5% gain over 15 minutes of exposure to the independent variable. Such a finding demonstrates that there is not a linear relation between the intervention and behavior change. This finding is significant because it means that more is not necessarily better. In addition, the parametric analysis suggests, from a practical standpoint, that 15 minutes seems to provide the best outcome for the effort involved.

The hallmark of parametric analyses is the systematic increase or decrease in the value of some dimension of the independent variable. Figure 5.3 shows such a manipulation in relation to the use of methylphenidate (Ritalin®) for a child with ADHD named Derrek. The dependent variable was the number of math problems solved by Derrek per

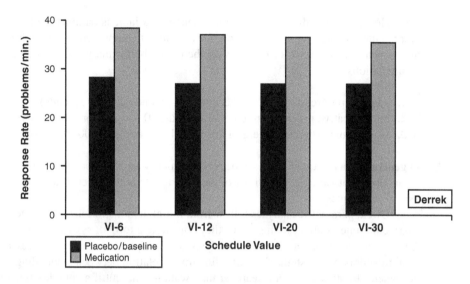

FIGURE 5.3 *Example of parametric analysis.* Problem responses per minute emitted by a child (Derrek) with attention deficit hyperactivity disorder were recorded. Black bars in the histogram represent instructional sessions in which Derrek received a placebo pill. Shaded bars represent instructional sessions in which Derrek received methylphenidate (MPH). The effects of the psychoactive drug were studied across parametric variations in the schedule of reinforcement for appropriate behavior (VI 6 seconds, VI 12 seconds, VI 30 seconds, or VI 60 seconds).

Source: From L. K. Murray and S. H. Kollins, "Effects of Methylphenidate on Sensitivity to Reinforcement in Children Diagnosed with Attention Deficit Hyperactivity Disorder: An Application of the Matching Law," *Journal of Applied Behavior Analysis,* 2000, *33,* fig. 2, p. 581. Copyright 2000 by the Society for the Experimental Analysis of Behavior. Reproduced by permission.

minute. In addition, the researchers (Murray & Kollins, 2001) alternated across school days between the child receiving a placebo and methylphenidate (MPH). What Murray and Kollins were particularly interested in was how the schedule of positive reinforcement that maintained Derrek's math work would interact with the placebo and MPH conditions. To accomplish this analysis, the authors parametrically varied the variable interval (VI) schedule of reinforcement (i.e., 6 seconds, 12 seconds, 30 seconds, or 60 seconds). The researchers found that MPH interacted with the VI schedule of reinforcement so that the denser the schedule of reinforcement, the more problems solved per minute. However, the different VI values of the reinforcement schedule had no differential effect on problem solving during placebo conditions.

Any aspect of the independent variable can be quantified and subjected to a parametric analysis. Possible dimensions for a parametric analysis might include the amount of exposure, the magnitude of exposure, or the density of exposures, among others. In addition, two (or more) different dimensions of an independent variable can be parametrically manipulated in relation to each other to establish how the dimensions interact. For example, researchers could vary the temporal dimension of VI reinforcement schedules and reinforcer magnitude (see Fisher & Mazur, 1997).

How a specific dimension of an independent variable is parametrically altered is another matter. Typically, researchers opt for a systematic approach to parametric variations in interventions. Options for how to vary the metric being analyzed include the following manipulations:

1. additive progression (e.g., 10 seconds, 20 seconds, and 30 seconds)
2. multiplicative progression (e.g., 10 seconds, 20 seconds, or 40 seconds)
3. logarithmic progression (e.g., 1 seconds, 10 seconds, or 100 seconds)

In general, which sequence is used depends primarily on logistical constraints on levels of the independent variable, sensitivity of the dependent variable metric, and the nature of the experimental question.

Often, parametric analyses follow from initial demonstrations of the effectiveness of a particular intervention. In this sense, they constitute a form of systematic replication. The reasons for conducting a parametric analysis are multiple. In some cases, a researcher may want to simply establish the form of a functional relation between responding and the environment. In other cases, a researcher may want to find out if a complex functional relation discovered in the laboratory also holds in applied settings (e.g., the effects of deprivation-induced shifts in dose-effect functions). In yet other cases, a researcher may want to know the cost-benefit ratio between the amount of an intervention and how much educational progress results. Each of these is a valid experimental question that makes use of parametric variations in the independent variable.

Component Analysis

Researchers also find it useful to "pull apart" independent variables. This approach is referred to as component analysis. The reason this type of question is asked is typically to discover what makes an independent variable work and/or why it works. When trying to identify what aspect of an intervention is necessary, researchers often remove one or more components of the independent variable. This is particularly important in educational research, because most interventions have multiple components. By removing a select number of elements, researchers can determine how that particular component(s) affects behavior.

Component analyses can be used to conduct efficiency experiments in the sense that they can identify the necessary components of an intervention. An example of a component analysis is provided in Figure 5.4. Medland and Stachnik (1972) studied an intervention called the "good behavior game" (Barrish, Saunders, & Wolf, 1969). This game was developed in the 1960s but is still used today because it is effective. In the Medland and Stachnik experiment, the independent variable was comprised of (1) rule statements, (2) a light box that signaled when the class was being "good" or "bad," and (3) a group contingency that provided differential reinforcement for meeting goals. The experiment was conducted in a fifth-grade general education classroom that had twenty-eight students. As shown in Figure 5.4, a baseline was established, with problem behaviors frequently occurring (e.g., talking out in class or not being in the assigned seat). The good behavior game was then introduced, with problem behaviors virtually eliminated. In session 36, one com-

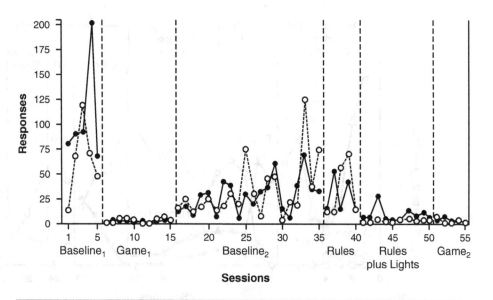

FIGURE 5.4 *Example of component analysis.* The experiment measured number of problem behaviors occurring during a class period. Each data symbol represents a different class "team." The component analysis occurred between Sessions 36 and 55. The treatment package (games 1 and 2) consisted of "rules," "lights," and access to a reward.

Source: From M. B. Medland and T. J. Stachnik, "Good-Behavior Game: A Replication and Systematic Analysis," *Journal of Applied Behavior Analysis,* 1972, *5,* fig. 1, p. 49. Copyright 1972 by the Society for the Experimental Analysis of Behavior. Reproduced by permission.

ponent of the intervention was introduced alone (i.e., rule statements), with little effect on classroom behavior. However, when two components of the original intervention were used (i.e., rule statements plus performance feedback), problem behaviors occurred at near zero levels and were the same as when the entire treatment package was used. These findings suggest that only two of the three intervention components were necessary for the independent variable to be effective. Although this analysis does not show why the intervention was effective in terms of specific behavioral processes influencing behavior, it does show which components are necessary for the intervention to be useful.

An example of a component analysis that did identify why an intervention was effective is provided in Figure 5.5 (page 74). In this experiment, Wacker and colleagues (1990) initially conducted an assessment that identified a child's problem behavior as occurring as a function of positive reinforcement in the form of access to a tangible object (i.e., a favored toy). Following this assessment, a treatment was developed called "functional communication training" (FCT) that prompted and reinforced the child to sign for the toy and placed hand biting on a schedule of negative punishment (i.e., removal of access to the toy). The results show that by session 18, the child was independently signing to gain access to the toy and not biting his hand. During sessions 19 through 29, a component analysis was conducted. The first component removed was the differential reinforcement and negative punishment contingencies, resulting in the child once again resorting to hand

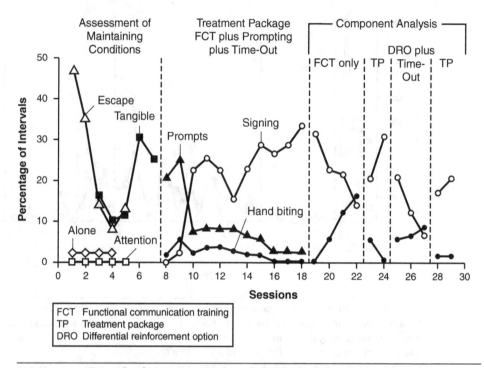

FIGURE 5.5   *Example of component analysis that identified why intervention was effective.*
The figure indicates the percentage of intervals in which various responses occurred. The
responses included hand biting, signing, and prompting by an adult. The component analysis
occurred between sessions 19 and 29. The treatment package (TP) included functional
communication training (FCT) and differential reinforcement of other behavior plus time-out.

Source: From D. P. Wacker, M. W. Steege, J. Northup, G. Sasso, W. Berg, T. Reimers, L. Cooper, K. Cigrand,
and L. Donn, "A Component Analysis of Functional Communication Training across Three Topographies of
Severe Behavior Problems," *Journal of Applied Behavior Analysis,* 1990, *23,* fig. 1, p. 424. Copyright 1990 by
the Society for the Experimental Analysis of Behavior. Reproduced by permission.

biting. This effect was reversed when the reinforcement and punishment components were
reinstated. Then, when the prompting and signing components were removed, a similar increase in problem behavior was observed. This analysis showed that each component of the
intervention was necessary for it to have a beneficial effect on communication and problem
behavior. Removing any one of these components rendered the intervention ineffective,
suggesting that each of the behavioral processes that comprised the intervention was necessary. That is, the reason the FCT intervention worked was because it placed problem behavior on extinction and differentially reinforced the occurrence of signing.

The general process is the same whether a research team uses component analyses to
identify (1) necessary versus superfluous components of an intervention or (2) the behavioral processes that make an intervention effective. The independent variable needs to be
operationalized and the individual elements identified. Then, the researchers need to decide
on an experimental plan for which component(s) will be removed and when (see Part Four).

This decision can be complex, because some elements of an independent variable are dependent on the presence of other elements. In such cases, the removal of one component may necessitate the removal of another component. Such situations will necessary constrain what can ultimately be said about the intervention, but at the same time they clearly identify for the researchers and future readers what interdependencies exist within the intervention package. This is important, because as with parametric analyses, component analyses typically follow demonstrative and comparative analyses. In the latter type of experiments, the focus is more on being effective than in systematically analyzing each aspect of an intervention.

Conclusion

When conducting research, a range of experimental questions can be posed. In this chapter, we have reviewed four general types of experimental questions: demonstration, comparative, parametric, and component. Explicitly stating experimental questions assists investigators to improve what they propose to study. Such a process typically results in refinements in the initial experimental question and an increased likelihood of experimental success. In addition, different types of experimental questions can be combined to pursue even more complex experimental analyses. The posing of experimental questions is an often-overlooked aspect of the experimental process but one that is integral to the process.

Part III

Measurement

6

Quantifying Behavior

Quantifying behavior is a fundamental aspect of the single-case research process. However, before discussing the quantification of behavioral events, it is important to ask, "What is behavior?" The answer may seem obvious, but there is actually a great deal of confusion in the behavioral sciences about what constitutes behavior. Mistakenly, many people believe that behavior is only comprised of the motoric acts a person engages in. Examples might include running across a playground, picking up a pencil, foot tapping, arm wrestling, turning on a computer, or sitting down in a chair. These are behaviors, but they are only a subsample of what constitutes behavior.

As noted in Chapter 2, John B. Watson (1924) originated an approach that has become known as classical behaviorism (Todd & Morris, 1994). In this approach to behavior analysis, Watson focused on overt behaviors that people engage in, as opposed to subjective inferences about what a person is thinking or feeling. This analytical strategy was an attempt to make the fledgling field of experimental psychology more objective by focusing on events that could be directly measured. Unfortunately, this approach had the unintended consequence of directing researchers' attention away from other interesting behaviors, like solving math problems, learning complex concepts, emotions, or the development of grammar and syntax. Hence, this approach has come to be called "black box psychology."

By the time that B. F. Skinner was actively doing research, it was becoming clear that confining behavior analysis to only overt motoric behaviors was too limiting (see Todd & Morris, 1995). Therefore, Skinner (1945, 1950) proposed what he referred to as radical behaviorism. In this new conceptualization, Skinner proposed that anything a person did should be an allowable datum for experimental analysis. That is, behavior was anything a person did, whether it occurred overtly or covertly. Thus, behavior analysis would include thoughts, problem solving, talking, emotions, bodily sensations, and brain activity. Indeed, Skinner (1985) foresaw the integration of behavior analysis and neuroscience as mutually compatible, scientific approaches to understanding human psychology. The only caveat Skinner proposed for radical behaviorism was that the event being analyzed had to be directly measurable and amenable to being operationalized.

Following the logic of radical behaviorism, in this book we will define behavior as "anything an organism does" (Catania, 1998, p. 380). However, in order for a behavior to be able to be counted—which is the whole point of measurement—it has to be amenable to certain circumstances. First, the behavior has to be defined so that it can be physically characterized. That is, an operational definition of the behavior needs to specify its key physical qualities. Second, the behavior needs to be rendered as a physically measurable event. In some way, the behavioral event needs to be measured by observational, electrical, or chemical methods. Finally, the measure of the behavioral event needs to be physically recorded in some manner. Such events could include marks on a piece of paper, digital storage on a hard drive, auditory recording, or written transcription, to name only a few. If these characteristics of behavior can be met, then anything a person does can be considered behavior and can be subjected to an experimental analysis (see Box 6.1).

Benefits of Counting Behavior

Assigning numbers to behavior has several benefits. Often referred to as direct measures of behavior, quantifying properties of responding for analysis is a benchmark characteristic of behavior analysis. There are multiple reasons that researchers using single-case designs insist on counting the behavior of people they are studying. One reason is the fallibility of human memory. It has been demonstrated across multiple disciplines that what people ob-

---

BOX 6.1 • *Why Cognitions and Mentalisms Do Not Count in Single-Case Designs*

Behavior analysts avoid cognitive and mentalistic references, not because they want to avoid what goes on inside a person but because such references do not have physical existence and hence are of little use in understanding what goes on inside someone's head, for example. Or, to put it another way, cognitions and mentalisms are only metaphors, not events. Metaphors, according to the Webster's *Ninth New Collegiate Dictionary,* are a figure of speech in which a word or phrase literally denoting one kind of object or idea is used in place of another to suggest a likeness or analogy between them (as in "drowning in money") <using ~, we say that computers have senses and a memory>; broadly : figurative language.

In general, cognitions and mentalisms are metaphors for events that occur in a person's nervous system or other tissues but that do not need to be physically demonstrated to exist. For example, a child does not remember her multiplication tables because she has a faulty short-term memory or she is unmotivated because she has poor self-esteem.

The figurative language of cognitive and mentalistic explanations is intuitive and satisfactory at a superficial level. However, explaining human behavior by references to things that do not exist as physical events is a risky approach to arriving at an understanding of why people do what they do (see Chapter 2). Because of this, behavior analysts have opted for the more conservative approach of focusing on material events that can be directly measured. Interestingly, recent developments in neuroimaging, often used in cognitive neuroscience, are rendering brain activity as physical entities that meet the requirements of directly measurable events. The neuroimaging of events can include electrical potentials from changes in cellular firing rates, visualization of changes in blood flow resulting from cell activity in certain brain nuclei, and radiological imaging of the activation of certain neurotransmitter receptors in various brain regions. Only time will tell whether physical events or metaphors have more explanatory power when trying to explain human behavior.

serve and later report often differs dramatically from what actually occurred. For example, eyewitnesses' accounts of events at a crime scene often differ substantially from one another, even though all individuals observed essentially the same events. Compounding this problem, the recall of events continues to become more variable over time (Ross, Reid, & Toglia, 2003).

If researchers had to rely on the memory of participants and/or observers, systematic progress would be extremely difficult because of the variability such an approach would introduce to the data. By directly measuring the behaviors of interest in a research study, investigators have a permanent product of what occurred and was recorded as the events unfolded. This provides an accurate recording of behavior and related events that does not change over time. It also has the additional benefit of being available for reanalysis.

A second reason to directly measure behavior is that it provides an unambiguous way of communicating experimental results to others. Because the behaviors were recorded as they occurred and are stored in a medium that does not change over time, the information can be shared with other researchers. This information sharing may come in the form of a graph, table, appendix, or some other medium, such as a Website, that allows access to the original data. This approach allows multiple individuals to look at the same data and arrive at their own conclusions about what happened to behavior during the experiment.

This very process also increases the accurate reporting of what occurred in a study. Because the data are directly measured and publicly reported, other individuals are allowed to scrutinize the research activities and the resulting data. This introduces a level of transparency into the research process that forces researchers to not overinterpret their findings. In general, this means that researchers will offer a relatively conservative interpretation of their findings, given that more adventuresome interpretations may be critically questioned by others.

The most compelling reason for directly measuring behavior is the opportunity it provides for exploring patterns of events. Although educational researchers sometimes study the effects of an independent variable in relation to a single dependent variable, often a more complex set of dependent measures are used. Given the richness and complexity of human behavior, this should not be surprising. By having permanent records of the actual behaviors that occurred during a study, researchers can study which behaviors regularly occurred before or after other behaviors in an attempt to better understand interdependencies among variables.

An early pioneer in behavior analysis, William N. Schoenfeld (1955) once referred to the complexity of human behavior and its interrelatedness with the environment, including other people's behaviors, as "the stream of behavior." As a person behaves, there is a continual sequence of antecedent and consequent events surrounding the behavior. Some of these events enter into functional relations with the behavior, resulting in some behaviors becoming more likely and others less likely. Discovering the nature of these events and their effects on behavior is the primary goal of behavior analysis.

An example of this stream of behavior is provided in Figure 6.1 (from Baer, 1986). This graphic shows the behavior of two people: a child and an adult. Each capital letter (e.g., *A* or *L*) is an individual topography of aggressive behavior (e.g., hitting others or screaming). Each lowercase letter (e.g., *b* or *c*) is a single topography of adult attention (e.g., saying "stop" or turning away from the child). Some of the child's behaviors co-occur among themselves (e.g., *N* and *P*), while other behaviors tend to occur less dependably with others (e.g., *E* or *Z*). Such patterns suggest some behaviors share certain functional proper-

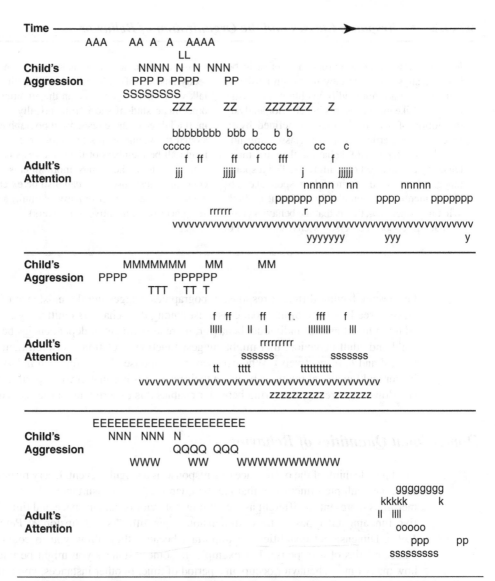

FIGURE 6.1 *Graphic examples of the kinds of contingencies that can operate between the clusters of topography, subsets, sequences, interresponse times, and concurrencies that make up both a child's "aggression" and an adult's "attention."* Time flows steadily from left to right. Each topography of the child's "aggressive" class is represented by uppercase letters and of the adult's "attention" class by lowercase letters. Each topography's duration is indicated by the unspaced repetition of its symbol letter (e.g., AAAA represents twice as long a duration as AA). Spaces between symbol letters indicate interresponse times.

Source: From D. M. Baer, "In Application, Frequency Is Not the Only Estimate of the Probability of Behavioral Units," 1986, in T. Thompson and M. D. Zeiler (Eds.), *Analysis and Integration of Behavioral Units* (pp. 117–136), fig. 1, p. 125. Hillsdale, NJ: Erlbaum Associates. Copyright 1986 by Lawrence Erlbaum Associates. Reproduced by permission.

BOX 6.2 • *Response Classes and the Organization of Behavior*

Response classes are of particular interest in behavior analysis because they reveal properties of
behavior that are not readily visible to the casual
observer. Like most concepts in behavior analysis,
the notion of a response class is defined by its
functional properties. Response classes are individual topographies of behavior that are maintained by a similar set of reinforcers. The response
topographies (i.e., the form of the response) can be
nearly identical or completely different or both.
What links them together is that the behaviors have
similar effects on the person's environment. For
example, an adolescent female may learn to correctly answer difficult questions in math class or
talk with a male friend to gain the attention of another male student she is romantically interested
in. If all three of these response topographies occasioned the young man's favorable attention, they
might all be members of the same response class.
And, just to make things more interesting, the
concept of response class can also be extended to
antecedents (e.g., discriminative stimuli) and consequences (e.g., negative reinforcers).

ties despite having different response topographies, suggesting the existence of response
classes (see Box 6.2). Similar patterns exist among the behaviors emitted by the adult. In
addition to patterns of individual behavior, there are sequential dependencies between the
child and adult behaviors that might suggest functional relations between their behavior
(e.g., Z and *b*, respectively). Whether there are response classes for each individual's behavior and functional relations between their responses is a matter for experimental analysis. However, directly measuring behavior enables this experimental process to occur.

Dimensional Quantities of Behavior

Most people think of the occurrence of a response as a singular event. Every response, however, has multiple dimensions that can be quantified for measurement. Each of these dimensions represents a different aspect of how behavior occurs in space and time. There are
five fundamental types of these dimensional quantities (see Johnston & Pennypacker,
1993). Dimensional quantities are important because they allow you to count different
characteristics of a response. For example, in some instances you might be interested in
how many times a behavior occurs in a period of time. In other instances, you might be interested in how much time is taken up by the occurrence of a response. In yet other situations, you might be interested in both characteristics of behavior. Identifying the
dimensional quantities used to describe patterns of behavior is a first step in developing
measurement systems when using single-case designs.

Figure 6.2 shows the hypothetical occurrence of a response. Along the horizontal
aspect of the figure, time is expressed in seconds. The vertical aspect of the figure denotes
the occurrence of individual responses. When a response occurs, the level of the line increases and remains increased for as long as the response occurs. When the response ends,
the line decreases and remains at that level until the behavior occurs again. This pattern of
behavior will be used to exemplify each of the following dimensional quantities.

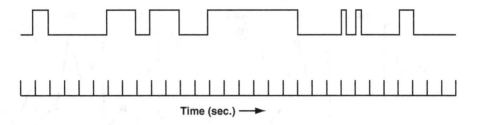

Time (sec.) ⟶

FIGURE 6.2   *Hypothetical occurrence of a response.* Along the vertical aspect of the figure, time is expressed in seconds. The horizontal aspect of the graph denotes the occurrence of individual responses. When a response occurs, the level of the line increases and remains increased for as long as the response occurs. When the response ends, the line decreases and remains at that level until the behavior occurs again.

Frequency (Rate)

Frequency counts of behavior are the most common dimensional quantity and the most intuitive. The frequency of a behavior can be defined as the number of occurrences of a response in a period of time. For example, a researcher could count the number of times a student talks to a peer during math class. If the class is always of a fixed duration, this datum could simply be reported as the number of times the student talks to a peer each day. Or, the researcher could report the frequency of behavior as indexed against some unit of time (e.g., number per minute). Either approach to summarizing this dimensional quantity is an index of its frequency.

Figure 6.3 shows how frequency is used as a dimension of responding to identify individual occurrences of a behavior. The figure shows that the onset of each response is counted as an occurrence of the behavior, regardless of other aspects of responding. In this instance, seven responses were counted. Again, this could be counted as seven occurrences during the fixed time of observation, or fourteen times per minute.

Another example of using frequency counts comes from a study by Christle and Schuster (2003), who analyzed a response card intervention for prompting active participation of

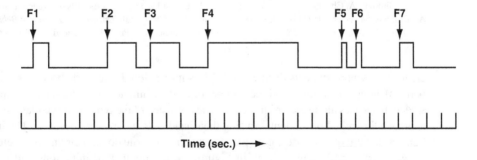

Time (sec.) ⟶

FIGURE 6.3   *Hypothetical example of frequency as a dimensional quantity.* Each F indicates the onset of a response that will be counted as an occurrence of the behavioral event. See Figure 6.2 for additional details.

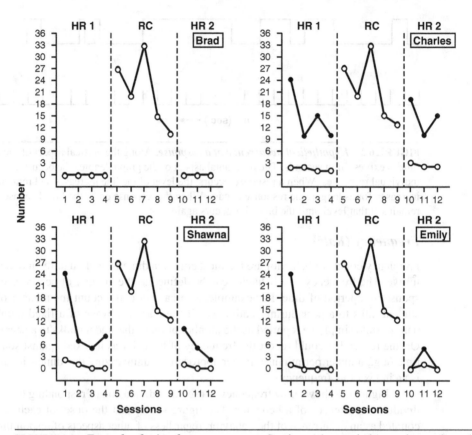

FIGURE 6.4 *Example of using frequency counts.* Sessions (class periods) are shown along the abscissa and the number of student-initiated opportunities to respond (closed circles) and student responses (open circles) along the ordinate. Baseline consisted of the typical whole-class instruction approach that relied on students' raising their hand (HR) to answer questions. The intervention was the use of response cards (RC) for students to write down their answers before initiating a response.

Source: From C. A. Christle and J. W. Schuster, "The Effects of Using Response Cards on Student Participation, Academic Achievement, and On-Task Behavior during Whole-Class Math Instruction," *Journal of Behavioral Education,* 2003, *12,* fig. 1, p. 158. Copyright 2003 by Human Sciences Press. Reproduced by permission.

elementary school students during whole-class instruction. Figure 6.4 shows sessions (class periods) along the abscissa and the number of student-initiated opportunities to respond and student responses along the ordinate. Baseline consisted of the typical whole-class instruction approach that relied on students' raising their hand (HR) to answer questions. The intervention was the use of response cards (RC) for students to write down their answers before initiating a response. As can be seen in Figure 6.4, the number of initiations and responses increased in frequency when the RC intervention was used.

It has become common practice to distinguish between frequency and rate of behavior, but this practice is more linguistic than substantive. Both terms refer to the number of occurrences of a response, with one noting occurrences in reference to a fixed amount of time (frequency) and the other expressing the frequency as occurrences per unit time (rate). Either way, the frequency of behavior is the dimensional quantity of interest, since occurrences per unit time is a fixed, rather than dynamic, quantity. Rather than engage in a tortured explanation of how to differentiate these two ways of counting responding, in this book they are considered to be the same (see also box 5.2 in Johnston & Pennypacker, 1993).

Counting the frequency of a behavior is an excellent and straightforward index of how many times a behavior occurs. In cases where this is the primary datum of interest, frequency is an appropriate dimensional quantity. However, in instances where the primary characteristic of behavior that is of experimental interest is the pacing of responding, how long responding occurs, or the physical force of responding, then other dimensional quantities would better characterize those behaviors. As is discussed later in this chapter, it is often wise to use multiple dimensional quantities to more completely characterize responding

Duration

Duration as a dimensional quantity allows for the estimation of the temporal extent of a response. Duration can be defined as the amount of time that elapses from the onset of a response to the offset of the same response. For example, a preschooler might begin to work at a particular activity center and continue working for 540 seconds. In this instance, her working at the activity center had a duration of 9 minutes. A researcher can summarize individual response durations (e.g., how long each response lasted), compute an average duration (e.g., mean duration of response), or note the percentage of time units occupied by responding (e.g., percentage of time).

Figure 6.5 presents a hypothetical example of duration as a dimensional quantity. In the figure, the duration of each response is indicated by a dashed line, noting the number of seconds from the onset of each response to its offset. In this example, response durations were 1, 2, 2, 6, 0.5, 0.5, and 1 seconds, a total duration of 13 seconds, with a total duration of 43% of the time.

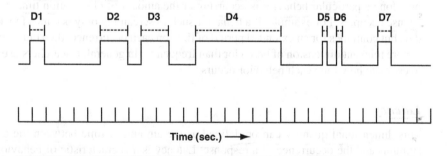

FIGURE 6.5 *Hypothetical example of duration as a dimensional quantity.* Each dashed line indicates the duration (D) from the onset of a response until the offset of the response. See Figure 6.2 for additional details.

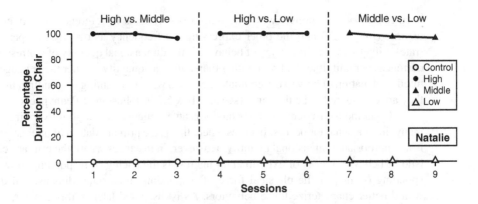

FIGURE 6.6 *Example of using duration as an index of behavior.* Sessions are shown on the *x*-axis, and the percent duration in chair is shown on the *y*-axis. The independent variables consist of rewards for working that were high preference, moderate preference, low preference, and control.

Source: From L. P. Hagopian, K. S. Rush, A. B. Lewin, and E. S. Long, "Evaluating the Predictive Validity of a Single Stimulus Engagement Preference Assessment," *Journal of Applied Behavior Analysis,* 2001, *34,* fig. 2, p. 478. Copyright 2001 by the Society for the Experimental Analysis of Behavior. Reproduced by permission.

Hagopian, Rush, Lewin, and Long (2003) present an example of using duration as an index of behavior. Hagopian et al. studied the duration of staying seated during an academic work task for a young woman with autism (see Figure 6.6). Over brief work sessions (*x*-axis), the percent duration in chair was measured (*y*-axis). The independent variables consisted of rewards for working that were high preference, moderate preference, low preference, and control. Each phase of the study assessed different combinations of rewards on Natalie's in-seat working. The duration of Natalie staying in her seat was highest when she was reinforced with high or moderate preference rewards, relative to the low preference or control conditions.

Duration is an appropriate dimensional quantity when a researcher is interested in how long a particular behavior is occurring or the amount of observation time that the response occupies. For example, if a behavior such as screaming only occurs a few times per day, but continues for an extended period of time on each occurrence, then duration may be a more relevant dimension of behavior than frequency. In general, researchers use duration to estimate how long each behavior occurs.

Latency

This dimensional quantity can be defined as the amount of time between the onset of a stimulus and the occurrence of a response. Latency is a characteristic of behavior that allows for the estimation of how long it takes for a behavior to occur in relation to some salient event in the environment. For example, a researcher may be interested in the amount of time that elapses between the ringing of the classroom bell signaling the start of class and

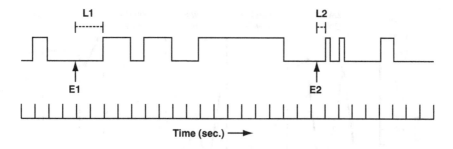

FIGURE 6.7 *Hypothetical example of latency as a dimensional quantity.* Each latency (L) is from an event of experimental interest (E1 and E2) to the first response. The dashed line indicates the number of seconds from the stimulus to the onset of a response. See Figure 6.2 for additional details.

the time it takes for a student to be seated. Reporting latencies can include each response latency or the average response latency.

Figure 6.7 shows a hypothetical example of response latency. The figure shows the occurrence of two events of experimental interest (E1 and E2) in relation to the occurrence of behavior. In this instance, 2 seconds elapsed between E1 and the response; in the second instance, the response did not occur until 1 second after E2. The average response latency was 1.5 seconds.

Figure 6.8 (page 88) shows a study by Wehby and Hollahan (2000). In this study, Wehby and Hollahan analyzed the effects of different sequences of requests on the latency to engaging in academic work for a girl with a learning disability (Meg). Across daily sessions (horizontal axis), the latency of responding was analyzed (vertical axis). When a series of requests that she was unlikely to comply with were made before asking her to start work (low P only), Meg had an average latency of 677 seconds before she began work. When a series of high-probability requests were made prior to asking her to do work (high P + low P), there was an average latency of 21 seconds before Meg began working. As shown in Figure 6.8, the high-probability response sequence reduced Meg's latency to begin work.

Latency is of interest as a dimensional quantity when the temporal relation between two different events is a focus of the experiment. In particular, researchers use latency to study how much time elapses before the occurrence of one event (e.g., a teacher's request) and the onset of some other behavioral event (e.g., compliance). Although such relations do not, in and of themselves, show a functional relation between events being measured, this characteristic of responding allows for the quantification of the temporal relation between events.

Interresponse Time

Douglas Anger (1956) was the first behavior analyst to use interresponse times (IRTs) as a dimensional quantity when he was a doctoral student studying with B. F. Skinner. Unlike latency, IRTs are estimates of the time that elapses between occurrences of a response. IRTs can be defined as the time that elapses between the occurrence of two instances of a

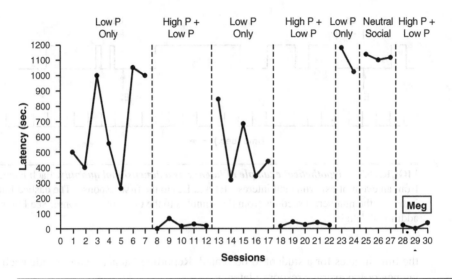

FIGURE 6.8 *Example of response latency.* Daily sessions (horizontal axis) and the latency of responding (vertical axis). Interventions included a sequence of low-probability requests (low P) and high-probability requests preceding a low-probability request (high P + low P).

Source: From J. H. Wehby and M. S. Hollahan, "Effects of High-Probability Requests on the Latency to Initiate Academic Tasks," *Journal of Applied Behavior Analysis,* 2000, *33,* fig. 1, p. 261. Copyright 2000 by the Society for the Experimental Analysis of Behavior. Reproduced by permission.

single response. The number of seconds that elapse between bites taken during lunch would be an example of an IRT. The first bite might have occurred at time 0, and the second bite might have occurred after 25 seconds. In this instance, there was an IRT of 25 seconds. IRTs can be summarized as individual occurrences, or the average time between responses.

A hypothetical example of IRTs as a dimensional quantity is displayed in Figure 6.9. In this example, there are a total of six IRTs (number of responses minus one), as indicated by the dashed lines between each response. Each IRT is denoted by a number. The IRTs,

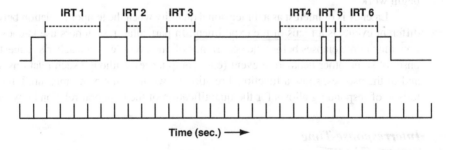

FIGURE 6.9 *Hypothetical example of interresponse time (IRT) as a dimensional quantity.* Each IRT is measured as the time that elapses from the onset of the behavior at one point in time and the onset of the next behavior. The dashed lines indicate the number of seconds from one response to the next response. See Figure 6.2 for additional details.

in succession, were 4, 1, 2, 3, 1, and 3 seconds in length. Overall, there was an average IRT of 2.3 seconds.

An example from the basic research literature of how IRTs can be used is provided by Lippman and Tragesser (2003). These authors studied the effect of magnitude of reinforcement on the choice making of college students. The arbitrary response selected for analysis was button pressing on a computer. The independent variables consisted of a positive reinforcement contingency that provided the largest magnitude of reinforcement either for brief IRTs or longer IRTs. Figure 6.10 shows how the reinforcement contingencies influenced response patterns. The percentage of responses (*y*-axis) that fell within certain IRT time bins (*x*-axis) is arrayed in the figure for each reinforcement contingency. The results of the Lippman and Tragesser study show that behavior was sensitive to reinforcer magnitude, with briefer IRTs or longer IRTs being emitted in accordance to the reinforcement schedules.

Quantifying behavior in terms of IRTs is particularly valuable when a researcher wants to establish how a response is distributed in time in relation to other occurrences of the same behavior. The value of such an analysis is that IRTs show whether behaviors occur in clusters (i.e., brief IRTs), are evenly distributed around some time parameter (e.g., paced responding), or occur in a bimodal or more complex distribution (e.g., two different temporal peaks). Although not often used as the only dimensional quantity for characterizing behavior, IRTs often provide a means of describing the temporal organization of responding that other dimensional quantities cannot provide.

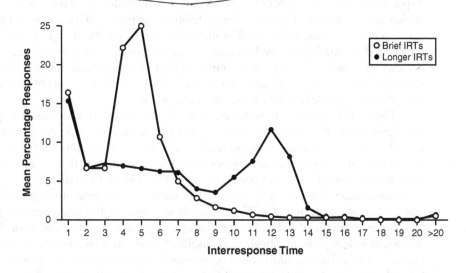

FIGURE 6.10 *Effect of magnitude of reinforcement on the choice making of college students.* The arbitrary response selected for analysis was button pressing on a computer. The mean percentage of responses is indexed against particular interresponse time (IRT) lengths. The independent variables consisted of a positive reinforcement contingency that provided the largest magnitude of reinforcement either for brief IRTs or longer IRTs.

Source: From L. G. Lippman and S. L. Tragesser, "Contingent Magnitude of Reward in Modified Human-Operant DRL-LH and CRF Schedules," *The Psychological Record*, 2003, *53,* fig. 4, p. 440. Copyright 2003 by Kenyon College. Reproduced by permission.

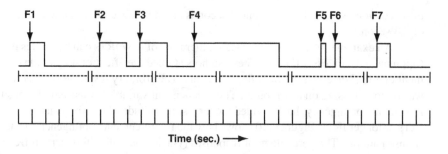

FIGURE 6.11 *Hypothetical example of celeration as a dimensional quantity.* Celeration is measured as the number of times that a particular response occurs in a unit of time indexed against unit of time. The dashed lines indicate the number of seconds from one response to the next response. In this example, the first unit time is fifteen seconds indexed against thirty seconds. See Figure 6.2 for additional details.

Celeration

Celeration is a dimension that allows for the quantification of the change in frequency of response over time. This index of responding is directly analogous to the concept of acceleration used in physics and engineering. Celeration is defined as the frequency of responding for a particular time unit divided by unit time. That is, it is the change in average IRTs for a period of time (e.g., seconds) as indexed against another time period (e.g., minutes). For example, correctly solving math problems could be characterized as the number per second per minute. This would allow for the analysis of changes in the rate of problem solving across one-minute intervals during math instruction.

Figure 6.11 presents a hypothetical example of celeration as a dimensional quantity. The figure shows the number of responses per five-second unit indexed against fifteen-second intervals. This arrangement allows for a description of the number of responses per second interval and how that rate changes every fifteen seconds. In this example, responding changed from 0.1 to 0.07 responses from one time unit to the next.

Kostewicza, Kubina, and Cooper (2000) present an example of using celeration to index behavior change over time. Kostewicza et al. examined the occurrence of aggressive thoughts and feelings of a newly arrived university graduate student. Counts of these behaviors, as well as pleasant thoughts, are displayed across days on a logarithmic scale (see Lindsley, 1991). The baseline rates of occurrence for these behaviors are shown in Figure 6.12. On average, the student counted forty to fifty pleasant thoughts or feelings during baseline and fewer angry or aggressive thoughts.

The analysis of celeration is particularly useful in educational contexts because it captures what we often talk about as fluency. Fluency is the well-practiced, fluid, accurate performance we try to establish in students (Johnson & Layng, 1996). Celeration accurately captures this pattern of responding by showing changes in behavior in relation to time. Celeration is also similar to what we have uncritically adopted in everyday usage as rate—that is, changes in the frequency of behavior in a period of time as it changes over time.

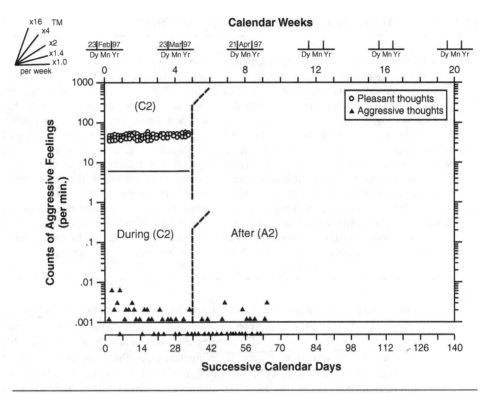

FIGURE 6.12 *Example of using celeration to index behavior change over time.*
The occurrence of aggressive thoughts and feelings of a new university graduate student as well
as pleasant thoughts are displayed across days on a logarithmic scale.

Source: From D. E. Kostewicz, R. M. Kubina, and J. O. Cooper, "Managing Aggressive Thoughts and Feelings
with Daily Counts of Nonaggressive Thoughts and Feelings: A Self-Experiment," *Journal of Behavior Therapy
and Experimental Psychiatry,* 2000, *31,* fig. 2, p. 183. Copyright 2000 by Pergamon Press. Reproduced by
permission.

Choosing Dimensional Quantities

As this chapter has shown, behavior is not a monolithic entity that is unidimensional. Instead, even in the analysis of a single topography of behavior, there are multiple facets to
each response that provide important information regarding various dimensions of its occurrence. Because of this multidimensionality of behavior, when designing a research
study, you need to make some important decisions about how to best characterize the responding you are interested in analyzing. This is not an easy decision, and there is no rule
book to refer to for a definite answer. Instead, researchers need to use their cumulative experience with the phenomenon being studied and their knowledge of other researchers' experiences with similar phenomena (see Box 6.3, page 92).

Adding to the difficulty in arriving at a decision about how to appropriately quantify
behavior is that individual behaviors typically do not occur alone, and in most research the

BOX 6.3 • *Are There Other Dimensional Quantities?*

Given the excitement engendered by discussions of dimensional quantities among researchers, the reader is undoubtedly thinking, "Are there other dimensional quantities that have not been discussed in this chapter?" The answer is yes. A dimensional quantity is a way of characterizing some physical aspect of a behavior in space and time. The dimensional quantities discussed in this chapter are those most commonly used in educational research and most relevant to educational contexts. However, there are other dimensional quantities and means of quantitatively analyzing them that are beyond the scope of this discussion. An example of another dimensional quantity is force. A response clearly generates properties that could be physically measured relating to the force of the behavior. For instance, responses might generate a certain number of newtons of force or obtain a certain number of decibels as a quantifiable unit. In addition, there is the largely untapped issue of characterizing behavior using ratios of dimensional quantities (see Johnston & Hodge, 1989). An example of ratios would be quantifying behavior as a ratio of frequency and duration. Overall, there is a great deal of research that remains to be done regarding new dimensional quantities, and the utility of using different ratios of these quantities to discover new aspects of responding.

primary experimental question is the interrelation of different behaviors. That interrelation may be between how two different topographies of behavior from the same individual enter into the same, or independent, response classes or how behaviors from different people enter into various reinforcement contingencies. As illustrated in Figure 6.1, the behavioral stream of a single individual is complex and that complexity is only multiplied by the interactions that person may have with others. Given this complexity, choosing the dimensional quantity(ies) that will adequately characterize the functional relations your experimental question is addressing is imperative.

The first rule of thumb in selecting dimensional quantities is to directly observe the behaviors you are interested in and look at different aspects of those responses. This need not be a highly technical task. All that is required is that you simply spend time in the situation you are interested in studying, watching people carefully and jotting down notes as appropriate. When you do this, what are you looking for? What is it about a particular response that seems relevant to your experimental question? Is it the pacing of the behavior, the rapidity with which it is emitted following a stimulus, how frequently it occurs, how it changes in frequency over time, or the persistence of the behavior when it does occur?

Once you have an idea about which dimensional quantities may be of most interest to your research question, discuss your observations with others you will be working with and/or researchers who are familiar with the area of research. Start by reviewing your experimental question and what it is you are hoping to learn by conducting your study. Are these relevant to your experimental question? Are the behaviors you are identifying good candidates for experimental analysis? Have you selected dimensional quantities that reflect meaningful characteristics of the behaviors of interest? By enlisting the feedback of others, you gain different perspectives on how to quantify behavior that may help you refine your ideas and improve how you are going about characterizing behavior in your study.

The next step is to choose multiple dimensions of responding. In laboratory research, it is common for a researcher to characterize behavior in terms of multiple dimensional quantities. This allows as complete a picture of behavior in relation to the experimental environment as is possible. However, a hallmark of laboratory research is the automated recording of behavior, and this recording usually occurs in highly simplified environments. The settings in which educational research is conducted are often more complex and may not permit the ubiquitous recording of all possible dimensional quantities. However, with that said, selecting more than one dimension of behavior to study is a wise experimental tactic. For example, it might be that the frequency and duration of a particular response interact and that one, the other, or both might be particularly sensitive to the intervention you are going to analyze.

The final arbiter in all research regarding the adequacy of the decisions you make—whether about hypotheses, measurement, or experimental design—is the data that are obtained. Do they show orderliness? Are they interpretable? Do they reveal something about the phenomenon you are studying that has not previously been revealed? Unfortunately, these questions cannot be answered a priori, but instead, like all operant behavior (and research, itself, is a form of operant behavior), you have to learn from the consequences of your behavior. The phenomenon you are studying and the data that result from your choice of experimental arrangements will be the ultimate guide about the adequacy of your choices and how you should proceed in future studies attempting to systematically replicate your results.

7

Recording Systems

A rigorous approach to measurement is the foundation of behavioral approaches to educational issues. Measurement is a necessary component of any effort to empirically study a phenomenon. Measurement involves choosing dimensional quantities, using recording systems to document behavior and stimuli, and conducting integrity checks on data collection. The reason such care is taken with measurement issues is that accurately documenting the level of a dependent variable is required to reveal the potential effects of an independent variable. For example, if you were to measure events with ±35% accuracy of the actual level, then any effect produced by the experimental variable would have to have an effect larger than ±35% to be revealed. If the independent variable did not produce such an effect, its influence on behavior would be masked by the variability induced by poor measurement. However, if you measure events that are within ±5% of the actual value, then more subtle effects produced by an intervention can be detected.

A key component in developing a rigorous approach to measurement is the recording system to be used (Thompson, Felce, & Symons, 1999). A recording system includes several different components. First, the system needs to adequately code the behaviors and stimuli of interest. That is, what is being recorded needs to accurately reflect what the experimenters are trying to study. This may seem obvious, but in practice it is extraordinarily challenging. Second, the system needs to accurately document the events of interest. Some type of measurement technique needs to be used to record what events occurred or did not occur. Third, some physical medium needs to permanently capture the recording of events. Fourth, events need to be sampled that reflect the scope of the experimental question. Finally, the recording system needs to be implemented and maintained. This includes recording behaviors and stimuli as accurately as possible and continually updating the recording system to preserve this level of precision. If all of this can be accomplished, then data will be gathered that can be analyzed in a meaningful way (see Part Five).

The process of recording events involves incorporating each of these aspects into the daily activities of a research study. Recording systems are a means to an end in the sense that without an adequate system, no study can yield interpretable results. Therefore, recording responses and stimuli occupies a somewhat unique role in all fields of research. Because of its importance, some scholars choose to specialize in the study of recording systems in

94

and of themselves (e.g., Kipfer, 1998; Trout, 1998; Whaley, 1973), while others use the products of this work as tools to pursue other experimental questions.

This chapter discusses how behavior and stimuli are recorded. This information will be presented in a linear manner that reflects the process from start to finish. The discussion will cover developing observational codes, selecting measurement techniques, choosing a medium for recording, sampling behavior, and training observers. The focus will be on the dependent variables used in an experiment. Then a separate, but related, issue—recording the independent variable(s) used in a study—will be addressed.

Developing and Using a Recording System

Observational Codes

The first step in developing a recording system is to develop an observational code. This refers to the types of behaviors and other events that will be the focus of observations. Carefully developing an observational code is important because it provides the framework for what events can be documented during the experiment. If something is left out of the observational code or is poorly conceptualized, the result may require the experiment to be re-conducted with an improved recording system. Therefore, this initial step in developing a recording system should be given considerable attention (Bijou, Peterson, & Ault, 1968).

What will be recorded? Generally, two categories of events need to be identified. First, the behaviors of interest need to be selected. This can include not only the behavior of the focal student, but also the responses of other individuals in that person's environment. Behaviors could include completing math problems, the occurrence of stereotypical behavior, steps used to solve a puzzle, types of greetings used, and so on. As was noted in Chapter 6, the limitation on what can be considered a behavior is the ability to operationalize and directly measure the response. The second general type of event included in observational codes are stimuli. Like behavior, stimuli can take on a potentially infinite number of topographies. Anything that is not a behavior, but occurs, can be considered a stimulus. Examples include the presentation of materials, presence of certain objects, sounds that might occur, and so on. Like behaviors, stimuli need to be operationalized and directly measured.

The particular behaviors and stimuli to be included in a recording system are derived from the experimental question. If you are studying how students solve math problems, then the focus of your observational code will be on various behaviors and stimuli associated with solving math problems. Similarly, if you are studying aggression, the focus of your observations will be on types of aggressive behaviors and associated stimuli. One important way of identifying what behaviors and stimuli might be of interest is to repeatedly observe the situations you want to study and take notes about what occurs. Another source for identifying relevant events comes from previous experiments on similar topics. The observational codes that other researchers have developed may be adequate for your purposes or may need to be adapted to fit your experimental interests. If appropriate, you should not hesitate to use previously developed observational codes; doing so will allow you to readily integrate the findings from various studies at the level of the data collected.

Whatever behaviors and/or stimuli are used, they will need to be defined into discrete categories (Sulzer-Azaroff & Mayer, 1991). It does not make sense to simultaneously record social interactions and positive verbal statements, because the latter is a subset of the former. Instead, researchers developing observational codes need to make sure their operational definitions of behaviors and stimuli are nonoverlapping. For example, social interactions could be subdivided into positive, negative, or neutral verbal statements. An additional issue is whether the observational code will contain elements that are exhaustive or open ended (Bakeman & Gottman, 1997). An exhaustive code defines events so that all events have a category for being recorded. The previous example of positive, negative, or neutral verbal statements is an example of an exhaustive set of categories. An open-ended category system focuses on particular events and does not attempt to inclusively define a logically exhaustive set. For example, if a researcher were only interested in greetings to other peers and this was sufficient to address the experimental question, there would not be a need to use a more complex observational code.

The simplest observational code that could be developed would focus on a single response. More complex codes can include dozens of behaviors and stimuli. Tang, Patterson, and Kennedy (2003) provide an example of a very basic system. These researchers studied students with severe disabilities who engaged in a single topography of stereotypical behavior (e.g., hand waving). Because the experimental question was to identify the environmental causes of the behavior, a more complex observational code was not necessary. On the other end of the continuum is an observational code developed by Walker and colleagues (e.g., Shinn et al., 1987) to study antisocial behavior in school settings. This observational code includes multiple categories for student behaviors, types of environmental contexts, various stimulus events, and how others react to the behaviors of a focal student. As in many aspects of research, the application of Occam's razor is an important consideration. The observational code needs to identify relevant behaviors and stimuli in order to adequately address the experimental question. However, the more complex the code, the harder it is to train observers and obtain acceptable levels of interobserver agreement (see Chapter 8). Basically, the observational code should be as simple as possible, but no simpler.

Measurement Techniques

Once an observational code has been established, researchers must determine which dimensional quantity or quantities they will need to document the occurrence of each response and stimulus represented in the code (see Chapter 6). For example, if screaming is the response of interest, would frequency or duration or both dimensions be the most appropriate way of representing the response? If the behavior is brief, then frequency might be an appropriate index. If each time the behavior occurs it lasts an extended period of time, then duration may be a more relevant dimension. Or, it might be concluded that both indexes of screaming need to be used to adequately characterize the nature of the behavior. Deciding what dimension(s) of responses and stimuli to measure requires that researchers be familiar with the behavior they will be recording prior to developing a recording system. Such a process needs to occur for each response and stimulus included in the observational code. It is possible that different dimensional quantities need to be selected for different responses and stimuli.

After dimensional quantities have been selected for the observational code, researchers will need to decide what measurement techniques they will use. Two general categories of measurement techniques can be used to sample behavior and stimuli. The first requires direct measures, and the second requires indirect measures. Direct measures sample events through observation of the behaviors and/or stimuli themselves. That is, the events are directly observed. This can be contrasted with indirect measures, which sample events via products of events and/or stimuli. For example, in a vocational work setting, the number of dishes washed could be used as an indirect measure of dishwashing. It should be noted that direct versus indirect measurement is a different topic than automated versus manual recording (see Box 7.1).

Once dimensional quantities and a general measurement technique are selected, the type of data collection procedure needs to be selected. The following sections discuss seven different procedures that are well established in the behavior-analytic research literature. These discussions will describe the data collection procedure, illustrate its use, and discuss its advantages and disadvantages (see also Springer, Brown, & Duncan, 1981).

Event Recording.   Event recording documents individual occurrences of a response or stimulus during an observation period. Each time an event of interest occurs, the instance is recorded. At the end of an observation, the number of events for a particular category can be counted and the total number of occurrences reported as a measure of the behavior of interest. Figure 7.1 (page 98) shows an example of an event recording system. The observation period was twenty minutes, and the number of questions asked and questions correctly answered during a classroom lecture were recorded. The figure shows that twelve questions

BOX 7.1 • *Automated Recording in Educational Settings*

A hallmark of the experimental analysis of behavior is the use of an automated apparatus to record the occurrence of responses and stimuli. For example, each time a lever is pressed or a food pellet delivered in an operant conditioning chamber, each event is separately recorded by a computer (see Catania, 1998). Such an arrangement allows the events that occur during an experiment to be recorded without human intervention (e.g., recording discrete events using paper and pencil). This arrangement removes the possibility of human error from the recording of events of experimental interest, although it does not remove the possibility of hardware or software errors.

In educational settings there is a long history of using human observation to record the behaviors and stimuli of interest (see Bijou et al., 1968). This is because educational environments do not easily lend themselves to automated recording. For example, it would be extremely difficult to find a mechanical means of recording the occurrence of social initiations or obscene gestures in school hallways. Such behaviors, however, can be easily recorded by human observers. This aspect of educational settings has required researchers since the 1960s to develop sophisticated recording procedures that rely on humans to record behaviors and stimuli. Because of this feature of educational settings and the history of using human observers, this chapter focuses on this approach to recording events. However, with the increasing use of computer software and Web-based applications, it is likely that there will be an increase in the use of automated recording in educational settings in the future.

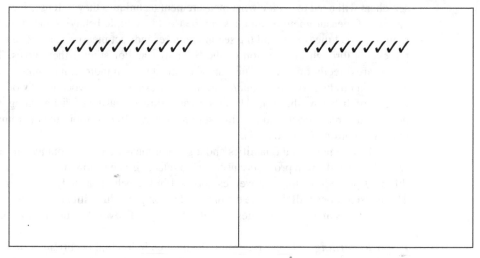

Number of Teacher Questions	**Number of Correct Student Answers**
✓✓✓✓✓✓✓✓✓✓✓✓	✓✓✓✓✓✓✓✓✓

√ = Occurrence of an event.

FIGURE 7.1   *Example of event recording.* The observation period was twenty minutes, and the number of questions asked and questions correctly answered during a classroom lecture was recorded.

were asked during the lecture, and nine correct answers were observed. In this instance, the event recording system documents two separate events.

The observation period used with event recording can be of either a fixed (e.g., 50 minutes) or variable length (e.g., 45 to 60 minutes). In some instances, particularly in classroom settings, a fixed observation length is not possible, because the length of instruction may vary from one day to the next. In such cases, researchers typically choose to use a variable length of observation that matches the duration of the educational activity being studied. For instances in which a fixed amount of time is used, the dependent variable can be reported as the number of occurrences or can be transformed into the number of occurrences per standard time unit (e.g., second, minute, or hour). If the observation period is variable in length, the number of occurrences per observation needs to be transformed using a standard time unit. For example, the data in Figure 7.1 could be reported as twelve and nine occurrences, respectively, or as 0.6 and 0.45, respectively, because a fixed observation time was used.

Event recording works best with discrete behaviors that have brief durations. Event recording can be used with frequency as a dimensional quantity. If a time-based element is added to event recording (i.e., time of occurrence for each event is documented), then this measurement technique can also be used to document interresponse time (IRT) or celeration.

The advantages of event recording include:

- It can be used to record multiple topographies of behavior and stimuli as discrete events.

- It is easy to use if a limited number of discrete events are being recorded. The more categories of events added, the more complex the recording system becomes. (This is true of all the measurement techniques we will discuss.)
- It provides an unambiguous estimate of how often a particular behavior or stimulus occurred during an observation.

The disadvantages of event recording include:

- It requires continuous observation. An observer is required to monitor the setting throughout the time period being observed.
- It confounds duration with frequency for events that vary in length, either within a category or between categories.

Permanent Product Recording. Permanent product recording is similar to event recording, except that the events of interest are recorded at the end of a period of time or after some task is completed. For example, instead of observing a child solve each of the math problems on a worksheet, the worksheet could be collected at the end of the work period, and the number of problems attempted and correct answers could be recorded. An example of this is shown in Figure 7.2. In this example, twenty-five problems were attempted and nineteen solved correctly.

Permanent product data can be reported in ways similar to event recording in terms of absolute numbers versus ratios of events and time. In addition, in situations such as that

Number of Problems Attempted	Correct Answers
✓✓✓✓✓✓✓✓✓✓✓✓ ✓✓✓✓✓✓✓✓✓	✓✓✓✓✓✓✓✓✓✓ ✓✓✓✓

√ = Occurrence of an event.

FIGURE 7.2 *Example of permanent product recording.* Instead of observing a child solve each math problem on a worksheet, the worksheet can be collected at the end of the work period, and the number of problems attempted and correct answers can be recorded.

presented in Figure 7.2, a percentage can be derived from the data. That is, twenty-five problems were attempted and nineteen correctly solved, meaning that 76% of the questions were correctly answered.

Permanent product recording works best with behaviors and stimuli that have some discrete outcome that remains once the events have ended. As with event recording, this makes permanent product recording particularly useful for documenting frequency as a dimensional quantity. However, if the time at which an event is produced can be documented in some manner, it is also possible to focus on IRT or celeration.

The advantages of permanent product recording include:

• It permits noncontinuous recording of behavior and stimulus events. An observer can engage in other activities during the time when the experimental events are occurring.
• It allows the products to be inspected and permits an error pattern analysis to be conducted (see Bellamy, Horner, & Inman, 1979). Such an analysis can be used to identify the type of mistakes that are made and to provide an overall estimation of accurate performance.

The disadvantage of permanent product recording is:

• Responses and stimuli must produce a tangible by-product, otherwise the measurement technique cannot be used.

Duration Recording.   The most direct measure of the dimensional quantity, duration, is to use the measurement technique, duration. Duration recording documents the amount of time that elapses between the onset of an event and the end of the same event. Figure 7.3 shows an example of a completed data sheet used for duration recording. The figure represents the amount of time required to swim a single lap during a physical education class that required students to swim ten laps each day. The duration of each of the ten laps was recorded in Figure 7.3.

In the example from Figure 7.3, a fixed number of events were required (i.e., ten laps), and the duration of each lap was the dependent variable of interest. These data should be summarized by the central tendency of the data (i.e., mean, mode, and/or median) and some estimate of the range (i.e., absolute or relative) (see Chapter 16). For example, the mean length of a lap was 50.3 seconds (range, 47.1 to 58.6 seconds). In situations where a variable number of events can occur, it can be useful to document the base rate (i.e., the number of occurrences of the event) of events along with the average and range of durations. If an observational situation has a fixed or variable amount of time, then a percentage of the overall time an event was observed to occur can be derived. For example, talking out of turn in a mathematics class might be observed to occur during 23% of the total class time using duration recording.

The advantage of duration recording is:

• The precise estimation of the temporal extent of behaviors and stimuli can be established. This can include the amount of time each occurrence of an event lasts or the total amount of observation time a behavior occurs.

Duration (seconds) of Each Lap Swum

Lap 1 = 48.7

Lap 2 = 49.0

Lap 3 = 47.1

Lap 4 = 47.3

Lap 5 = 47.8

Lap 6 = 48.2

Lap 7 = 49.3

Lap 8 = 52.8

Lap 9 = 53.7

Lap 10 = 58.6

FIGURE 7.3 *Example of a completed data sheet used for duration recording.* The figure represents the amount of time required to swim a single lap during a physical education class that required students to swim ten laps each day.

The disadvantages of duration recording include:

- The technique requires continuous observation.
- The technique also requires the use of some type of timing device (e.g., a stopwatch).
- In situations where frequent, brief events are being recorded, this technique may be cumbersome and inaccurate.

Latency Recording. Latency recording, like duration, is closely linked to a specific dimensional quantity, in this case latency. With latency recording, the time between the onset of a stimulus or behavior and the subsequent onset of the target response is recorded. An example of data reflecting latency recording is shown in Figure 7.4 (page 102). The data sheet shows the number of seconds that elapsed between a teacher request and a student complying with the request. During the observation, six different requests were made, with a median latency to compliance of 7.15 (range, 4.8 to 45.1).

In some instances, the experimental situation may be arranged so that a fixed number of stimulus presentations is presented; in other cases, the number may be allowed to vary under naturalistic conditions. In either situation, the central tendency and some measure of variability can be reported, because the total latency (in seconds) can be divided by the number of stimulus presentations.

Latency (seconds) to Student Compliance

Request 1 = 5.3

Request 2 = 45.1

Request 3 = 12.4

Request 4 = 8.1

Request 5 = 6.2

Request 6 = 4.8

FIGURE 7.4   *Example of a completed data sheet used for latency recording.* The data sheet shows the number of seconds that elapsed between a teacher request and a student complying with the request.

The advantage of latency recording is:

• It provides an index of the temporal relation between one event and another.

The disadvantages of latency recording include:

• It requires continuous observation.
• It requires the use of some type of timing device (e.g., a stopwatch).
• If stimulus presentations are not fixed, the number of events may vary considerably from one observation to the next.
• The response of interest may have no causal relation to the stimulus presentation, and the relation between the two variables may be only correlational.

Partial-Interval Recording.   Rather than recording discrete events as they occur (as has been done with each of the previous four recording techniques), the remaining three techniques use sampling strategies to estimate the occurrence of stimuli and behaviors. That is, they divide observations into discrete intervals of time and note the occurrence or nonoccurrence of particular events. This process does not provide for an exact recording of what occurred but instead provides an approximation of what stimuli and behaviors were observed.

In the case of partial-interval recording, if an event of interest is observed to occur at any time within a specific time interval, the interval is scored as an occurrence of the stimulus or response. If the same event occurs multiple times within the interval, it is still scored simply as an occurrence. If the event of interest is not observed during the interval, then it is scored as a nonoccurrence of the stimulus or response. Figure 7.5 (left-hand panel) shows an example of partial-interval recording. In this example, one behavior was recorded (e.g., hitting another student) during the observation (left side of figure). When the behavior was observed, an X was marked in the interval box. The figure shows that eight out of ten intervals were scored as occurrences of the response, using partial-interval recording. Such an outcome would be summarized as the response having occurred during 80% of observation intervals.

The length of an interval is an important consideration when using partial-interval recording. Overall, the smaller the interval, the more accurate the estimate of the occurrence of the behavior will be (Powell, Martindale, & Kulp, 1975). To illustrate this concept, a sensitive interval would be one second. This would very accurately track when a behavior did,

Behavior	Partial	Whole	Momentary
▮	X		X
▮	X		
▮	X		X
▮	X		X
▮	X		X
▮	X	X	X
▮	X		
▮	X		
Outcome:	*80%*	*10%*	*50%*

FIGURE 7.5 *Example of partial-interval (left-hand panel), whole-interval (center panel), and momentary-interval recording (right-hand panel).* On the far left side of the figure is real-time onset and offset of the behavior being observed. When the behavior met the requirement for an occurrence, an *X* was marked in the interval box. The percentage of intervals scored is summarized at the bottom of the figure.

or did not, occur. This can be compared with a time interval of one minute. A one-minute interval would overestimate the occurrence of an event, because the event would only need to occur once in the interval to be scored as an occurrence. However, using very brief intervals (e.g., one second) would make the recording of events difficult, if not impossible. Therefore, by convention, researchers tend to use intervals that are five, ten, or fifteen seconds in length, with shorter intervals being preferable to minimize inflation of the estimated occurrence of behavior. In addition, there is an important interaction between the interval length and the duration of the event being recorded (Repp, Roberts, Slack, Repp, & Berkler, 1976). The briefer the event being analyzed, the shorter the interval should be so as not to inflate how often the behavior is occurring.

 The advantages of partial-interval recording include:

- It provides an estimate of the occurrence of behaviors and stimuli without requiring that every event be recorded.
- It does not require continuous observation.

 The disadvantages of partial-interval recording include:

- It requires some type of cueing device to signal the observer when an interval begins and ends.
- It overestimates the occurrence of the response if larger intervals are used, particularly with brief events.

Whole-Interval Recording.   A second approach to interval estimates of behaviors and stimuli is whole-interval recording. In this approach, the event of interest has to occur throughout the entire interval to be scored as an occurrence. If responding occurs for most, but not all, of the interval, the interval is scored as a nonoccurrence. An example of whole-interval recording is presented in Figure 7.5 (center panel). In relation to the behavior that occurred, the only interval in which responding was scored as occurring was for the seventh interval. Even though behaviors were observed in multiple intervals, only once was the behavior observed to occur continuously throughout an interval. The result is an estimate that behavior occurred during 10% of the intervals.

Clearly, the behavior of interest occurred more than 10% of the time during the observational period. The existence of such discrepancies is a particular concern with whole-interval recording procedures. For behaviors that occur briefly, this approach to measurement underestimates the actual occurrence of behavior. This characteristic of the procedure is exacerbated if longer intervals are chosen. So, again, with interval measurement procedures there is an interaction between the duration of behavior and interval length (Repp et al., 1976). For this reason, whole-interval recording is typically used only when the behavior and/or stimuli being observed are of long duration. Because of these limitations, whole-interval recording procedures are rarely used by researchers (Kelly, 1977).

 The advantage of whole-interval recording is:

- It can provide an estimate of the occurrence of behaviors and stimuli that have long durations without requiring that every event be recorded.

The disadvantages of whole-interval recording include:

* It requires continuous observation.
* It requires some type of cueing device to signal the observer when an interval begins and ends.
* It underestimates the occurrence of the response if larger intervals are used, particularly with brief events.

Momentary-Interval Recording.   The final type of interval recording system to be discussed is momentary-interval recording, which is also referred to as time sampling or momentary time sampling (e.g., Harrop & Daniels, 1986). Using this approach, observations only occur for a subset of an interval. Hence, only a part of (i.e., a moment) of the entire interval is observed. Typically, the nonobservational part of the interval is referred to as the "wait" component, and the observational part is referred to as the "record" component. For example, a researcher may select a ten-second interval in which there are five-second wait and five-second record components. In this instance, the observer would not observe during the first five seconds of the interval and then record the occurrence of events for the final five seconds of the interval. Most often, the record component uses a strategy similar to partial-interval recording (i.e., the event need only occur once), but it is possible to use this recording technique using a whole-interval criterion.

Figure 7.5 (right-hand panel) shows the use of a ten-second momentary-interval recording procedure with nine-second wait and one-second record components. The result was that five out of ten intervals were scored as the behavior occurring, producing an estimate of 50% of the intervals. Using momentary-interval recording, intervals of five, ten, or fifteen seconds are typically used, but intervals of thirty seconds or one minute (or more) can be used to estimate the occurrence of behavior. Typically, the longer the overall observation time, the larger the interval can be. Interacting with this is the length of the record component, which often ranges from one second for shorter intervals to fifteen seconds for longer intervals.

A particular advantage of momentary-interval recording is that one observer can record the behavior of multiple individuals during the same observation session. For example, if a researcher is using a fifteen-second interval with ten-second wait and five-second record components, then the observer could monitor up to three different students at a time. The observer could do this by observing each student for five seconds, then shifting her attention to the next student for five seconds, then observing the third student for the same time period, and then begin the process over again.

The advantages of momentary-interval recording include:

* It allows for a potentially efficient use of observer time for simultaneously recording multiple participants.
* It does not require continuous observation.

The disadvantages of momentary-interval recording include:

* It requires some type of cueing device to signal the observer when an interval begins and ends.

- It can underestimate or overestimate the occurrence of events as a function of event duration and frequency and the length of wait and record components.

Recording Medium

An issue closely related to the selection of measurement techniques is the medium used to record behavior and stimuli. After developing an observational code and selecting a measurement technique, there must be some means of capturing events in some fashion for later analysis. Typically, researchers either directly observe sessions or they record them using videotape or some other digital medium. The advantage of collecting data while directly observing the session is primarily one of efficiency. Once the session is finished, the data have already been collected and are ready for the next step, data analysis (see Part Five). The advantage of capturing the session on videotape is that the events are available for repeated analysis. This means that if the observational code needs to be altered, all sessions can be rescored using the revised protocol. In addition, because the sessions are captured for repeated viewing, more elaborate observational codes can be used. The primary disadvantages of recording sessions for later scoring are the time involved and the fact that not all events occurring in a setting can be captured with a videocamera or other device.

A related decision is whether to use a paper-and-pencil or computerized system. Paper-and-pencil systems, as the name implies, use readily available technologies to record behavior and stimuli. Advantages of paper-and-pencil systems include the ease with which they can be created and used. An alternative is to use a computer-based data acquisition program that includes software and hardware for collecting and recording information (Kahng & Iwata, 1998). Advantages of computer-based systems are (1) the ability to quickly summarize data, (2) the ability to download data onto other computers for data analysis, and (3) the ease of simultaneously recording multiple behaviors (via a keypad or keyboard). However, most instances of data collection do not require computer-based systems, and the majority of data analyses reported in published studies can be recorded using paper-and-pencil systems (see Miltenberger, Rapp, & Long, 1999).

Sampling Settings

An important decision regarding recording systems is what settings (and the behaviors and stimuli that occur within them) will be sampled for observation. There are two general types of settings in which educational research is conducted: natural settings and analogue settings. Natural settings are those settings in which the behaviors of interest are expected to occur in a student's typical life. They include home, community, and school settings in which the person lives, works, and is educated (Kennedy, 2003). Such settings are the primary goal of any applied research endeavor, because it is behavior change in a person's natural settings that is the ultimate goal of any educational research effort. However, it is often necessary to conduct a series of studies under more controlled circumstances before the findings can be extrapolated to natural settings. Such studies are often referred to as being conducted in analogue settings, although these situations can also be referred to as clinic, pull-out, or laboratory settings. In analogue settings, the goal is to reduce the number of extraneous variables that can influence behavior in order to analyze more fundamental functional relations (Wacker, 2000). If experimenters conducting research in analogue settings are successful, the end result will be a better understanding of behavior that can be used in natural settings to improve student outcomes. Currently, there is a great deal of professional and policymaker interest in extending analogue research findings to natural settings, and this process is referred to variously as research-to-practice or translational research (see Lerman, 2003; Malouf & Schiller, 1995; Nunes, Carroll, & Bickel, 2002).

As can be deduced from the previous statements, the matter of what settings need to be sampled is derived from the experimental question being addressed in a single-case analysis. If the experimental question is focused on revealing basic properties of behavior, then analogue settings are likely (but not necessarily) the preferred choice. Typically, analogue settings sample limited amounts of time and are chosen for the convenience of the researchers. For example, using brief experimental designs (Chapter 13), individual sessions may last only five or ten minutes, and as few as three or four sessions may be necessary to show a functional relation. Because the goal of research in analogue settings is the discovery of behavioral processes, the length and number of sessions are defined by how long it takes to reveal the behavioral process and demonstrate a functional relation.

In natural settings, the issue of sampling settings is more complex, and the best solution to the problem is to base your sampling procedures on the scope of experimental questions. If the experimental question focuses on learning a certain type of mathematics performance in an algebra class, then the focus of the investigation should be on solving mathematics problems in that classroom. If the experimental question addresses the generalization of mathematical problem solving, then a larger set of contexts may be appropriate. If your experimental question is one that focuses on the entire school day or behaviors that occur at home or in the community, then those environments also need to be sampled. This does not mean that these settings have to be observed all of the time, only that the observations that are conducted need to reflect what occurs in those settings.

What you choose to sample will define how broadly you can draw conclusions about your findings. This is a fundamental rule in selecting the setting(s) to be sampled in a study. An important issue is whether the settings sampled match your experimental question; what can be concluded will be limited to what settings you sample. For example, if you want to study mathematical problem solving during the school day, but you only sample behaviors from a single classroom setting, then your conclusions will be limited to behavior change observed in that single classroom setting. Any conclusion above and beyond these will only be speculation.

In addition, the amount of time sampled in the chosen settings should adequately represent the settings of experimental interest. The optimal choice is to observe the entire time period of experimental interest. If mathematical problem solving in algebra class is the focus of a study, then observing problem solving during the entire class period might be optimal. However, for instances where resources do not permit exhaustive sampling (i.e., observing the entire time period of interest), then selective sampling is necessary. A rule of thumb is that the sampling done should closely match what would be observed if an exhaustive sampling had been conducted. Ideally, this sampling strategy would be empirically demonstrated (i.e., a direct comparison would be conducted). However, when an empirical demonstration is not feasible, researchers often revert to logical argument to show that the sampling strategy was adequate to address the experimental question. The former is more convincing; the latter, more common.

Finally, a related issue is the occurrence of the responses and stimuli of interest. The amount of time sampled should allow for the responses and stimuli to occur multiple times. If the observational time frame is too restricted, then the responses and stimuli of interest will not be adequately sampled. This is typically not a concern for frequently occurring behaviors (e.g., solving mathematics problems), but it can be a significant procedural challenge when dealing with behaviors or stimuli that occur infrequently (e.g., refusing to accept a car ride from a stranger). Often, the only realistic solution to studying infrequently occurring responses and stimuli is to resort to analogue settings that can simulate the occurrence of these events to generate a rate of occurrence that is acceptable for analysis.

Training Observers

Observer errors, whether using computerized or paper-and-pencil recording systems, are the primary source of error in observational data. Because of this fact, researchers need to train observers to collect data on behaviors and stimuli with the greatest accuracy and fidelity possible. This section discusses steps that researchers can follow to help ensure that their data are collected with the greatest possible integrity.

The first step in training observers is fairly obvious. You need to identify and select individuals who can serve as data collectors. There is no specific rule about who can or cannot serve as observers, but there are some general characteristics and logistical issues that should be considered. A general set of requirements is that each observer needs to be punctual, commit the effort to learn the observational code, accept critical feedback about the quality of observations, and show the appropriate etiquette for the settings being observed. An additional positive characteristic is that the individual is willing to stay with the research team for an extended amount of time (i.e., several years) so that the effort of training novice observers is minimized. Beyond these requirements, anyone willing to serve as a research assistant can effectively collect high-quality direct observation data.

Following the selection and hiring of observers, university-approved ethics training needs to be conducted. All institutions of higher education or research institutes have an institutionally sanctioned training program for new research staff that has been approved by funding agencies (e.g., the National Institutes of Health). The training typically involves issues of confidentiality, observer etiquette, data storage and reporting, and accuracy of information.

The next step is to systematically train observers. The first requirement is that each observer memorize the observational code and the definition of each event in the code. This should be followed by discussion of examples that are positive and negative instances of events in the observational code. Once observers verbally understand the observational code, they need to be introduced to the recording system and recording medium that will be used. Often, observers practice by observing videotaped examples of the types of situations they will be observing. Typically, this entails watching a videotaped example; discussing individual occurrences of behavior and stimuli; and coming to agreement on their categorization, how the events would be physically recorded, and so on. Observers then independently and silently score the video examples. These data are analyzed using an index of interobserver agreement (see Chapter 8) to estimate the extent to which two observers are consistent with each other. Typically, training continues until a minimum of 85% interobserver agreement is reached, although the higher the agreement, the better.

At this point, observational sessions in the settings where data will be collected can be conducted. At important issue to be aware of when first entering an environment is that of observational reactivity. Reactivity stems from how people in a classroom or other educational setting change their behavior when novel observers are introduced into the situation. This change in behavior can result in spurious baseline data. Therefore, initial observations are generally considered in vivo training opportunities (i.e., nonexperimental data) to allow observers and those being observed to adapt to the data collection process.

An additional element of observer training is periodic retraining (or "recalibration"), typically using the original training materials. The reason for this retraining is to avoid what is referred to as observer drift. Observer drift occurs when, during the course of an experiment, the definitions that observers are using implicitly or explicitly change. For example, in baseline, observers may score any hand-to-head contact as an instance of self-injury, but as the experiment unfolds, what is recorded might change to only hand-to-head events that look forceful. This drift in the coding criterion would likely result in a decreased number of events being recorded, which could undesirably alter the experimental outcomes and interpretation of the data. To minimize the occurrence of observer drift, periodic retraining is conducted to help ensure that the original definitions are used throughout a study.

Recording Independent Variables

Typically, data are collected only in regard to the dependent measures used in a study. This is a necessary set of procedures that allows researchers to monitor the dependent variables of interest. However, rarely do researchers collect quantitative information on their independent variables (Gresham, Gansle, & Noell, 1993). Indeed, Gresham et al. estimated that only 9% of published studies present data on the independent variable. As was noted by Peterson, Homer, and Wonderlich (1982), "a curious double standard has developed in operant technology whereby certain variables (e.g., social behavior, smiling, and attention) routinely have operational definitions and some measure of observer reliability when the observed behavior is the target response or dependent variable, but no such rigor is applied as antecedents or consequences to the target behavior, as independent variables" (pp. 478–479). This oversight is indeed strange, given the rigor and precision that is the hallmark of single-case designs. For researchers not to measure the status of their interventions relative to changes in behavior seems an important oversight. Such measures allow for an assessment of the integrity of the independent variable during the conduct of an experiment.

The primary concern when data are not collected regarding the status of the independent variable is that the researchers cannot objectively establish the degree to which an intervention is implemented with fidelity. Without this information, we can only assume that the independent variable was implemented with precision and consistency. However, given the complexities of educational settings, this is probably a fallacious assumption. In the absence of this type of information, researchers and consumers cannot assess the degree to which variation in the dependent variable covaries with the independent variable in anything other than a binomial manner. That is, we have to follow the researchers' verbal statements that the intervention is present or absent, but we do not have data that allow measurement along a continuous scale. It would seem like the collection of data regarding the independent variable would be desirable in terms of quantitatively estimating the presence and extent of the independent variable and how dependent and independent variables covary during a study.

When researchers do collect data on their independent variables, this information is often referred to as treatment integrity, intervention fidelity, or implementation reliability data. The collection of this type of information requires several steps be taken by researchers. First, the independent variable needs to be operationally defined. Second, dimensional quantities need to be selected that adequately characterize the intervention. Third, a recording system needs to be developed to gather information regarding the independent variable. Fourth, a recording medium needs to be identified. Finally, observers need to be trained in the use of the recording system and achieve a consistent level of interobserver agreement.

An example of a study where data were collected regarding dependent and independent variables is provided by Kennedy (1994). As shown in Figure 7.6, two variables were tracked in relation to student behavior: problem behavior and social affect. In addition, two variables were tracked in relation to teacher behavior: task demands and social comments. Because task demands and social comments were the two primary elements of the independent variable, this arrangement constitutes a treatment integrity check. During baseline, task demands occurred at a consistent rate, as did the problem behaviors of Edgar, Sally, and Ernest. Positive affect (student behavior) and social comments (teacher behavior) were low during baseline. The independent variable consisted of the teacher making frequent social comments and gradually increasing the number of demands. Over time, demands were increased to baseline levels, but problem behaviors occurred at much lower rates than in baseline. This arrangement allowed for the documentation of how student and teacher behavior covaried during the study.

By documenting the degree to which an independent variable is implemented with fidelity (i.e., the degree to which it was designed to be implemented), researchers gain the ability to more closely track changes in behavior relative to implementation and withdrawal of interventions. This process allows for more definitive statements to be made regarding the interrelation between interventions and dependent measures. Not only does this allow more precise conclusions to be drawn, it also allows for the potential analysis of parametric variations in the independent variable and how they may, or may not, influence behaviors of educational interest.

Conclusion

This chapter has reviewed the basics of recording systems, one element involved in the development and use of measurement systems to estimate the occurrence of experimental events. In combination with the chapters on dimensional quantities (Chapter 6) and interobserver agreement (Chapter 8), this chapter provides the basis for gathering quantitative information regarding dependent and independent variables. Because of the importance of observational data to applied research in educational settings, the issues discussed in Part Three of this book need to be carefully adhered to. Otherwise, the data being collected, no matter how elegant they may look in graphic form (see Chapter 15), will not be of interest because they will not accurately reflect the events that were of experimental interest.

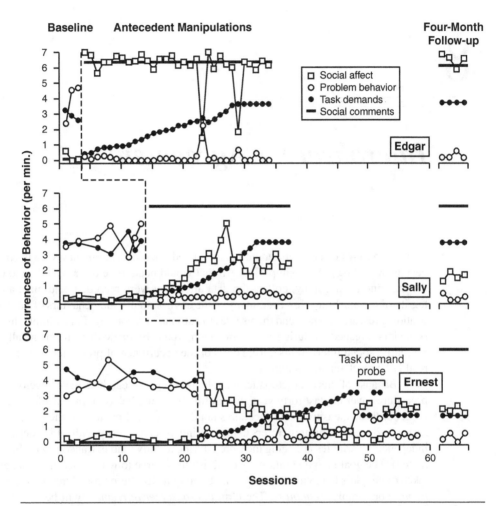

FIGURE 7.6 *Example of data collection regarding dependent and independent variables.*
Frequency of occurrence is plotted along the vertical axis, and sessions along the horizontal axis
for three students, Edgar, Sally, and Ernest. Two variables were tracked in relation to student
behavior: problem behavior and social affect. In addition, two variables were tracked in relation
to teacher behavior: task demands and social comments. Because task demands and social
comments were the two primary elements of the independent variable, this measurement
arrangement constitutes a treatment integrity check.

Source: From C. H. Kennedy, "Manipulating Antecedent Conditions to Alter the Stimulus Control of Problem
Behavior," *Journal of Applied Behavior Analysis,* 1994, *27,* fig. 2, p. 166. Copyright 1994 by the Society for the
Experimental Analysis of Behavior. Reproduced by permission.

8

Interobserver Agreement

If all recordings of behavior could be automated, then measurement issues in single-case designs would be greatly simplified. All that would need to be done would be to calibrate the machine for accuracy, collect the data after they were recorded, and maintain the integrity of the machine. However, many of the environments and behaviors of interest in educational research do not lend themselves to automated recording. For example, most of the behaviors engaged in during recess or lunch would be difficult to mechanically record. Similarly, social interactions during class or the occurrence of problem behaviors may not readily be mechanically recorded.

Because of this characteristic of applied settings, researchers have developed a set of procedures over the last forty years to carefully measure behavior in real-life settings. One aspect of these measurement procedures not discussed in Chapter 7 is the issue of *interobserver agreement*. This term refers to monitoring the consistency with which dependent and independent variables are being measured during a study (and extraneous variables, if warranted). The goal is to quantitatively establish the degree to which measures that are being taken of people's behavior are consistent. Synonyms for these procedures are *interrater reliability* or, simply, *reliability*. The term *interobserver agreement* will be used to refer to these procedures as a matter of convention; the terms are interchangable.

This chapter reviews interobserver agreement procedures, particularly as they relate to the assessment of dependent variables (although they equally apply to independent variables, see Chapter 7).

Why Collect Interobserver Agreement?

When behavior cannot be automatically recorded, researchers using single-case designs rely on human beings to score when a particular behavior occurs or does not occur. By its very nature, this process introduces unwanted variability into the measurement process. This variability takes the form of not recording with perfect consistency the occurrence or nonoccurrence of each of the variables of interest. The introduction of human error into the recording process requires that certain steps be taken by researchers to monitor and assess the types of errors that might be occurring.

Collecting interobserver agreement data allows researchers to monitor and assess the integrity with which information regarding variables is being recorded. Typically, two trained observers independently record the behaviors of interest at the same time using the same measurement procedures. The independence of those observations is important because it ensures that what is being recorded is the sole product of the person producing the recording. This independence allows for an objective comparison of how two different people capture the occurrences and nonoccurrence of behavior using the measurement system. By doing this, a researcher can estimate the degree to which two separate people using the recording procedure agree on what occurred or did not occur.

Notice the careful language that is being used in the discussion of interobserver agreement data. When discussing interobserver agreement, people use words like *agreement, reliable,* and *consistent* to describe how the data are interpreted. Researchers avoid using terms like *accuracy, exactness,* or *truthfulness.* This is because even though two individuals can independently record behavior and perfectly agree on its occurrence and nonoccurrence, they both could be equally inaccurate in their recording of behavior (Deitz, 1988). Hence, interobserver agreement data allow an assessment of the consistency with which two observers agree about the recording of behavior, but it is not a measure of the accuracy of their recordings.

For interobserver agreement data to be collected, both observers should be trained on the use of the same behavioral code and recording system. If this rather obvious criterion is met, then the independent recording of the same behavioral situation allows a researcher to assess the degree to which different observers agree. This is important for at least three reasons.

First, estimating interobserver agreement can be used as a training standard for new data recorders. After a new observer has been trained on an observational code and recording procedure, having that person record behavior at the same time as an experienced data collector allows for a quantitative index of agreement. This facilitates being able to estimate the degree to which the new observer is recording behavior in a similar manner to more experienced observers. A strategy such as this allows for a consistent standard to be established regarding when new observers have been adequately trained in observational techniques.

The second—and primary—reason to collect interobserver agreement data is to estimate how consistent data recorders are when collecting data during the experiment. This allows for an unambiguous estimation of the degree to which various observers during a study were able to use the measurement system to record behavioral events. Presenting this information to others allows them to judge the degree to which data were collected with consistency among observers. The higher the degree of interobserver agreement, the more consistent observers were in their use of the measurement system. That is, changes in the status of a variable (e.g., a dependent variable) are likely due to changes in the experimental situation (e.g., introduction of the independent variable) rather than variability introduced by different observers. This information is typically reported in the Method section of a manuscript (see Box 8.1, page 114).

A third reason to collect interobserver agreement information is to avoid observer drift. Observer drift occurs when the original definitions used by observers in a behavioral code shift during the course of a study (Kazdin, 1977). For example, the behavior, hitting head against objects, might be operationally defined as contact of a person's head with any object. However, over the course of the study, observers might begin to judge intentionality and

BOX 8.1 • *Where Do Researchers Report Interobserver Agreement Data When Publishing Their Findings?*

Occasionally, researchers mistakenly report inter-observer agreement outcomes in the Results section of a manuscript, rather than in the Method section. Along with artificially separating the interobserver agreement procedures and formulas from the resulting data, this practice also mischaracterizes what these data represent. Interobserver agreement data are not the result of an experimental analysis, like the percentage of intervals of a behavior or the duration of an event. Instead, interobserver agreement data are integrity checks on how the observational system is being used to collect information. Because of this, interobserver agreement data are procedural checks on the consistency with which the measurement system was used and are therefore not results of the study but an integral part of the procedures used to conduct the investigation. Given this observation, it is most accurate to report agreement procedures, formulas, and outcomes in a section at the end of the Method section titled Interobserver Agreement.

record precursor behaviors (e.g., moving the head toward an object) as if they were head hits. This drift in the use of the definition could seriously threaten the integrity of data being collected. To help keep observer drift from occurring, ongoing review of observational codes by observers and the collection of interobserver agreement are typically used. In addition, some researchers use videotapes of events at the start of a study for retraining observers as a means of ensuring consistency not only among observers but within observers over time.

Different Formulas for Calculating Interobserver Agreement

The previous sections of this chapter provided a general idea of what interobserver agreement is and why this type of data is collected. This section discusses various approaches to summarizing and calculating interobserver agreement data (see Page & Iwata, 1986). The review of formulas will be selective and not encompass either correlational approaches or complex statistical approaches (see Box 8.2). Instead, what will be reviewed are approaches to estimating interobserver agreement that are currently used in single-case research—that is, approaches to calculating interobserver agreement that researchers have found useful in conducting research.

Table 8.1 presents a hypothetical data set that will be used to illustrate the different approaches to calculating interobserver agreement. Data were recorded using a ten-second partial-interval recording procedure. There are ten intervals of observation present in the table. Two observers (1 and 2) independently recorded the response of interest. The first time a response was observed to occur in an interval was recorded as an *R*. In the first interval, neither observer recorded a response. In the second interval, both observers recorded the occurrence of a response. During the third interval, only observer 1 recorded the occurrence of a response, and so on. Overall, observer 1 recorded five occurrences of the response, as did observer 2.

BOX 8.2 • *Interobserver Agreement, Correlations, and Kappa*

Two additional approaches to calculating interobserver agreement are not discussed in this book, even though there are precedents for doing so. However, each is not discussed for a different reason. The first is the use of correlation coefficients (typically, Pearson product-moment coefficients) to estimate interobserver agreement. An important flaw in the use of correlation coefficients to compute interobserver agreement is that extremely high correlations can be obtained even if the observers never actually agree on an occurrence of behavior. As long as the two scores increase or decrease their estimates in a similar proportion, the correlation between what is recorded will be very high.

A second type of interobserver agreement not discussed in the text is kappa (*k*). The *k* statistic was initially developed by Cohen (1960) and suggested for use in calculating interobserver agreement by Hartmann (1977). The goal of using

k in interobserver agreement calculations is an intellectually valid one: the statistic controls for some of the base rate issues inherent in the recording of behavior. By base rate, what is meant is the probability of occurrence associated with a particular behavior. If behaviors occur very frequently (i.e., have a high base rate), the chance that two observers will randomly agree a behavior occurred is increased relative to behaviors that occur less frequently. This statistical phenomenon inflates the estimation of interobserver agreement. The *k* statistic compensates for base rate issues by introducing a correction for random agreements. Although *k* has certain merits, it is rarely reported in the research literature relating to single-case designs. Therefore, although the goals associated with the use of this statistic are meritorious, its lack of use by researchers argues against its utility in estimating interobserver agreement.

Total Agreement

A relatively straightforward way of calculating interobserver agreement is to use a total agreement approach (also known as the frequency-ratio approach). Using a total agreement strategy, a researcher sums the total number of responses recorded by each observer, divides the smaller total by the larger total, and multiplies the amount by 100%. The formula for total agreement is

$S \div L \times 100\%$ where S is the smaller total and L is the larger total

Using the data in Table 8.1 to calculate total agreement would require the following steps.

TABLE 8.1 *Hypothetical Data on the Occurrence and Nonoccurrence of a Single Response (R)*

	Ten-second Intervals									
	1	*2*	*3*	*4*	*5*	*6*	*7*	*8*	*9*	*10*
Observer 1		R	R			R		R	R	
Observer 2		R		R		R		R	R	

1. Observer 1 recorded five responses.
2. Observer 2 recorded 5 responses.
3. Since the values are equivalent, either can serve as the numerator or denominator.
4. The result of dividing 5 by 5 is 1.
5. Multiplying 1 by 100% equals 100%.

Therefore, using total agreement as an index of interobserver agreement for the data in Table 8.1 results in an outcome of 100% agreement.

A benefit of total agreement is that it is easy to conceptualize and calculate. A second benefit is that it can be used to calculate interobserver agreement in instances where observers have not accurately aligned their intervals (i.e., one observer began recording during the first interval, but the second did not begin until the third interval). A third advantage of using total agreement is that it is relatively sensitive to overall levels of responding.

With those benefits noted, however, there is an important limitation to using a total agreement approach for estimating interobserver agreement. Although this approach to interobserver agreement does provide an index of the overall occurrence of behavior, it does not provide an estimation of whether both observers ever agreed on the occurrence of individual instances of behavior. Therefore, you can arrive at high levels of agreement but have never agreed on the occurrence of a single behavior. For example, if the pattern of data collection shown in Table 8.1 during intervals 3 and 4 were repeated throughout an observational session, using total agreement as an estimate of interobserver agreement, the outcome would be 100% agreement. Clearly, this is an issue of concern in terms of interpreting what the datum actually represents.

Interval Agreement

An approach to calculating interobserver agreement that takes into account when behavior occurs is interval agreement. This approach to estimating interobserver agreement is also referred to as combined, point-by-point, or overall agreement (Kazdin, 1982). Interval agreement requires an interval or event system of measurement be used to record behavior. To calculate interval agreement, the recording of behavior is compared between the two observers on an interval-by-interval basis. If both observers recorded the response as occurring or not occurring in a particular interval, it is scored as an agreement. If one observer recorded the occurrence of a response in an interval, but the secondary observer did not, this is considered a disagreement. Then the total number of agreements is divided by the total number of agreements plus disagreements, and the sum is multiplied by 100%. The formula for interval agreement is

$$A \div A + D \times 100\% \text{ where } A \text{ is agreements and } D \text{ is disagreements}$$

This approach requires the following steps:

1. Score each interval as an agreement or disagreement.
2. Sum the number of agreements.
3. Sum the number of disagreements.

4. Divide the number of agreements by the number of agreements plus disagreements.
5. Multiply the quantity from step 4 by 100%.

Using the data from Table 8.1 would result in the following calculations: agreements were scored for eight of the intervals and disagreements were scored for two of the intervals. Dividing eight by ten results in 0.8. Multiplying this product by 100% results in an interobserver agreement score of 80%.

Clearly, interval agreement is more precise than total agreement for estimating interobserver agreement. That precision stems from the interval-by-interval basis for comparing the data. Such a procedure allows for overall estimation of how two observers scored behavior but does so based on specific time units. Because of these positive features, interval agreement has become one of the most commonly used indexes of interobserver agreement.

Interval agreement does have a drawback that relates to the base rate of behavior (see Box 8.2). Because this approach to interobserver agreement scores agreements on an interval-by-interval basis, at very high or low occurrences of a response, it may not adequately represent whether observers actually agreed on the occurrence or nonoccurrence of responding (Bijou, Peterson, & Ault, 1968). For example, if behavior was scored only once during an observation similar to Table 8.1 and the observers disagreed on its occurrence, interval agreement would still be very high (i.e., 90%). However, in this case the observers would never have agreed on the occurrence of the response. A similar inflation of the interobserver agreement index occurs when behaviors occur very frequently. Because of this concern, researchers have developed a more stringent interobserver agreement scoring strategy called occurrence/nonoccurrence agreement.

Occurrence/Nonoccurrence Agreement

An even more stringent approach to estimating interobserver agreement is to calculate interval agreement for both the occurrence and nonoccurrence of a behavior. Referred to as occurrence/nonoccurrence agreement, this approach allows for the calculating of two agreement coefficients: one for the occurrence of the response and one for the nonoccurrence of the response. This strategy does not suffer from inflation by extremely high or low rates of events because the dual reporting structure of the interobserver agreement measure allows for the separation of the occurrence and nonoccurrence of the same event (Hawkins & Dotson, 1975).

The formula for occurrence/nonoccurrence agreement is the same as interval agreement, except two separate calculations are conducted: one for the occurrence and one for nonoccurrence of behavior. Each statistic is then reported separately (cf. Johnson & Bolstad, 1973). To calculate interval agreement, one observer is designated as the primary observer (e.g., observer 1 in Table 8.1) and the other observer as the secondary observer (e.g., observer 2 in Table 8.1). To calculate occurrence agreement, each time a response is recorded by the primary observer, a check is made regarding whether the secondary observer also recorded an occurrence. If both observers scored the occurrence of a behavior, then an occurrence agreement is tallied. If observer 1 scored an occurrence and observer 2 scored a nonoccurrence, then an occurrence disagreement is tallied. The remainder of the calculation is the same as for interval agreement.

To calculate nonoccurrence agreement, each time a response is scored as not occurring by the primary observer, a check is made regarding whether the secondary observer scored the interval as a nonoccurrence. If both observers scored the nonoccurrence of a behavior, then a nonoccurrence agreement is tallied. If observer 1 scored a nonoccurrence and observer 2 scored an occurrence, then a nonoccurrence disagreement is tallied. Again, the remainder of the calculation is the same as for interval agreement.

Using this process with the data from Table 8.1, occurrence agreement would result in the following outcomes being tallied: occurrence agreement for intervals 2, 6, 8, and 9 and occurrence disagreement for interval 3. Using the interval agreement formula, we would calculate four divided by five (four plus one) multiplied by 100% equals 80%. Nonoccurrence agreement for intervals 1, 5, 7, and 10 and occurrence disagreement for interval 4. Using the interval agreement formula, we would calculate four divided by five (four plus one) multiplied by 100% equals 80%. The result would be reported as the observers obtaining 80% occurrence agreement and 80% nonoccurrence agreement for the behavior of interest.

A variation on the separate reporting of occurrence and nonoccurrence agreement outcomes was proposed by Hawkins and Dotson (1975). These authors proposed deriving a mean from the occurrence and nonoccurrence agreement outcomes (which would be 80% in our example) and using this product as an estimate of interobserver agreement. This approach is referred to as mean occurrence/nonoccurrence agreement. Although mentioned here for completeness, this approach to combining interobserver coefficients is rarely reported in the research literature.

Occurrence/nonoccurrence agreement is an increasingly common means of reporting interobserver agreement (Kelly, 1977; Page & Iwata, 1986). It is the most rigorous of the commonly used approaches to interobserver agreement and, because of this characteristic, is the preferred means of calculating interobserver agreement. Sometimes, for thoroughness, researchers will report both interval agreement (as an overall index of interobserver agreement) and occurrence/nonoccurrence agreement to fully characterize the degree to which consistency was obtained by different observers during a study.

Additional Interobserver Agreement Approaches

There are several additional approaches to calculating interobserver agreement that are used by researchers, depending on the characteristics of the dimensional quantities of behavior and recording systems being used.

Exact Agreement.   Repp, Dietz, Boles, Dietz, and Repp (1976) proposed an approach to scoring event-by-interval data referred to as exact agreement. Using this approach, a researcher scores whether two observers scored the same number of behavioral events during each interval of observation. Table 8.2 shows a hypothetical data set we will use to calculate exact agreement. To calculate exact agreement, we would use the interval agreement formula. Using the data from Table 8.2, we would score intervals 1, 2, 5, 7, 8, and 10 as agreements and intervals 3, 4, 6, and 9 as disagreements. Therefore, six divided by ten multiplied by 100% equals 60%.

TABLE 8.2 *Hypothetical Data for the Event-by-Interval Recording of a Single Response*

	Ten-second Intervals									
	1	*2*	*3*	*4*	*5*	*6*	*7*	*8*	*9*	*10*
Observer 1		3	1			6		1	2	
Observer 2		3		1		4		1	1	

Note: The number within each interval is the frequency of occurrence.

The strength of this approach to interobserver agreement is also its greatest weakness. That is, because the criterion for an agreement is so rigorous, it is difficult to obtain a satisfactory level of interobserver agreement. (For this reason, we will not discuss the possibility of creating formulas for occurrence/nonoccurrence exact agreement!)

Duration or Latency Agreement. To calculate interobserver agreement for either duration or latency data, researchers use the total agreement approach discussed previously. For example, the total duration of behavior recorded by observer 1 might equal 300 seconds and 264 seconds for observer 2, which would result in 88% interobserver agreement. Similarly, if the total latency of behavior recorded by observer 1 was 75 seconds and 84 seconds for observer 2, the result would be 89% interobserver agreement. Whether calculating duration or latency agreement using this method, the same limitations discussed previously apply and need to be taken into account when interpreting interobserver agreement outcomes.

Event or Permanent Product Agreement. As with duration or latency, when calculating event or permanent product agreement, the total agreement approach is warranted. For example, if forty-two behavioral products were scored by observer 1 and forty were scored by observer 2, then 95% interobserver agreement would be obtained. Even with its liabilities, total agreement is the most appropriate statistic to use with event or permanent product data.

Levels and Frequencies of Interobserver Agreement

So far we have been discussing why to collect interobserver agreement data and methods for calculating the estimates. At this point, it is time to examine what outcome levels are acceptable for interobserver agreement and how frequently this information needs to be gathered. Each of these concepts will be explored separately, but given their nature, an appropriate treatment of this topic requires an elaboration of how they interrelate.

Acceptable Interobserver Agreement Outcomes

Given the formulas just discussed and the various numbers derived from the calculations, the question is raised of how high these levels should be. Or, said another way, how high do the percentages have to be to be considered acceptable levels of observer consistency? The convention used in applied research is that a minimum of 80% interobserver agreement needs to be achieved. However, this is only a convention. There is no scientific justification for why 80% is necessary, only a long history of researchers using this percentage as a benchmark of acceptability and being successful in their research activities.

There are, of course, factors that make the 80% standard either too high or too low (Kazdin, 1982). When using an observational code with multiple behaviors that have complex definitions, researchers often accept slightly lower interobserver agreement outcomes. Similarly, if the environments in which observations are conducted are very complex or challenging for collecting data, lower estimates might be acceptable. The base rate of each behavior is also very important. High levels of agreement on behaviors that occur nearly continuously are not as impressive as when the same level of agreement is achieved for behaviors that occur at moderate or low rates. Each of these factors needs to be considered when weighing the acceptability of a particular interobserver agreement outcome.

Two additional factors need to be considered: (1) the type of interobserver agreement formula being used and (2) the sensitivity of behavior change relative to the independent variable. Obviously, if the same data set is considered and two agreement formulas are used that differ in the degree of stringency, there will be different interobserver agreement estimates. For example, in the previous section, for the data presented in Table 8.1, an outcome of 100% was obtained using total agreement, and an outcome of 80% resulted from using interval agreement. Therefore, it is critical that when reporting interobserver agreement data, the specific formula be reported in the text, so other researchers can judge the level obtained in relation to the statistic used to make the calculations. A final issue that requires consideration is the degree to which behavior changes from baseline to intervention. If there is a high degree of variability from one condition to the next or the level of behavior change is small across conditions, interobserver agreement outcomes will need to be higher. This is because the variability produced by the inconsistencies of observation may become greater than the effect of the independent variable.

Percentage of Observations

How many observational sessions need to have interobserver agreement data collected to adequately assess the consistency of measurement? Again, there is no scientifically defensible standard that has been arrived at. There are, however, conventions that have evolved over the last forty years of applied research using single-case designs. In general, when discussing or reporting interobserver agreement data, the overall number of sessions included for agreement checks is expressed as a percentage. The current convention is that 20% of observations is a minimal percentage and 33% is preferable.

Interactions between Levels and Frequencies of Interobserver Agreement

As should be clear by now, the collection of interobserver agreement data is a necessary and integral aspect of single-case research, and the interpretation of these data is largely based on convention. Along with the previously mentioned variables that influence how often to collect interobserver agreement data and what level should be achieved, there is one more consideration. In general, the higher the level of agreement obtained by observers, the lower the overall percentage of sessions that need to have agreement checks included. Or, stated conversely, the lower the level of agreement, the more sessions that need to be included in agreement checks. Overall, it is best to keep the purpose of interobserver agreement in mind when making decisions about how high and how often. That is, this type of data is collected to allow the researcher to estimate the consistency with which data are being collected and to use this information to arrive at an appropriate interpretation of the data that emerge from an investigation.

Conclusion

Interobserver agreement data provide an important means of assessing the consistency with which the dependent and independent variables analyzed in a study are measured. Although agreement data does not establish whether observers' recordings are veridical, interobserver agreement information does allow for an estimate of whether different individuals could use a measurement system to collect similar information. A variety of formulas can be used to collect this information, each of which varies in its level of rigor. In addition, there are a number of conventions that have developed regarding how often interobserver agreement data are gathered and what level of agreement should be obtained. However, there is no scientifically defensible standard other than to observe that the conventions allow researchers to effectively engage in research activities that are replicable by others.

Part **IV**

Design Tactics

9

A-B-A-B Designs

The previous three parts explored general approaches to experimentation, the use of single-case designs, establishing functional relations, replication, and how to define and measure behavior. This part covers the design tactics used in single-case research to establish experimental control over the dependent variable by the independent variable. To review the previous definition, single-case designs are used to demonstrate experimental control over the behavior of a single participant. This individual participant serves both as the control and experimental subject (to borrow phraseology from group comparison designs). In addition, repeated sampling of the dependent variable occurs over time to establish patterns of behavior in baseline and intervention phases.

One design tactic that is at the heart of single-case designs in both frequency of use by researchers and how experimental control is established over behavior is the A-B-A-B design. But first, a review of more rudimentary designs discussed in Chapter 3 may be helpful. The central logic for all experimentation, whether single-case design or some other approach, is the logic of planned comparisons (see Chapter 1). In general, planned comparisons take the form of two experimental conditions being compared to each other. Implicit in this definition is that some type of dependent variable is established and, at a minimum, is assessed in the presence and absence of an independent variable. Differences between the two phases can be attributed to the independent variable if certain preconditions are met.

In single-case designs, these preconditions are concisely referred to as the establishment of a functional relation. For single-case designs, all planned comparisons fall into the logic of how to arrange baseline (A) and intervention (B) conditions. In its most elemental form, all single-case designs are arrangements of A-B conditions. For example, establishing a baseline of reading fluency provides the opportunity to compare the same student's reading when she is receiving some type of intervention. However, with an A-B arrangement, attributing any differences between the two conditions to the influence of the independent variable is premature. This interpretative limitation is necessary because of possible threats to internal validity (see Chapter 3).

To control for threats to internal validity, or at least minimize the possibility that extraneous variables are influencing experimental outcomes, researchers using single-case designs use the concept of replication—or, to be precise, within-participant direct replication (see Chapter 4). That is, following an A-B sequence of experimental conditions, the researcher then reverts to the A condition to see if the original baseline pattern of behavior can be reestablished with the removal of the independent variable. If this is the case, then confidence that a functional relation is being established between independent and dependent variables increases. This type of experimental sequence is referred to as an A-B-A design.

A-B-A-B Designs

An A-B-A design is the minimal type of experimental arrangement that can establish experimental control in single-case research. However, if the experimental situation permits, researchers prefer to reintroduce the independent variable at least one more time. Such an arrangement constitutes an A-B-A-B design. Thus, when using an A-B-A-B design, the researcher begins with a baseline, introduces an intervention, returns to baseline, and then reintroduces the same intervention. If levels of the dependent variable(s) covary with the presence and absence of the independent variable, then a high degree of experimental control has been established over responding.

Researchers prefer to use A-B-A-B designs instead of A-B-A designs for at least two reasons. First, the A-B-A-B design allows for two separate instances of replication. The first possible replication occurs when the baseline is reintroduced (i.e., A-B-A). If successful, the baseline pattern of responding is reestablished following the removal of the independent variable. The second replication occurs when the intervention is reintroduced (i.e., A-B-A-B). Again, if successful, the initial experimental effect is reestablished for a second time. This A-B-A-B arrangement allows for the replication of both baseline patterns of behavior and intervention effects.

A second reason that researchers prefer using A-B-A-B designs to A-B-A designs is the applied nature of educational research. By its definition, applied behavior analysis focuses on "applications of the experimental analysis of behavior to problems of social importance" (inside front cover, *Journal of Applied Behavior Analysis,* vol. 1 to present). Implicit in this statement is that researchers are focusing on instances in which a person is faced with a situation in which they and/or others are distressed because of the occurrence of too many or too few behaviors. Therefore, if an intervention improves this problematic situation, it is ethically appropriate to end a study in a manner that permits the participant to receive the most beneficial intervention (i.e., A-B-A-B).

An example of an A-B-A-B design is presented in Figure 9.1 (page 126). In this study by Gillat and Sulzer-Azaroff (1994), the effect of a school principal's behavior on the classroom teaching practices of educators were studied. The dependent variable was comprised of three sets of practices that principals can engage in that improve educators' performances: goal setting, nonverbal (written) feedback, and praise (see Daniels, 1989; Sulzer-Azaroff & Mayer, 1991). Baseline consisted of the principal visiting the educators' classrooms as typically would occur during her daily administrative duties. The independent variable was comprised of having a consultant train the principal in organizational behavior management skills, having the principal implement a self-monitoring system, and having the experimenters provide her with daily feedback regarding her performance (see Hayes et al., 1985, regarding why self-monitoring systems work). During the initial baseline,

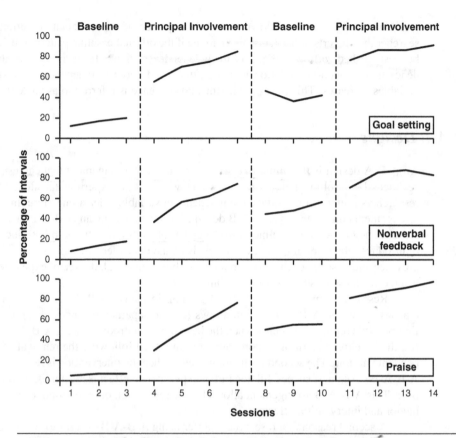

FIGURE 9.1 *Example of an A-B-A-B design.* The effect of a consultant's intervention on the performance feedback provided by a school principal to educators was explored using an A-B-A-B design. The vertical axis represents the percentage of intervals in which the principal used goal setting, nonverbal feedback, or praise when interacting with her educators. The intervention was comprised of having the consultant train the principal in organizational behavior management skills, having her implement a self-monitoring system, and having the experimenters provide her with daily feedback regarding her performance.

Source: From A. Gillat and B. Sulzer-Azaroff, "Promoting Principals' Managerial Involvement in Instructional Improvement," *Journal of Applied Behavior Analysis,* 1994, *27,* fig. 1, p. 120. Copyright 1994 by the Society for the Experimental Analysis of Behavior. Reproduced by permission.

the principal infrequently engaged in the target behaviors. During the initial intervention phase, she increased her use of goal setting, nonverbal feedback, and praise. The principal's performance feedback then decreased when the intervention was withdrawn (see Box 9.1), generally replicating the previous baseline. Then, when the independent variable was rein-troduced, her performance improved a second time. The result was the establishment of a functional relation between the principal's performance feedback and the consultant's in-tervention using an A-B-A-B design.

A second example of an A-B-A-B design is provided by Lancioni et al. (2002) and is shown in Figure 9.2. The behavior of interest was the activation of an optic microswitch to

BOX 9.1 • *Do We Reverse or Withdraw Independent Variables?*

A recurrent theme in this book is the precise use of language to minimize ambiguity or miscommunication. Using words that imply something that is not present can be misleading and result in the misinterpretation of research findings. However, adding to the difficulty in language use is that multiple terms are often used synonymously in a particular field of research, even though their dictionary meanings imply different things. Such is the case with the language relating to A-B-A-B designs. In particular, two terms are often used synonymously to refer to the act of moving from the B to A phases of the design. Those terms are reversal and withdrawal. It is common to read a passage such as "a reversal of the intervention to baseline was conducted." Equally common are phrases such as "the intervention was withdrawn and the proce-

dures returned to baseline." There is a historical distinction in the use of the two terms in relation to A-B-A-B designs. The term *reversal* was initially used by Baer, Wolf, and Risley (1968) in reference to the effect on behavior that occurs when the independent variable is removed. That is, levels of the behavior should reverse to baseline patterns of responding. However, Leitenberg (1973) noted that the term *withdrawal* was more accurate, because it described the procedural act of removing the intervention without presuming that a change in behavior will occur. Whatever their histories and distinctions are, currently both terms are used interchangeably when describing A-B-A-B designs, even though they imply slightly different meanings. Apparently, this distinction is more academic than practical.

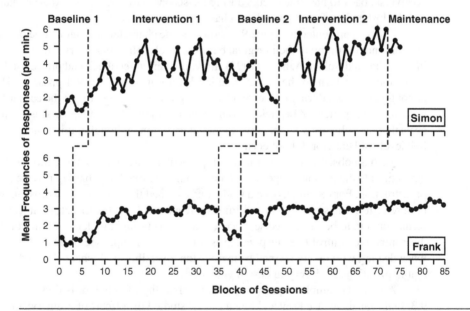

FIGURE 9.2 *Example of an A-B-A-B design.* The behavior of interest was the activation of an optic microswitch to communicate the choices of a student with severe multiple disabilities. Two students participated: Simon and Frank. Multiple observational sessions, lasting ten minutes each, occurred per day.

Source: From G. E. Lancioni, N. N. Singh, M. F. O'Reilly, D. Oliva, S. Baccani, and A. Canevaro, "Using Simple Hand-Movement Responses with Optic Microswitches with Two Persons with Multiple Disabilities," *Research and Practice for Persons with Severe Disabilities,* 2002, *27,* fig. 1, p. 278. Copyright 2002 by TASH. Reproduced by permission.

communicate the choices of a student with severe multiple disabilities. Two students participated: Simon and Frank. Multiple observational sessions, lasting ten minutes each, occurred per day. Initial baseline observations showed that behaviors occurred approximately once per minute. When systematic instruction was used as an intervention, Simon's microswitch use increased to 3.7 responses per minute (rpm) and Frank's switch use increased to 2.6 rpm. Without the intervention, both responses decreased in frequency during the second baseline phase. During the second intervention phase, Simon and Frank's communication increased to 4.5 and 2.8 rpm, respectively. The results of Lancioni et al.'s use of the A-B-A-B design demonstrated that students with the most significant disabilities can learn to use augmentative communication systems if provided with systematic instruction.

Reversibility of Behavior

An important design issue when using A-B-A-B designs is whether the behavior change produced during the initial B phase will return to baseline levels during the second A phase. This issue has been referred to the reversibility of behavior (Sidman, 1960). Because the logic of an A-B-A-B design is predicated on behavior changing from the first baseline to the first intervention phase and then changing back to baseline levels during the second baseline, reversibility of behavior is critical to the integrity of this experimental design. If no reversal back to baseline occurs during the second baseline phase, experimental control may be lost and no functional relation has been demonstrated.

The data presented in Figure 9.1 showed some characteristics indicative of dependent variables not returning to their original baseline levels following intervention. Specifically, in the Gillat and Sulzer-Azaroff (1994) study, nonverbal feedback and praise used by principals did not return to the initial baseline level during the second phase B. However, although behaviors during the second baseline phase were higher than the earlier baseline, a change in the pattern of behavior was observed from the B to A phases. This strongly suggests that the behavior was sensitive to the intervention, although a full return to the baseline levels of behavior did not occur.

Such an observation is not unusual, particularly when the intervention introduces a new skill into the person's repertoire. Once a skill is learned, it is hard to reverse the effects of instruction. For example, once a student has learned that the written words *cat* and *kissa* both refer to felines in English and Finnish, respectively, it is difficult to unlearn this information. Or, to be more precise, once a behavior is brought under stimulus control, such discriminative control over responding is difficult to disrupt (see Sidman, 1994). Hence, when dealing with newly learned behaviors, the reversibility of what is learned has important implications for how you design your study.

A second example of problems with reversibility of behavior is illustrated in Figure 9.3. In this analysis, De Prey and Sugai (2002) studied the effects of a supervision and precorrection intervention on the problem behaviors of a class of sixth-graders. The classroom management strategy was studied in relation to the percentage of intervals in which minor behavioral infractions occurred during the social studies class. During the initial baseline phase, De Prey and Sugai documented consistently high levels of minor behavior problems (range, 89 to 100% of sessions). The intervention reduced these occurrences to approximately 50% of intervals by the tenth through thirteenth sessions. When the intervention was

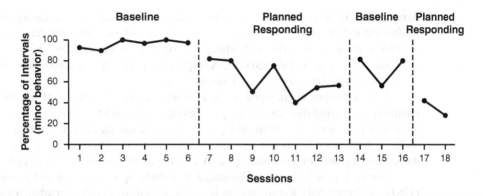

FIGURE 9.3 *Example of an A-B-A-B design.* The focus of the study was the effects of a supervision and precorrection intervention on the problem behaviors of a class of sixth-graders. The classroom management strategy was studied in relation to the percentage of intervals in which minor behavioral infractions occurred during the social studies class.

Source: From R. L. De Prey and G. Sugai, "The Effect of Active Supervision and Precorrection on Minor Behavioral Incidents in a Sixth-Grade General Education Classroom," *Journal of Behavioral Education,* 2002, *11*, fig. 1, p. 261. Copyright 2002 by Human Sciences Press. Reproduced by permission.

withdrawn, behavior problems in the classroom became more variable than during the final sessions of the first intervention phase, but the behaviors did not return to baseline levels and substantially overlapped with the previous intervention phase. However, when the classroom management techniques were reintroduced, clear decreases in minor behavior problems were observed.

The data in Figure 9.3 highlight two issues that should be considered in the use of A-B-A-B designs. First is the issue of reversibility. In the De Prey and Sugai study, the reversal in the pattern of behavior during the second baseline was modest. In fact, their experimental control relied primarily on the changes in behavior that occurred during the first intervention and the precipitous drop in behavior that occurred during the second intervention phase. This means that two data points (sessions 17 and 18) are the primary basis for claiming experimental control. This observation raises the second consideration. When behaviors only partially reverse in an A-B-A-B experiment, it is often more convincing if additional baseline and intervention phases are conducted. This additional direct replication of an experimental effect is referred to as A-B-A-B-A-B design (depending on the number of phase repeats). Given the experimental results displayed in Figure 9.3, additional repeats would have added to the believability that the intervention was the primary source of behavioral control.

B-A-B Designs

In some instances when a researcher seeks to conduct an experiment in educational settings, an intervention may already be in place. This might occur because an innovative teacher has developed an intervention that appears to be effective and wants to test this hypothesis following the initial intervention. In other instances, an intervention may have been implemented prematurely with the establishment of experimental control only possible by using a variant of the A-B-A-B design type. A single-case design that is particularly effective in instances such as these is the B-A-B design.

B-A-B designs begin when an intervention has already been implemented. Experimental control using this type of design relies on the dependent variable being sensitive to the withdrawal or reversal of the independent variable during the B to A phase change. In addition, behavioral levels need to change again when the intervention is reintroduced in the second B phase. In this sense, the B-A-B is the inverse of the A-B-A design.

Use of a B-A-B design is illustrated in a study by Robinson, Newby, and Ganzell (1981) (see Figure 9.4). Robinson et al. began their analysis of behavior when a token economy had been established to increase the number of classroom assignments completed by students with behavior problems. During the initial intervention phase, students completed an average of thirty-five assignments per day. When the intervention was withdrawn, the average number of completed assignments decreased to four per day. Replicating the previous intervention effect, assignment completion increased to forty per day during the second intervention phase. This B-A-B analysis demonstrated that the academic performance of the students was better when a token economy was used by the classroom teacher, relative to no token economy being used.

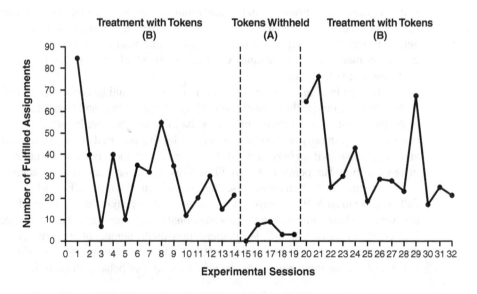

FIGURE 9.4   *Example of a B-A-B design.* The study explored the effects of a token economy system on the number of classroom assignments completed by students with behavior problems.

Source: From P. W. Robinson, T. J. Newby, and S. L. Ganzell, "A Token System for a Class of Underachieving Hyperactive Children," *Journal of Applied Behavior Analysis,* 1981, *14,* fig. 1, p. 311. Copyright 1981 by the Society for the Experimental Analysis of Behavior. Reproduced by permission.

A second example of using a B-A-B design comes from the work of Pace and Toyer (2000). In this clinical example (see Figure 9.5), the authors were presented with the case of a girl with severe disabilities whose parents had started her on an iron and multivitamin nutritional intervention. The girl's case was referred to the clinic because she emitted a behavior referred to as pica (i.e., eating indigestible objects), which can be life threatening. Her parents reported significant improvements in the girl's pica since they had begun the vitamin therapy. When Pace and Toyer assessed the occurrence of pica during the initial B phase, very few instances of pica were observed. When the multivitamin component of the intervention was removed and the girl again was assessed in the clinic, she engaged in more instances of pica. This effect was reversed when the multivitamin was again given to her on a regular basis. Using a B-A-B design, Pace and Toyer provided provocative evidence that nutritional issues may be related to some cases of pica.

When using B-A-B designs, an additional baseline can be added to further replicate findings (i.e., B-A-B-A). Such direct replications can further increase the believability that a functional relation has been established between dependent and independent variables. If this pattern of direct replication is continued (e.g., B-A-B-A-B), then the B-A-B design begins to acquire many of the properties of the A-B-A-B design. A primary limitation of the B-A-B design is that there is no initial baseline pattern of behavior. This limits a researcher's ability to make statements about how the intervention impacted the previous

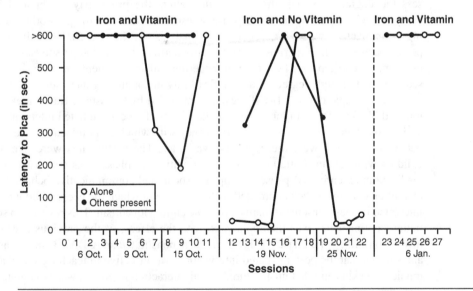

FIGURE 9.5 *Example of a B-A-B design.* The study focused on the effects of a multivitamin nutritional supplement on the occurrence of pica. The dependent variable was the latency to the first occurrence of pica, which was studied when an adult was present or absent.

Source: From G. M. Pace and E. A. Toyer, "The Effects of a Vitamin Supplement on the Pica of a Child with Severe Mental Retardation," *Journal of Applied Behavior Analysis,* 2000, *33,* fig. 1, p. 621. Copyright 2000 by the Society for the Experimental Analysis of Behavior. Reproduced by permission.

pattern of behavior. That is, there is no evidence that the behavior was problematic prior to intervention, although if experimental control is demonstrated, behavior is worsened during the subsequent baseline phase. With this interpretative limitation of B-A-B designs noted, they are useful in situations where the analysis of previously implemented interventions are of interest to educational researchers.

A-B-C and Associated Designs

An important variation of the A-B-A-B design is the A-B-C and associated designs. In the A-B-C design, an additional condition is added to the A-B-A-B analysis. That is, the C element in the A-B-C design provides the researcher with an additional opportunity to analyze how various interventions influence behavior. For example, using the principal feedback study discussed previously, we could extend this analysis by adding a written-feedback-only phase, provide the feedback only once a week, or assess the effects of a system that was Internet based. If any one of these additional analyses had been added to the Gillett and Sulzer-Azaroff (1994) study, there would have been a C phase of the experimental design.

What makes A-B-C-B designs of particular interest to researchers is the opportunity to move beyond demonstration experiments, which are typically the focus of A-B-A-B designs. That is, contrasting a baseline with an intervention phase allows a researcher to assess the degree to which the intervention alters the previously established baseline. However, with the addition of a C phase, a researcher now has the possibility of conducting component, parametric, or comparative analysis (see Chapter 5). Not only can a single person be used as the experimental and control participant, but that person can also be used as a contrast participant. These types of experimental arrangements provide single-case researchers with a high degree of tactical flexibility in conducting analyses.

An example of an A-B-C-B design is provided by Goldstein, Kaczmarek, Pennington, and Shafer (1992). Figure 9.6 show the results of a peer-mediated intervention analysis by Goldstein and colleagues. The frequency with which communicative acts and social behaviors occurred were the dependent variables. The participants were five preschool children with autism. Initially, a baseline condition (A phase) was contrasted with peer-mediated intervention (B phase) to improve social and communicative behavior. This intervention phase was then contrasted with a C phase in which the peers without disabilities interacted in a less structured manner with the child with autism. This reversal in social initiation contingencies was then compared with the effects of the previous peer-mediated instruction strategy (B phase). This arrangement constituted an A-B-C-B single-case design and showed that the peer-mediated intervention was effective in teaching social and communicative skills and that unstructured social interaction in groups was not enough to produce these results.

Such an A-B-C-B arrangement of experimental conditions allows certain conclusions to be drawn but also limits the ability to draw other conclusions. The A-B-C-B design permits strong statements about possible functional relations between the B-C-B components of the study. This is because the effects that might occur from changing from the B to C phase are replicated by returning to the B phase. The general logic is the same as an A-B-A or B-A-B design. However, less can be said about the relation between A and B

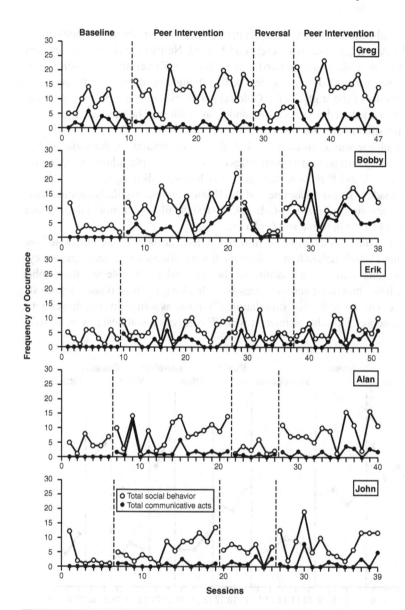

FIGURE 9.6 *Example of an A-B-C-B design.* The frequency with which communicative acts and social behaviors occurred were the dependent variables. The participants were five preschool children with autism. Initially, a baseline condition (A phase) was contrasted with peer-mediated intervention (B phase) to improve social and communicative behavior. This intervention phase was then contrasted with a C phase in which the peers without disabilities interacted in a less structured manner with the child with autism.

Source: From H. Goldstein, L. Kaczmarek, R. Pennington, and K. Shafer, "Peer-Mediated Intervention: Attending to, Commenting on, and Acknowledging the Behavior of Preschoolers with Autism," *Journal of Applied Behavior Analysis,* 1992, *25,* fig. 2, p. 297. Copyright 1992 by the Society for the Experimental Analysis of Behavior. Reproduced by permission.

phases, since no replication of the A phase occurs. In addition, the ability to draw conclusions between the A and C phases is severely constrained. Neither the A or C phases were replicated, nor were they directly compared with each other. Therefore, when using an A-B-C-B design or its associated designs, a great deal of thought needs to be employed when interpreting the results of the study. In the Goldstein et al. example, the primary comparison is between peer-mediated and reversal conditions, with less interpretative emphasis placed on other possible juxtapositions.

There are multiple variations on the A-B-C design. Depending on the variation produced, a different set of interpretative possibilities occur. For example, adding an additional comparison between A and B phases, such as in a A-B-C-B-A-B design, permits clearer statements to be made regarding baseline and the B intervention. Similarly, adding additional A and C phases, such as in a A-B-C-B-A-C-A design, allows for more interpretation of the relation between the baseline and C phases.

Figure 9.7 provides an example of how the A-B-C design can be elaborated on. Kennedy and Souza (1995) studied how various conditions influenced the self-injurious eye poking of a young man with severe disabilities. Their dependent variable was the number of eye pokes per hour, measured across successive school days. Three phases were compared: (1) baseline with no additional stimulation, (2) music as a stimulus to interact with, and (3) a videogame as a stimulus to interact with. The experimental design was an A-B-

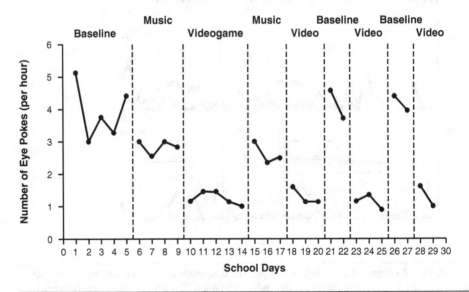

FIGURE 9.7   *Example of an A-B-C-B-C-A-C-A design.* The dependent variable was the number of eye pokes per hour, measured across successive school days. Three phases were compared: (1) baseline with no additional stimulation, (2) music as a stimulus to interact with, and (3) a videogame as a stimulus to interact with.

Source: From C. H. Kennedy and G. Souza, "Functional Analysis and Treatment of Eye Poking," *Journal of Applied Behavior Analysis,* 1995, *28,* fig. 3, p. 33. Copyright 1995 by the Society for the Experimental Analysis of Behavior. Reproduced by permission.

C-B-C-A-C-A-C arrangement. Eye poking was highest in baseline, lowest in the videogame condition, and at a moderate level in the music condition. Because replicated comparisons were conducted for various pairing of phases (i.e., B versus C, and A versus C), statements could be made about functional relations between each of the first two phases analyzed and the C phase.

In addition to the many permutations of A, B, and C phases that can be arranged, additional phases can also be added to the A-B-A-B design logic. For example, D and E phases could added to extend the analytical scope of a study, permitting even more comparisons among independent variables. However, there is a limit to how elaborate such a design can be. For meaningful comparisons to be made among all conditions, the addition of each new phase must produce a multiplicative effect on the number of comparisons that can be conducted. Because of this feature of A-B-C-B designs, the use of too many additional phases to the analysis can render the experimental design intractable.

Strengths and Limitations

A-B-A-B designs are an extension of A-B-A designs. A-B-A-B designs allow researchers to compare two conditions within a single individual. The number of replications conducted is primarily a function of the clarity of the data. In some instances, an A-B-A-B sequence is sufficient; in other conditions, an A-B-A-B-A-B sequence (or more repeats) may be necessary to demonstrate a functional relation. B-A-B designs, a variant of the A-B-A-B design, can be used to demonstrate the effects of a previously established intervention. In addition, this design type allows for the comparison of additional phases, using A-B-C and associated designs. Because of this flexibility, the A-B-A-B single-case design is frequently used by researchers.

There are, however, some limitations of this design type. First, if a behavior is not reversible, an A-B-A-B design is not appropriate (see Box 9.1). For instances in which behavior change is not reversible, researchers typically opt for another single-case design, such as the multiple baseline (Chapter 11) or repeated acquisition designs (Chapter 12). Second, if reversal of the behavior to baseline levels is deemed unacceptable because of the risks involved, a multiple baseline design is preferred over an A-B-A-B or other types of single-case designs. Finally, if a large number of conditions need to be compared or multiple repeats of a smaller number of conditions are necessary, then A-B-A-B designs may become intractable, particularly in educational settings. In these instances, researchers typically use multielement (Chapter 10) or brief experimental designs (Chapter 14).

10

Multielement Designs

In this chapter, we discuss the use of multielement designs in single-case research. More than any other type of single-case design tactic, the multielement design has had a diverse set of nomenclature attached to it. Terms referring to this design type have included alternating treatments design (Barlow & Hayes, 1979; Barlow & Hersen, 1984), multielement design (Sidman, 1960; Ulman & Sulzer-Azaroff, 1975), multiple schedule design (Agras, Leitenberg, Barlow, & Thomson, 1969; Hersen & Barlow, 1976; Leitenberg, 1973), multitreatment design (Kazdin, 1982), and simultaneous treatment design (Browning, 1967; Kazdin & Geesey, 1977). As is discussed in Box 10.1, most of these terms are not accurate or only refer to a subset of designs discussed in this chapter. Therefore, multielement designs will be used to refer to this design tactic because of its historical precedence, technical accuracy, and inclusiveness.

Chapter 9 explored the gradual alternation between A and B phases of a study as a means of establishing experimental control. These A-B-A-B designs can be used to develop functional relations under a range of circumstances. However, one limitation of A-B-A-B design and its variants makes other single-case designs, such as the multielement design, a desirable alternative. Specifically, A-B-A-B designs become intractable when a range of conditions need to be experimentally analyzed. An advantage of designs such as multielement designs is that they make the comparison of multiple conditions feasible.

Multielement Designs

Multielement designs alternate between conditions as a means of demonstrating experimental control. In particular, these designs rely on response differentiation between or among conditions to establish a functional relation. That is, in at least two of the conditions being analyzed, responding needs to occur at distinctly different levels to demonstrate a functional relation. In its most simplified arrangement, a multielement design could be used to study the effects of two conditions—baseline (A) and intervention (B)—on behavior. Using this design approach, a researcher would then alternate between the A and B conditions from session to session. This rapid alternation between conditions is then analyzed to assess whether levels of

BOX 10.1 • *Various Names and Meanings for Multielement Designs*

Multielement designs have been referred to using a variety of terms, some more accurate than others. The term *multielement design* was actually coined by basic researchers working in operant laboratories during the 1950s, and the term was codified in Sidman's *Tactics of Scientific Research,* which described research practices in the experimental analysis of behavior during this time period. Because of this history, Ulman and Sulzer-Azaroff (1975) used the term *multielement design* to introduce applied researchers to this novel experimental tactic. However, at the same time, other applied researchers were developing new designs, some very similar to multielement designs, and were naming them within the contexts of their own research efforts. This resulted in terms such as *alternating treatments designs, multiple-schedule designs, multitreatment designs,* and *simultaneous treatment designs.* However, the use of *multielement designs* has persisted and is the preferred term in contemporary single-case research because it is more encompassing and accurate than the other terms. For example, *multiple-schedule designs* actually refers to the use of a multiple schedule of reinforcement that requires alternation between distinct reinforcement contingencies and discriminative stimuli (see Ferster & Skinner, 1957), something that does not apply to all multielement designs. Similarly, *simultaneous treatments designs* refers to choice procedures that allow participants to select which interventions they experience. In contemporary parlance, such designs are part of what is referred to as *concurrent operant designs* (see Chapter 14). Because a range of single-case designs can be used to compare multiple treatments, the term *multitreatment design* has been viewed as too vague. The term *alternating treatments design* has a somewhat more complex history and will be discussed in a later subsection of this chapter. So, although some readers may disagree, this text has adopted the use of *multielement designs* as the preferred term for this type of single-case design.

behavior under each of the two conditions are differentiated. If response differentiation occurs between the A and B conditions, then a functional relation has been demonstrated.

An example of the use of multielement designs is provided by Heckaman, Alber, Hooper, and Heward (1998), who studied the number of disruptive behaviors emitted by Jimmy, a child with autism (see Figure 10.1, page 138). The two conditions compared instruction on easy tasks (A) versus difficult tasks (B). The researchers switched between the two conditions a total of six times. The result was a pattern of disruptive behavior consistently higher during the difficult task condition when compared to the easy task condition. The results suggest that Jimmy's problem behavior was associated with task difficulty. Such a design allows for multiple direct replications of the experimental effect within a participant over a brief period of time.

Figure 10.2 (page 138) shows a more elaborate multielement design. In this study by Taylor, Alber, and Walker (2002), three different conditions were analyzed. The dependent variable of interest was the reading comprehension of students with learning disabilities. The first condition, self-questioning, required students to answer a set of prescribed questions after reading a passage. The second condition, story mapping, had students draw a graphic representation of what they had just read in a passage. The third condition, no intervention, required students to read the passage with no supplemental aids. These different reading conditions were alternated across days. The data show that the highest number of test questions answered correctly were in the self-questioning condition, followed by the story mapping condition, and no intervention condition.

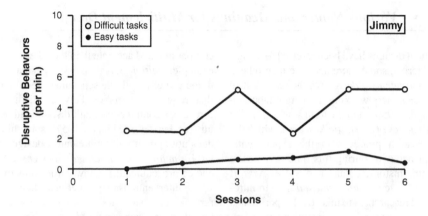

FIGURE 10.1   *Example of basic multielement design.* The graph is arrayed as the number of disruptive behaviors per minute for a child with autism (*y*-axis). The two conditions compared instruction on difficult tasks versus easy tasks. The researchers switched between the two conditions a total of six times (*x*-axis).

Source: From K. A. Heckaman, S. Alber, S. Hooper, and W. L. Heward, "A Comparison of Least-to-Most Prompts and Progressive Time Delay on the Disruptive Behavior of Students with Autism," *Journal of Behavioral Education,* 1998, *8,* fig. 1, p. 187. Copyright 1998 by Human Sciences Press. Reproduced by permission.

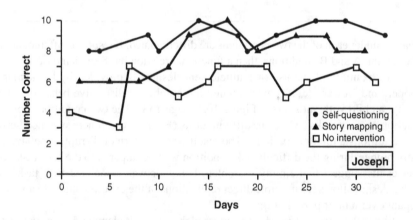

FIGURE 10.2   *Example of multielement design.* The dependent variable of interest was the reading comprehension of students with learning disabilities (vertical axis). The first condition, self-questioning, required students to answer a set of prescribed questions after reading a passage. The second condition, story mapping, had students draw a graphic representation of what they had just read in a passage. The third condition, no intervention, required the student to read the passage with no supplemental aids. These different reading conditions were alternated across days (horizontal axis).

Source: From L. K. Taylor, S. R. Alber, and D. W. Walker, "The Comparative Effects of a Modified Self-Questioning Strategy and Story Mapping on the Reading Comprehension of Elementary Students with Learning Disabilities," *Journal of Behavioral Education,* 2002, *11,* fig. 1, p. 79. Copyright 2002 by Human Sciences Press. Reproduced by permission.

Another example of a multielement design is shown in Figure 10.3. In this study by Iwata, Dorsey, Slifer, Bauman, and Richman (1982/1994), the self-injurious behaviors of children with developmental disabilities were studied to identify possible reinforcers maintaining the behavior. Four distinct conditions were analyzed: (1) removal of task demands contingent on self-injury (academic), (2) no interaction or other stimulation (alone), (3) adult attention contingent on self-injury (social disapproval), and (4) an enriched environment with toys and adult attention (play). Figure 10.3 shows that each of the four children's self-injury displayed a different pattern across conditions. For child 1, self-injury occurred only in the academic condition. For child 2, the pattern of self-injury is largely undifferentiated. The self-injury of child 4 was highest during the alone condition, and the behavior of child 5 was highest during the social disapproval condition. Using this multielement design, Iwata et al. were able to demonstrate that each child's self-injury had a distinct set of

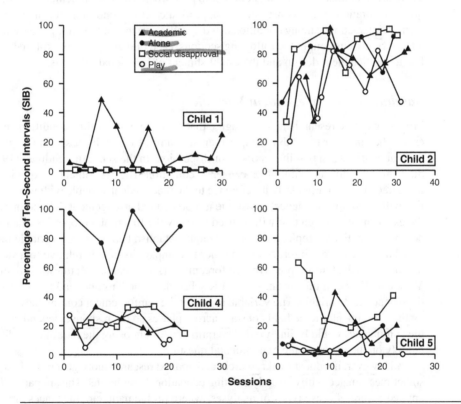

FIGURE 10.3 *Example of multielement design.* The figure shows percentage of intervals with self-injurious behaviors (y-axis) across sessions (x-axis). Four distinct conditions were analyzed: (1) removal of task demands contingent on self-injury (academic), (2) no interaction or other stimulation (alone), (3) adult attention contingent on self-injury (social disapproval), and (4) an enriched environment with toys and adult attention (play).

Source: From B. A. Iwata, M. F. Dorsey, K. J. Slifer, K. E. Bauman, and G. S. Richman, "Toward a Functional Analysis of Self-Injury," *Journal of Applied Behavior Analysis,* 1994, *27,* fig. 2, p. 205. Reprinted from *Analysis and Intervention in Developmental Disabilities,* 1982, vol. 2, pp. 3–20. Copyright 1994 by the Society for the Experimental Analysis of Behavior. Reproduced by permission.

conditions under which it occurred, suggesting that each child's behavior might need an individually tailored intervention plan.

Each of the experiments just reviewed used a multielement design to establish a functional relation within a single participant. Although each experiment used different dependent measures and studied different experimental conditions, all shared features common to multielement designs. Each set of authors identified distinct experimental conditions, alternating among them from session to session, and observed the degree of response differentiation that resulted. This general set of requirements forms the basis of multielement designs.

Tactical Issues and Multielement Designs

There are a number of issues that come into play when using multielement designs that require elaboration. What constitutes an appropriate set of conditions for analysis, how to identify interactions among conditions, and specific variants of the multiple baseline design all deserve discussion. In the following sections, each of these issues is explored as they relate to multielement design and the establishment of functional relations.

Baseline versus Independent Variables

Most single-case researchers would agree that some type of baseline condition needs to be established in order to establish experimental control. But, as discussed in Chapters 3 and 5, what constitutes a baseline is open for discussion. In the sense that Sidman (1960) used the term, a baseline is an initial experimental condition. The experimenter explicitly defines its characteristics, particularly in reference to the independent variable with which the baseline will be compared. Hence, a baseline is a procedural arrangement defined in relation to the experimental design that will be used to study the functional properties of an independent variable. For example, a researcher might establish behavior on a variable ratio (VR) schedule of positive reinforcement in order to compare its effects relative to a variable interval (VI) schedule of positive reinforcement (see Catania, Matthews, Silverman, & Yohalem, 1977). In this instance, the VR schedule is the baseline, and the VI schedule is the independent variable. The variable aspect of the reinforcement contingency was chosen by the experimenter to be held constant across phases so the response-dependent nature of the contingency could be analyzed. The rationale for choosing the baseline condition rests entirely on the nature of the experimental question.

However, in educational research, and applied research more generally, baselines are sometimes equated with currently existing educational conditions. This, in part, reflects the applied nature of these types of analyses, where problematic circumstances are often the starting point to test an intervention. Nonetheless, this does not imply that baselines are a priori the currently existing situation. Instead, what constitutes an appropriate baseline is directly referenced to the experimental question and the hypothesis being studied. If a demonstration question (Chapter 5) is of experimental interest, then a preexisting baseline (e.g., poor classroom teaching practices) may be appropriate to show that the intervention improves behavior. If other types of experimental questions are being asked (e.g., comparative, component, or parametric), an appropriate baseline condition may be constituted by some other arrangement.

An example of what is an appropriate baseline can be illustrated by a study focusing on the on-task behavior of three students with attention deficit hyperactivity disorder. Flood, Wilder, Flood, and Masuda (2002) used six different conditions in a multielement design to better understand what conditions increased or decreased on-task behavior (see Figure 10.4). None of the conditions selected by Flood et al. was a "typical" classroom arrangement. Instead, these authors selected a set of conditions that they hypothesized

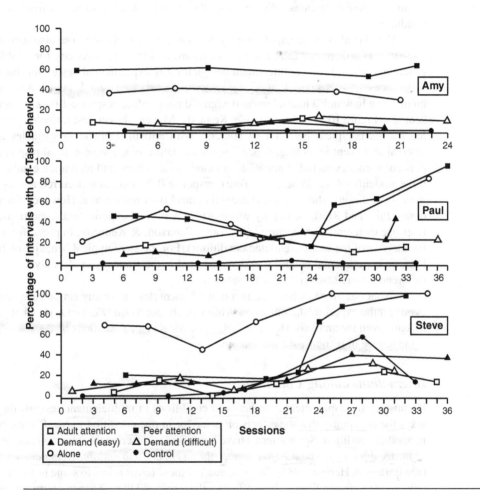

FIGURE 10.4 *Example of determining baseline.* The figure shows analysis of off-task behavior for three students with attention deficit hyperactivity disorder (Amy, Paul, and Steve). The dependent variable was the percentage of intervals with off-task behavior. Six independent variables were included in the analysis (i.e., adult attention, being alone, control, difficult demands, easy demands, and peer attention conditions).

Source: From W. A. Flood, D. A. Wilder, A. L. Flood, and A. Masuda, "Peer-Mediated Reinforcement plus Prompting as Treatment for Off-Task Behavior in Children with Attention Deficit Hyperactivity Disorder," *Journal of Applied Behavior Analysis,* 2002, *35,* fig. 1, p. 202. Copyright 2002 by the Society for the Experimental Analysis of Behavior. Reproduced by permission.

might contribute to problem behaviors (e.g., difficult demands, being alone, adult attention, or peer attention conditions) and contrasted them with conditions not hypothesized to contribute to problem behaviors (e.g., easy demands or control conditions). These latter two conditions were selected because they were likely to produce low levels of off-task behavior and could serve as comparisons for the conditions that were more likely to increase off-task behavior. In a sense, the easy demand and control conditions could be considered a baseline for comparison with the other conditions. More important, the constitution and selection of these conditions followed from the experimental question, not from preexisting conditions.

Flood et al.'s inclusion of the easy demand and control conditions also served to produce response differentiation among conditions, an outcome necessary for establishing a functional relation. In a multielement design (or any experimental design for that matter), differences between conditions are necessary to show experimental control. An example of an instance in which a multielement design did not produce response differentiation is presented in Figure 10.5. In this example, Kennedy, Meyer, Shukla, and Knowles (2000) studied the stereotypical behavior of students with autism. Dependent variables included interval and event recording, depending on the nature of the stereotypical response. Independent variables included attention, demand, no attention, and recreation conditions. For three students (Brad, James, and Tom), response differentiation occurred among experimental conditions, showing experimental control over responding. However, for two students (Julie and Rita), stereotypy was elevated across all experimental conditions, and no response differentiation occurred (see Tang, Paterson, & Kennedy, in press, for a follow-up analysis of the undifferentiated conditions). For the stereotypical behavior of Julie and Rita, no experimental control was demonstrated in the Kennedy et al. analysis because no differences were observed across conditions.

What constitutes a baseline in a multielement design (or any single-case design) depends on the experimental question. What you choose to study depends on what you want to learn from the analysis. However, what is critical is the conditions be chosen to produce some degree of response differentiation.

Interactions among Conditions

Because of the rapid alternation between conditions in multielement designs, there is always the possibility that the effects on behavior in one condition may influence behavior in another condition. Several terms have been used to describe this phenomenon, including *sequence effects, carry-over effects, alternation effects,* and *multiple treatment interference* (see Barlow & Hersen, 1984). Because each of these terms refers to some instance of an interaction among conditions, these effects will be referred to by a generic term, suggested by Hains and Baer (1989)—namely, *interaction effects.*

A hypothetical example of an interaction effect can be derived from the experiment depicted in Figure 10.3. It is possible that in such an experimental sequence, exposure to the academic condition prior to the play condition could influence behavior in the latter condition if high levels of responding were seen in the former condition. This might occur because of behavioral momentum from the academic to play condition or a disruption in stimulus control exerted by the play condition (Nevin, 1996; Nevin, Milo, Odum, &

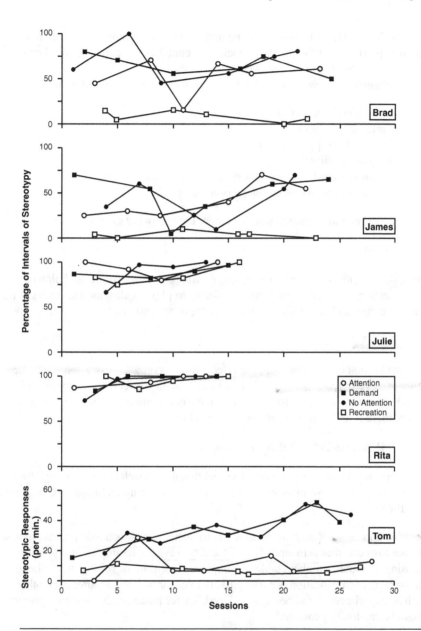

FIGURE 10.5 *Example of lack of response differentiation.* The percentage of intervals or responses per minute of stereotypical behavior by five students with autism (Brad, James, Julie, Rita, and Tom) is shown. Experimental conditions included attention, demand, no attention, and recreation conditions. There is a lack of response differentiation for Julie and Rita.

Source: From C. H. Kennedy, K. A. Meyer, T. Knowles, and S. Shukla, "Analyzing the Multiple Functions of Stereotypical Behavior for Students with Autism: Implications for Assessment and Treatment," *Journal of Applied Behavior Analysis,* 2000, *33,* fig. 1, p. 563. Copyright 2000 by the Society for the Experimental Analysis of Behavior. Reproduced by permission.

Shahan, 2003). The net result might be that the level of behavior observed in the play condition is partly an artifact of the sequence of conditions (i.e., academic then play), rather than an absolute product of the play condition itself.

Schematically, we can model this phenomenon using the following symbols:

A = academic condition
B = alone condition
C = social disapproval condition
D = play condition
- = movement from one condition to another with no interaction effect
* = the occurrence of an interaction effect.

In the experimental sequence just discussed, the following events occurred.

B-C-A*D

Thus, the condition sequence alone, social disapproval, academic, and play occurred, with an interaction effect occurring from academic to play conditions. However, in this example, if the play and academic conditions are reversed, no interaction effect is observed.

B-C-D-A

Such an arrangement shows that the effects of one condition on another are due to the sequence in which they occur, in addition to the absolute effects the individual condition has on behavior. Or, we might find that any time a condition is preceded by the academic condition, there is an interaction effect as shown below.

C-B-A*D or A*C-D-B or D-A*B-C

In many areas of psychology, the traditional approach to "controlling" for interaction effects has been to use randomization or counterbalancing techniques (Campbell & Stanley, 1963).

Randomization. Randomization refers to using some stochastic process to assign a sequence to events that is independent of the actual events. Examples of how to do this would be using a random numbers table, a computer algorithm, or rolling dice. The logic is that, on average, each condition is equally likely to occur before and after each other condition, with no experimenter bias being introduced. So, for instance, the sequence presented below might be randomly generated.

C-B-A-D-A-C-D-B-D-A-B-C

In this sequence, each condition is presented three times in a multielement design. Therefore, the influence of a possible interaction effect is randomly distributed across the experiment. However, a researcher versed in single-case design methods would quickly point out that no control of the sequence effect has been established. Instead, what has occurred is that from a statistical perspective, the change in behavior produced by the interaction effect has been equally distributed across conditions. If the A condition always produced an interaction with the condition that followed it, the following interaction sequence below would occur.

C-B-A*D-A*C-D-B-D-A*B-C

Counterbalancing.   Counterbalancing takes a more direct approach to equally distributing possible interaction effects across conditions. Counterbalancing is a technique that has the same goal as randomization but arranges the sequence of conditions in a planned manner. For example, a researcher might choose to use a Latin Square counterbalancing technique (Reese, 1997) in which each condition appears in each ordinal position once and each condition precedes and follows each condition once. Using our example from Figure 10.3, the following sequence below could be generated:

A-D-B-C-D-C-A-B-B-A-C-D-C-B-D-A

However, like the randomization technique, if interaction effects are present, the following interaction action effects would still occur:

A*D-B-C-D-C-A*B-B-A*C-D-C-B-D-A

Analysis of Interaction Effects.   Although randomization and counterbalancing techniques equally distribute the interactive effect across conditions, there is no control for this effect from an experimental standpoint (see Box 10.2, page 146). All that is accomplished is the statistical averaging of the effect across conditions. In instances where interaction effects might occur, single-case researchers (e.g., Hains & Baer, 1989) have suggested that the appropriate approach to understanding these effects is to conduct an experimental analysis of the phenomenon. That is, when interaction effects are suspected in an experiment, that effect then becomes the focus of the analysis (even though such an analysis was not initially the experimental question). One of the more elegant aspects of single-case designs is that they permit such experimental flexibility, allowing the researcher to explore a phenomenon as it is revealed rather than having to rigidly follow a planned experimental sequence (e.g., McGonigle, Rojahn, Dixon, & Strain, 1987; Shapiro, Kazdin, & McGonigle, 1982).

An example of this process of following your data is exemplified by Berg et al. (2000). Berg and colleagues conducted a functional analysis of problem behavior for a young child with multiple disabilities and problem behavior. During previous analyses, these authors had noticed possible interaction effects for the child's problem behavior. In particular, they had noticed that in some assessments adult attention was a positive reinforcer for problem behavior, but in other assessments the same attention was a neutral stimulus. Berg et al. hypothesized that previous exposure to adult attention before an assessment session might decrease the value of adult attention as a reinforcer. This behavioral process is referred to as an establishing or motivating operation (see Laraway, Snycerski, Michael, & Poling, 2003; McGill, 1999). To test this hypothesis, the authors systematically manipulated the amount of adult attention prior to sessions analyzing whether adult attention functioned as a positive reinforcer for problem behavior. Figure 10.6 (page 146) shows the percentage of intervals in which self-injury was observed during sessions testing whether adult attention influenced this behavior. Two types of conditions were analyzed: (1) the child was alone before the

BOX 10.2 • *Are Randomization or Counterbalancing Useful in Multielement Designs?*

Any introductory course on experimental psychology will teach you the importance of randomization and counterbalancing when designing an experiment. In fact, these techniques are often referred to as "control" techniques in such contexts. However, this is a logic based on group comparison designs and the statistical analyses associated with their use. If interaction effects occur, then randomizing or counterbalancing will evenly distribute those effects across conditions so that their mathematical presence will equally influence the data in all other conditions. However, in single-case designs, or any inductive approach to experimentation, such an experimental tactic is not a control technique in the sense that experimental control is established. For researchers using single-case designs, control techniques are associated with the establishment of a functional relation between variables to explain why some behavioral effect occurs. If an interaction effect occurs, it is the result of a behavioral process that is uncontrolled within the existing experimental arrangement. In single-case designs, such in-

stances are invitations for further experimental analysis and discovery. Or, as Murray Sidman wrote in *Tactics of Scientific Research* (1960), "variability is not mere noise in the system. It is the major datum" (pp. 197–198).

Interestingly, single-case researchers have adopted the convention of randomizing the sequence of experimental conditions when using multielement designs. Presumably, the benefit of doing this is that a researcher is attempting to distribute possible interaction effects evenly across the experimental analysis. If interaction effects are present and robust, then the sequence of events should be revealed through visual analysis of the data. However, some researchers, particularly in behavioral pharmacology (which, by definition, is the study of interaction effects), have adopted the convention of using fixed sequences of conditions and reversing the sequence to assess for the presence of interaction effects. Which approach is more scientifically useful in educational settings remains to be seen.

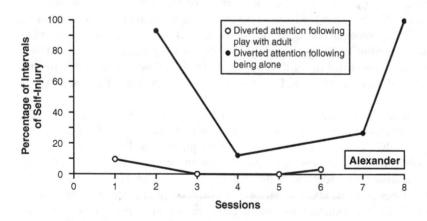

FIGURE 10.6 *An experimental analysis of an interaction effect.* The percentage of intervals in which self-injury was observed during sessions that tested whether adult attention influenced this behavior. Two types of conditions were analyzed: (1) the child was alone before the attention assessment or (2) the child played with an adult before the attention assessment.

Source: From W. K. Berg, S. Peck, D. P. Wacker, J. Harding, J. McComas, D. Richman, and K. Brown, "The Effects of Presession Exposure to Attention on the Results of Assessments of Attention as a Reinforcer," *Journal of Applied Behavior Analysis,* 2000, *33,* fig. 2, p. 469. Copyright 2000 by the Society for the Experimental Analysis of Behavior. Reproduced by permission.

attention assessment or (2) the child played with an adult before the attention assessment. The results showed that prior exposure to adult attention decreased the reinforcing value of adult attention during the functional analysis. Berg et al. not only noticed an interaction effect but also were able to successfully analyze the interaction and explain why it occurred.

Graphic Analysis of Data.   One strategy that can assist in identifying interaction effects involves the graphic analysis of data (see Chapter 16). When plotting data from a multielement design in a graph so the data can be visually analyzed, a researcher has two options. The data points can be plotted so separate sessions overlap (see Figure 10.1), or the data can be arrayed to show each session in sequence (see Figure 10.2). One value of plotting the data in sequence is that you can see which sessions preceded or followed other sessions. This approach to visualizing information allows for easier detection of interaction effects when using multielement designs.

Alternating Treatments Design

Alternating treatments design (ATD) is a variant of multielement design. As introduced in the late 1970s (Barlow & Hayes, 1979), ATD is a special instance of the broader set of designs discussed in this chapter. As noted by Barlow and Hayes, "in the typical design [i.e., ATD], after a baseline period, two treatments (A and B) are administered, alternating with each other, and the effects on one behavior are observed" (p. 200). This description of ATD was accompanied by Figure 10.7. In the figure, a baseline period (phase 1) was followed by a second phase in which two independent variables were administered in a multielement design, with the more effective intervention continuing into phase 3. Interestingly, Barlow and

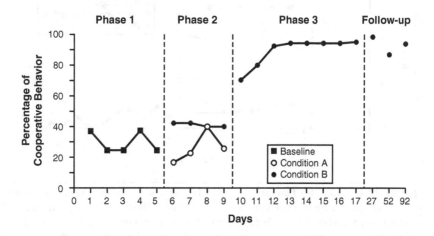

FIGURE 10.7 *Example of alternating treatments design (ATD).* The baseline period (phase 1) was followed by a second phase in which two independent variables were administered in a multielement design, with the more effective intervention continuing into phase 3.

Source: From D. H. Barlow and S. C. Hayes, "Alternating Treatments Design: One Strategy for Comparing the Effects of Two Treatments in a Single Subject," *Journal of Applied Behavior Analysis,* 1979, *12,* fig. 1, p. 201. Copyright 1979 by the Society for the Experimental Analysis of Behavior. Reproduced by permission.

Hersen (1984), in their influential single-case design text, included a chapter titled "Alternating Treatments Design" that expanded the scope of the original ATD to encompass what had previously been referred to as multielement designs. (This chapter and terminology had not been present in their earlier edition, Hersen & Barlow, 1976.) Also of historical interest, in a contemporaneous and similarly influential text on single-case designs, Kazdin (1982) included a similar chapter but titled it "Multitreatment Designs."

Clearly, such a procedural arrangement is consistent with multielement design logic, but the inclusion of a baseline and a final phase using a single intervention are conditions that limit the scope of the design. In fact, these conditions present substantial interpretative limitations when using ATD. First, the instigation of an experiment with a baseline that is not replicated in subsequent phases of the study makes the pattern of behavior difficult to interpret. Since the only analysis of behavior under baseline conditions is during the start of the study and is not repeated, there is no attempt to return to baseline conditions. Second, the inclusion of the final phase in which the more effective intervention is in place is a positive aspect of the design from an applied standpoint, but, as in baseline, these data are somewhat difficult to interpret because of the lack of any additional experimental manipulations. However, the second phase of ATD is a classic multielement design and can be used to demonstrate experimental control.

An augmentation to ATD that improves at least the first concern previously mentioned is shown in Figure 10.8. In this figure, Kennedy and Souza (1995) used a modified ATD to analyze the eye poking of a young man with severe disabilities. In keeping with the

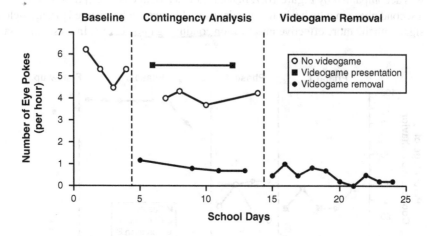

FIGURE 10.8 *Example of augmented ATD.* In this figure, a modified ATD was used to analyze the eye poking of a young man with severe disabilities. In keeping with the ATD tactic, these authors established a baseline and then introduced two interventions. However, in this design, the baseline phase of the investigation was extended into the second phase, allowing comparisons among the independent variables and baseline. The study ended with an extended phase in which the most effective intervention was assessed.

Source: From C. H. Kennedy and G. Souza, "Functional Analysis and Treatment of Eye-Poking," *Journal of Applied Behavior Analysis,* 1995, *28,* fig. 4, p. 34. Copyright 1995 by the Society for the Experimental Analysis of Behavior. Reproduced by permission.

ATD tactic, these authors established a baseline and then introduced two interventions. However, in this design, the baseline phase of the investigation was extended into the second phase, allowing comparisons among the independent variables and baseline. The study ended with an extended phase in which the most effective intervention was assessed. This design arrangement allowed for a comparison of baseline and interventions, although the extended third phase was largely nonanalytical.

Strengths and Limitations

Multielement designs have a long and distinguished history in the experimental analysis of behavior (Sidman, 1960). Relatively early in the development of behavior analysis, this design tactic was introduced to applied researchers (Ulman & Sulzer-Azaroff, 1975). Their use provides researchers with a powerful analytical tool for exploring behavioral processes. As long as response differentiation occurs across at least one condition, then experimental control can be readily demonstrated.

Multielement designs allow researchers to analyze two or more experimental conditions using a single participant. In recently published reports, it is not unusual for authors to compare five or six different experimental conditions. Such flexibility allows a researcher to build in high levels of experimental control-and-contrast conditions that are not permitted by other single-case designs. For this reason alone, multielement designs are an important analytical tool. However, not only does this design type encompass a large number of experimental comparisons, the rapid alternation between or among conditions allows for this analytical process to unfold rapidly when compared with other design tactics.

There are, of course, limiting conditions to the use of multielement designs. The primary design limitation of multielement designs rests on the issue of behavioral reversibility. If a change in behavior produced by an independent variable cannot be reversed by the withdrawal of the intervention, then multielement designs are not a suitable design alternative (see Chapter 11). A second limitation in using multielement designs is the potential for interaction effects, where the effect on behavior of baseline and/or independent variable conditions is influenced by the presence or juxtaposition of other conditions. But, as argued by Haines and Baer (1989), the inducement of interaction effects can provide for the opportunity for additional analyses of the behavioral processes that cause interaction effects (which may be educationally useful). However, in instances where interaction effects may be a concern, then A-B-A-B (Chapter 9), multiple baseline (Chapter 11), or combined designs (Chapter 14) might be preferable alternatives.

11

Multiple Baseline Designs

Unlike A-B-A-B or multielement designs, the use of a multiple baseline design does not require the withdrawal, reversal, or repeated alternation of conditions. Instead, as the name implies, two or more baselines are concurrently established and the independent variable is sequentially introduced across the baselines. This means that once an intervention is introduced, it is not removed. Multiple baseline designs are an important alternative in instances in which the effects of the independent variable cannot be reversed once behavior is exposed to it. In addition, because the design logic is based on an A-B sequence for each baseline, such designs have the logistical advantage of requiring fewer changes in an educational setting than other $N = 1$ designs. Because of this characteristic, some researchers consider the absence of a return to baseline to be ethically more desirable (e.g., Barlow & Hersen, 1984; Kazdin, 1982; Tawney & Gast, 1984) (see Box 11.1).

BOX 11.1 • *Are Multiple Baseline Designs Ethically Preferable to Other Single-Case Designs?*

One concern about A-B-A-B and multielement designs is that the return to baseline may not be ethically desirable. This is because the baseline condition may have exposed the person to some undesirable situation, such as bullying by peers or the occurrence of self-injurious behavior. Following a successful intervention that improves the problematic situation, a return to the undesirable situation could be considered ethically unacceptable, since it would reexpose the person to negative circumstances. This has led some researchers to prefer multiple baseline designs to other types of single-case designs. However, this preference is relative, not absolute. One of the drawbacks of a multiple baseline design, by definition, is the prolongation of baseline conditions for the lower tiers of the design. For the behaviors, people, and so on that are exposed to the lower tiers of a multiple baseline design, an extended exposure to the problematic situation is required. For instances that may expose a participant to prolonged baseline conditions, an A-B-A-B or multielement design may minimize the person's exposure to the undesirable situation. Indeed, if exposure to a baseline condition is a clear ethical concern, then single-case designs, such as multielement or brief designs, that minimize the number of baseline sessions may be the most desirable alternative.

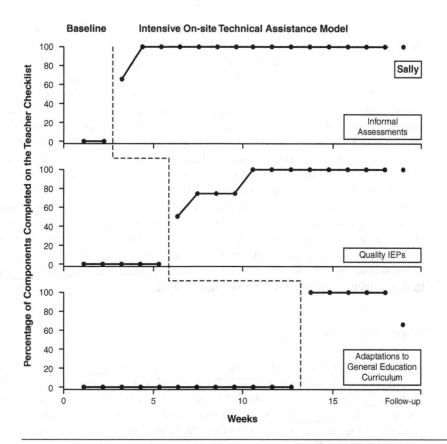

FIGURE 11.1 *Example of a multiple-baseline-across-behaviors design.* The dependent variable was the percentage of components correctly completed for each of three teaching skills: (1) informal assessments, (2) quality IEPs, and (3) adaptations to the general education curriculum. The intervention was an intensive on-site technical assistance intervention to improve the teaching practices of a special educator, Sally.

Source: From N. M. Clark, L. S. Cushing, and C. H. Kennedy, "An Intensive On-Site Technical Assistance Model to Promote Inclusive Practices for Students with Severe Disabilities," manuscript submitted for publication.

An example of a multiple baseline design is provided in Figure 11.1. This study, by Clark, Cushing, and Kennedy (2003), used an intensive on-site technical assistance intervention to improve the teaching practices of a special educator, Sally. The dependent variable was the percentage of components correctly completed for each of three teaching skills: (1) informal assessments, (2) quality IEPs, and (3) adaptations to the general education curriculum. Each of these teaching skills comprised an individual tier of the multiple baseline design, making this a multiple-baseline-across-behaviors design.

In a multiple baseline design, as previously noted, the independent variable is sequentially administered across different tiers or baselines. The logic of the design requires researchers to simultaneously evaluate different patterns of behavior as the design is implemented. For instance, in Figure 11.1, the first baseline (i.e., informal assessments) was stable over two weeks. When the intervention was implemented, there was an immediate increase in the educator's correct use of informal assessment. However, there was no change in the level of behaviors on the other two tiers of the multiple baseline design at the same point in time. This shows that only behaviors directly receiving the intervention were influenced by it. In week 6, the intervention was implemented for the second baseline (i.e., quality IEPs), and this dependent variable then increased over several weeks. In addition, behavior on the first baseline continued to maintain at high levels with the independent variable in place, but behaviors on the third tier (i.e., adaptations) remained at low levels while still in baseline. Hence, only behaviors that had received intervention improved. Finally, in week 13, the intervention was applied to the behaviors represented on the third tier of the multiple baseline design, and improvements were immediately observed.

Figure 11.1 illustrates the basic logic of a multiple baseline design. Individual baselines are established, consistent response patterns are observed, and then the independent variable is systematically introduced to one baseline at a time. The researcher waits until a clear change in the pattern of behavior occurs for the baseline receiving the intervention, with the other tier(s) remaining stable. The process is then repeated with the second tier and so on. If changes in the dependent variable occur only when the independent variable is introduced, then a functional relation is demonstrated.

Basic Multiple Baseline Designs

Traditionally, multiple baseline designs have been described as occurring across behaviors, people, settings, stimuli, or times (Baer, Wolf, & Risley, 1968). That is, the tiers of the multiple baseline design can be comprised of a range of events that might be associated with a particular experimental question. An example of a multiple baseline design across behaviors was presented in Figure 11.1. An example of a multiple-baseline-across-people design is shown in Figure 11.2. "People" can refer to students, educators, administrators, family members, related services professionals, and so on. In this study by March and Horner (2002), the percentage of academically engaged time served as the dependent variable, and behavioral interventions derived from the reinforcers maintaining off-task behavior was the independent variable. Participants were three middle-school students (Andy, Bill, and Cathy) whose teacher noted that their problem behaviors interfered with their class work. Baselines were established concurrently for each of the three students' behavior, and the intervention sequentially introduced one tier at a time and only after a change in the pattern of behavior from baseline had been demonstrated. This experimental design represents an initial experimental effect in an A-B sequence for Andy that was replicated once for Bill and once for Cathy (see Box 11.2, page 154).

Another example of a multiple baseline design is shown in Figure 11.3 (page 154). This figure shows a multiple-baseline-across-settings design. The study by Kennedy, Cushing, and Itkonen (1997) analyzed the effects of a peer support program on the social contacts between a student with severe disabilities (Max) and his peers without disabilities in two general education classes. This experimental design represents the minimal number of tiers a multiple baseline can have and still show a replicated effect (i.e., two) (see Chapter 3). In the Kennedy et al. study, stable baselines were established, and the independent variable was introduced sequentially across the class periods. In each instance, the intervention was associated with an increase in the number of social contacts and the number of peers interacted with. Hence, a functional relation was established.

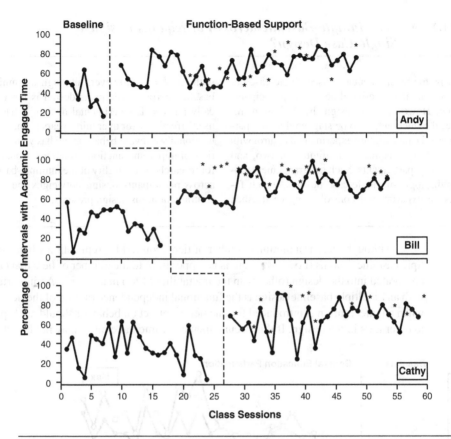

FIGURE 11.2 *Example of a multiple-baseline-across-participants design.* The percentage of academically engaged time served as the dependent variable, and behavioral interventions derived from the reinforcers maintaining off-task behavior was the independent variable. Participants were three middle-school students (Andy, Bill, and Cathy) whose teacher noted that their problem behaviors interfered with their class work.

Source: From R. E. March and R. H. Horner, "Feasibility and Contributions of Functional Behavioral Assessment in Schools," *Journal of Emotional and Behavioral Disorders,* 2002, *10,* fig. 2, p. 167. Copyright 2002 by ProEd. Reproduced by permission.

When multiple-baseline-across-stimuli designs are used, anything that might serve as a stimulus for interaction could be incorporated into the design (e.g., toys or computer games). If a multiple-baseline-across-time design is used, then other factors (such as setting, people, and behaviors) are held constant, while the intervention is sequentially implemented across different times of the day. In general, any event that is of experimental interest can be incorporated into a multiple baseline design. As long as the event meets the requirements for operationalization discussed in Chapter 7, then it can be used as a tier in a multiple baseline design. In addition, as was shown in Figure 4.3 (page 55) in Chapter 4, multiple baseline designs can also incorporate combinations of behaviors, people, settings, stimuli, or times into the tiers of the design.

BOX 11.2 • *Is a Multiple-Baseline-across-Participants Design a Single-Case Design?*

Perhaps the most frequently used single-case design is the multiple-baseline-across-participants design. However, this design, by definition, requires the intervention to be staggered across participants. Demonstrating experimental control with such a design requires a minimum of two, and often more, participants. Such an arrangement violates the logic of single-case designs, which focuses on experimental control being established with an $N = 1$. However, although the multiple-baseline-across-participants design is not technically an $N = 1$ experimental design, it has been used effectively for over thirty years to analyze educationally relevant behavior and has yielded a variety of important functional relations. Apparently, for researchers, the utility of the multiple-baseline-across-participants design outweighs the logical contradiction this design presents.

Although there is a minimal number of tiers required for replication when using multiple baseline designs (i.e., two), there is no upper limit to the number of tiers that can be incorporated into the design (other than the tractability of too many tiers). An important issue with any multiple baseline design is the functional independence of each of the tiers. That is, when an intervention is introduced for one tier, its effect on behavior should not "spill over" to other tiers in the design. If this occurs, then experimental control may not be achieved.

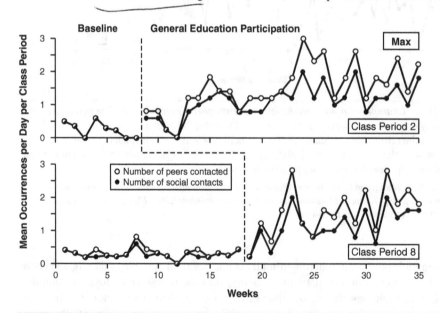

FIGURE 11.3 *Example of multiple-baseline-across-settings design.* The study measured effects of a peer support program on the social contacts between a student with severe disabilities (Max) and his peers without disabilities in two classes. This experimental design represents the minimal number of tiers a multiple baseline can have and still show a replicated effect.

Source: From C. H. Kennedy, L. Cushing, and T. Itkonen, "General Education Participation Increases the Social Contacts and Friendship Networks of Students with Severe Disabilities." *Journal of Behavioral Education,* 1997, 7. Copyright 1997 by Human Sciences Press. Reproduced with permission.

Another issue with establishing experimental control via multiple baseline designs relates to delayed intervention effects. Because introducing the intervention across tiers of the multiple baseline design requires the dependent variable to change its pattern of occurrence, delayed intervention effects can be a concern. If the next intervention is done too soon, a functional relation cannot be demonstrated. Conversely, if the effect of the independent variable is sufficiently delayed, then in some instances maturational processes (i.e., a threat to internal validity) may change the behaviors in other tiers of the design. If this occurs, then baselines would begin showing improvements in the absence of the independent variable and, again, experimental control would be compromised.

Multiple Baseline Design Variants

Variants of the multiple baseline design have emerged since the design was first used in the 1960s. We will discuss two general variations of the multiple baseline design in this section: (1) multiprobe multiple baseline designs and (2) nonconcurrent multiple baseline designs.

Multiprobe Multiple Baseline Designs

Horner and Baer (1978) introduced the multiprobe multiple baseline design as a way of making the multiple baseline design more efficient for researchers. In the standard multiple baseline design discussed in the previous section, data points are taken for each session in each tier of the multiple baseline design. For tiers that receive intervention later in the experimental sequence, a large number of data points are typically collected. The multiprobe multiple baseline design takes advantage of this situation by only intermittently collecting data during the execution of the experimental series. Because data are only collected intermittently, this saves the amount of effort required to record and score observational sessions.

Importantly, data are collected only intermittently during the experiment at times required for estimating trends and related patterns in the data within and between tiers. An example of this design is presented in Figure 11.4 (page 156). Schepis, Reid, Behrmann, and Sutton (1998) used a multiprobe multiple baseline design to study how to increase the communication of preschool children with autism. The dependent variables included the number of child communicative interactions per minute. The independent variable was a combined naturalistic instruction and augmentative communication intervention. The experimental design had four tiers, with exhaustive combinations of two children (Ben and Cory) and two activities (snack and play).

Across the forty-nine sessions per tier that were conducted by Schepis et al., an average of twenty data points was obtained for each tier. Several facets of this experimental design deserve comment. First, the baseline and intervention sessions were conducted on a regular basis, but data were collected only intermittently on the children's behavior. Therefore, the data represent a sampling of the overall performance of the children and activities in the baseline and intervention conditions. Second, data probes were taken intermittently, but consistently, across the study. Third, probe data were collected at strategic time points during the experiment. Specifically, data points were collected before and after the introduction of the independent variable for each tier of the multiprobe multiple baseline design. This allowed the researchers to estimate levels of the dependent variable at each time point

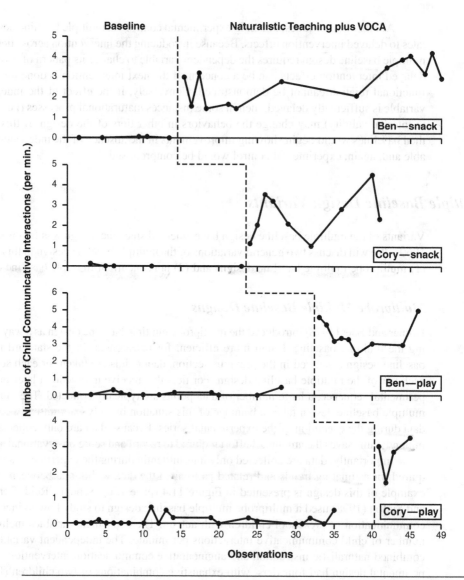

FIGURE 11.4   *Example of a multiprobe multiple baseline design.* The dependent variables included the number of child communicative interactions per minute, shown on the *y*-axis. The independent variable was a combined naturalistic instruction and augmentative communication intervention. The experimental design had four tiers, which combined two children (Ben and Cory) and two contexts (snack and play).

Source: From M. M. Schepis, D. H. Reid, M. M. Behrmann, and K. A. Sutton, "Increasing Communicative Interactions of Young Children with Autism Using a Voice Output Communication Aid (VOCA) and Naturalistic Teaching," *Journal of Applied Behavior Analysis,* 1998, *31,* fig. 1, p. 570. Copyright 1998 by the Society for the Experimental Analysis of Behavior. Reproduced by permission.

surrounding when the intervention was introduced. These characteristics are critical for demonstrating a functional relation with this type of design.

As can be seen in Figure 11.4, Schepis et al. met these design requirements. The children's communicative interactions only increased following the introduction of the naturalistic-teaching-plus-augmentative-communication intervention. At each time point that data probes were collected during baseline across the tiers, low levels of communication were observed. However, each time the intervention was introduced, communication increased for that particular combination of child and activity. Thus, experimental control was demonstrated even though less than 50% of the sessions had data collected on child behaviors.

A second type of multiprobe multiple baseline design was introduced by Tawney and Gast (1984). This type of design is particularly useful for studying generalization processes (Stokes & Baer, 1977; Horner, Dunlap, & Koegel, 1988). In this type of single-case design, data collection occurs at two time points—(1) baseline and (2) instructional sessions—for each tier of the multiple baseline design. In addition, two types of behavioral variables are included in each tier of the design: (1) target and (2) generalization behaviors. Baseline probes are collected on all target and generalization behaviors across tiers; then, an intervention is introduced to the first-tier target behaviors. When behavior change has occurred (e.g., response acquisition), probes are taken across all target and generalization behaviors to assess their status. This process is then repeated, in sequence, for the remaining tiers in the design.

An example of this design tactic was used in a study by Werts, Caldwell, and Wolery (2003). Figure 11.5 (page 158) shows the data from a child with a learning disability named Gabe. The behaviors of interest were the acquisition of three instructed labels for objects (labeled target behaviors, sets 1, 2, and 3) and three generalization words for different objects (labeled instructive feedback behaviors, sets 1, 2, and 3). Data were initially collected across all six behaviors of interest to estimate levels of expressive labeling. An intervention was then introduced that directly taught Gabe the set 1 target behavior and indirectly taught him the set 1 instructive feedback behavior. Once the instructional criteria were met on the set 1 target behavior, probes across all six behaviors were again conducted (with an additional probe added during instruction for the set 1 instructive feedback behavior). In this instance, only the set 1 behaviors were acquired, with set 2 and 3 behaviors remaining at baseline levels. This process was subsequently repeated on each set of behaviors, with label acquisition only occurring after instruction.

Multiprobe multiple baseline designs can be efficient experimental tools, as shown by the Schepis et al. and Werts et al. studies. Because data are intermittently collected at strategic time points within the multiple baseline design, the amount of effort required for data collection and scoring is minimized. A primary drawback to the use of these designs is that, because of the intermittent nature of data collection, this design type is less sensitive to abrupt changes in the level of behavior that might occur during baseline. In addition, if cyclical patterns of behavior are present, the intermittent sampling technique may not capture the occurrence of these patterns (see Fisher Piazza, & Roane, 2002).

Nonconcurrent Multiple Baseline Designs

A second variant of the multiple baseline design is the nonconcurrent multiple baseline design. As previously noted, all single-case designs are differing configurations of A-B conditions. In the multiple baseline design, the A-B conditions are staggered on different tiers

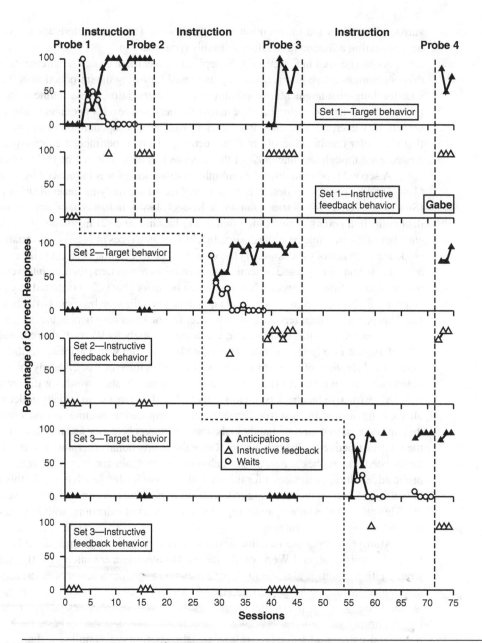

FIGURE 11.5 *Example of a multiprobe multiple baseline design.* Data shown are from a child with a learning disability named Gabe. The behaviors of interest were the acquisition of three instructed labels for objects (labeled target behaviors, sets 1, 2, and 3) and three generalization words for different objects (labeled instructive feedback behaviors, sets 1, 2, and 3).

Source: From M. G. Werts, N. K. Caldwell, and M. Wolery, "Instructive Feedback: Effects of a Presentation Variable," *Journal of Special Education,* 2003, *37,* fig. 2, p. 128. Copyright 2003 by ProEd. Reproduced by permission.

of the experimental arrangement. The design controls for a number of possible threats to external validity by staggering the introduction of the independent variable on different tiers and assessing for consistent effects.

A variation on this logic is the separation of the different A-B tiers in time. That is, instead of all the tiers being conducted concurrently, each of the tiers can be conducted at different time points. The differing A-B tiers can be completely separated in time (e.g., different months, semesters, or years), there can be partial overlap, or some tiers can be time synced, while others are temporally distant. Because of this temporal feature, such designs are referred to as nonconcurrent (Watson & Workman, 1981).

An example of this design type is presented in Figure 11.6 (page 160). Werle, Murphy, and Budd (1993) studied chronic food refusal in young children using a home-based intervention. The dependent variable was the number of bites taken by each child during a meal. The independent variable was the use of contingent praise and clear prompts to the child provided by parents during the meal. Figure 11.6 shows treatment integrity data from this study for the independent variable. Because this was an unusual problem and was potentially life threatening, the authors used a nonconcurrent multiple baseline design to assess a series of cases that came to their attention. The left-hand column shows that the training package increased parents' use of contingent attention when their children ate appropriately. The right-hand column shows an increase in the number of trained prompts used by parents during the feeding time. The data are arrayed concurrently by session number, even though each A-B analysis occurred separately.

A second example of the utility of nonconcurrent multiple baseline designs is presented in a hypothetical case by Harvey, May, and Kennedy (in press). In this instance, shown in Figure 11.7 (page 161), a nonconcurrent multiple baseline design was used to analyze a larger aggregate than is usually the focus of single-case research (i.e., each "individual" was a local education agency, namely, Watson, Freemont, and Washington). In this instance, the intervention focused on increasing teachers' use of effective instructional practices and a consistent general education curriculum. Each tier in this design was conducted in different school semesters. In addition, in this instance, the authors labeled the tiers with the calendar dates when each A-B analysis was conducted.

Another way of graphing data from a nonconcurrent multiple baseline design was presented by Waston and Workman (1981). In this paper, which originally introduced this design variant, the authors suggested graphing the data in a manner that reflects the temporal relation between each tier in the design. Figure 11.8 (page 162) shows an example of this graphic approach, using hypothetical data. Three participants were included in the analysis, with subject 1 receiving the first baseline and intervention series, then subject 2, and, finally, subject 3. There is some overlap between the three cases, but with differing baseline lengths. Whatever graphic approach shown in Figures 11.6, 11.7, or 11.8 is used, it is important that researchers specify in the reporting of their data when each set of A-B conditions was conducted so readers can judge possible temporal relations between or among the various tiers of the design.

A benefit of the nonconcurrent multiple baseline design is that is allows researchers to systematically study topics that might not otherwise be amenable to an experimental analysis (Harvey et al., in press). This includes rare cases, limited research resources, and the incorporation of larger individual units (e.g., schools, local education agencies, or state educational agencies) into single-case studies. This design variant controls for most threats

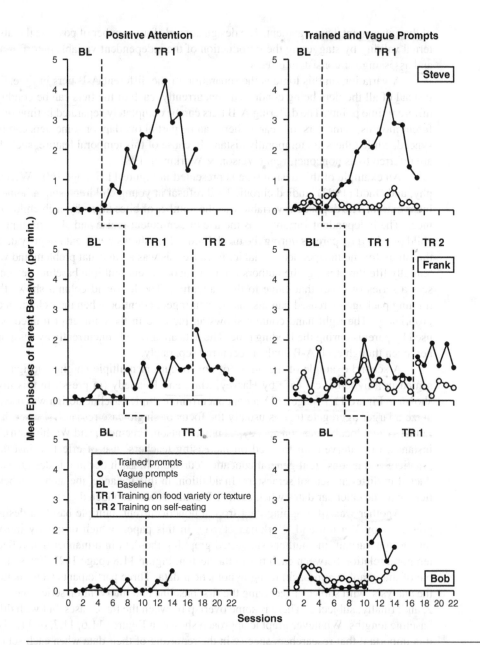

FIGURE 11.6 *Example of a nonconcurrent multiple baseline design.* The dependent variable was the number of bites of food taken by each child. The independent variable was the use of contingent praise and clear prompts to the child provided by parents. The graph shows treatment integrity data from this study for the independent variable.

Source: From M. A. Werle, T. B. Murphy, and K. S. Budd, "Treating Chronic Food Refusal in Young Children: Home-Based Parent Training," *Journal of Applied Behavior Analysis,* 1993, *26,* fig. 1, p. 428. Copyright 1993 by the Society for the Experimental Analysis of Behavior. Reproduced by permission.

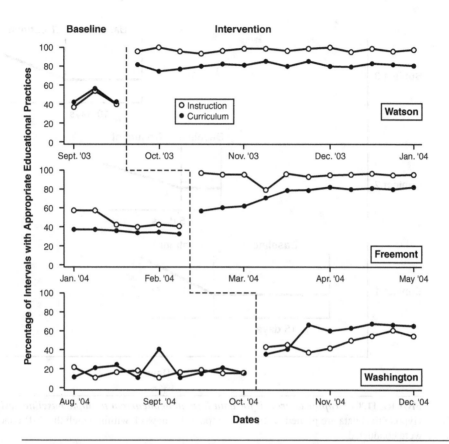

FIGURE 11.7 *Nonconcurrent multiple baseline design.* The specific dates are added along the abscissa. In this hypothetical study, the intervention focused on increasing teachers' use of effective instructional practices and a consistent general education curriculum. Each tier in this design was conducted in different school semesters.

Source: From M. T. Harvey, M. E. May, and C. H. Kennedy, "Nonconcurrent *N* = 1 Experimental Designs for Educational Program Evaluation." *Journal of Behavioral Education,* in press. Copyright by Human Sciences Press. Reproduced by permission.

to internal validity (e.g., maturation, test-retest sensitivity, and instrumentation changes), with the exception of history effects. Therefore, use of this design needs to be considered within the larger context of establishing experimental control and gaining access to experimental opportunities not typically considered amenable to single-case design analysis (or other types of experimental designs).

Strengths and Limitations

Multiple baseline designs are probably the most used type of single-case design. This is in part due to the simplicity of the design and its flexibility. Early on in the development of applied behavior analysis, there was an emphasis on developing experimental designs that

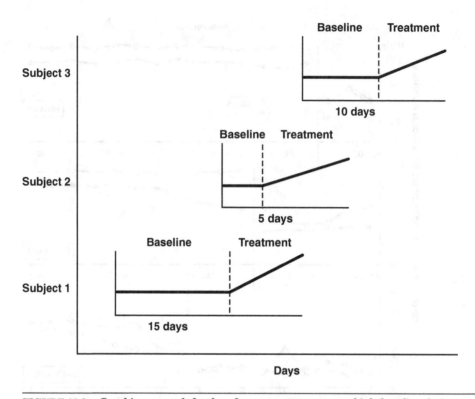

FIGURE 11.8 *Graphic approach for data form nonconcurrent multiple baseline design.*
Hypothetical data are plotted within the temporal framework within which the A-B conditions
were conducted.

Source: From P. J. Watson and E. A. Workman, "The Non-concurrent Multiple Baseline Across-Individuals
Design: An Extension of the Traditional Multiple-Baseline Design," *Journal of Behavior Therapy and
Experimental Psychiatry,* 1981, *12,* fig. 1, p. 258. Copyright 1981 by Pergamon Press. Reproduced by
permission.

could be used by practitioners in the settings where they worked. The multiple baseline design, whether across students, settings, behaviors, stimuli, or times, was an ideal analytical
tool that filled this need (see Barlow, Hayes, Nelson, 1984). In addition, because of the inherent flexibility in the timing of interventions and the ability to conduct analyses in a multiprobe or nonconcurrent fashion, this approach is easily adapted to applied settings.

        Another strength of the multiple baseline design is its utility. Multiple baseline designs
are the experimental tactic of choice in situations where behavior cannot be reversed, logistical constraints do not allow the removal of the intervention, or ethical concerns make removal of the intervention unacceptable. However, this strength is also the primary weakness
of the design. Because of its structure, it is difficult to conduct comparative, component, or
parametric analyses of independent variables using the multiple baseline design. In general,
its status as an analytical tool is limited to demonstrating the general effects of an independent variable on behavior. This means that multiple baseline designs are not very useful for
exploring basic behavioral processes. So, as with all the other analytical tactics covered in
Part Four, the utility of any particular design depends on the experimental question.

12

Repeated Acquisition Designs

The difficulty of reversing some types of learned behavior is an important issue in single-case designs. Because many $N = 1$ designs rely on the manipulation of reinforcement contingencies or the withdrawal of interventions, the reversal of behavior to baseline patterns is necessary to demonstrate response differentiation and experimental control. Multiple baseline designs are used to deal with the issue of reversibility by establishing two or more baselines and then sequentially introducing the independent variable one tier at a time. Such a design tactic amounts to a staggered set of A-B experimental conditions.

Repeated Acquisition Designs

When the reversibility of behavior is a question, an alternative design to the multiple baseline design is the repeated acquisition design. Initially introduced by Boren (1963) for basic research on learning processes, the repeated acquisition design allows for the analysis of skill acquisition under different experimental conditions (see also Boren and Devine, 1968). The defining characteristics of a repeated acquisition design are (1) the use of multiple equivalent learning tasks (2) in which acquisition can be studied repeatedly from one task to another (3) under at least two different experimental conditions. That is, the participant is exposed to a particular learning task and the rate of acquisition is documented during the same time period that the participant learns a new task under different experimental conditions. This process is then continued with new tasks until a clear difference is demonstrated between or among conditions. The result is an opportunity to study the effects of various experimental conditions on learning processes in such areas as reading, math, social studies, science, or physical skills.

An example of a repeated acquisition design is presented in Figure 12.1 (page 164). This figure shows a study of sight-word acquisition for four students with moderate-to-mild intellectual disabilities (see Barbetta, Heward, Bradley, & Miller, 1994). The dependent variable was the number of sight-words correctly read. Two different interventions were compared in terms of feedback when a word was incorrectly read: (1) immediate practice or (2) delayed practice. Each week, seven new words were randomly assigned to either the immediate practice or delayed practice intervention. Instruction then occurred on each set of words

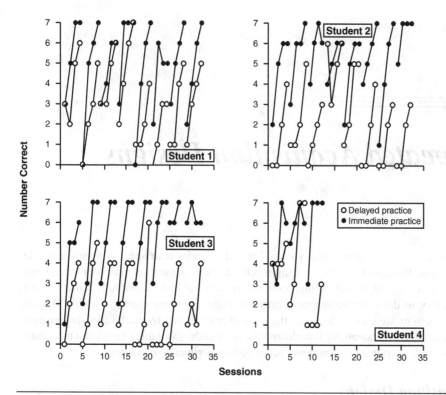

FIGURE 12.1 *Example of a repeated acquisition design.* This figure shows a study of sight-word acquisition for four students with moderate-to-mild intellectual disabilities. The dependent variable was the number of sight words read correctly. Two different interventions were compared in terms of feedback when a word was read incorrectly: (1) immediate practice or (2) delayed practice.

Source: From P. M. Barbetta, W. L. Heward, D. M. Bradley, and A. D. Miller, "Effects of Immediate and Delayed Error Correction on the Acquisition and Maintenance of Sight Words by Students with Developmental Disabilities," *Journal of Applied Behavior Analysis,* 1994, *27,* fig. 1, p. 178. Copyright 1994 by the Society for the Experimental Analysis of Behavior. Reprinted by permission.

using the prespecified instructional technique. On day 1, delayed feedback instruction occurred on word set 1, then immediate feedback instruction occurred on word set 2. The next day, delayed feedback instruction occurred again for word set 1, with immediate feedback instruction being provided for word set 2. This process was repeated until at least one set of words had been acquired. The next week, a new set of words was chosen; the words were randomly assigned to the two instructional conditions, and the acquisition process repeated.

Figure 12.1 shows that students 1, 2, and 3 received eight different reading word sets comparing the delayed versus immediate feedback interventions, while student 4 was taught three word sets. For students 1, 3, and 4, the immediate feedback strategy always produced more rapid sight-word acquisition. This is shown by the response differentiation that occurred between each set of words under the two experimental conditions. For example, all seven words were correctly read in the immediate feedback condition for student 1 by session 3, but only six words were read correctly by session 4 for the same student. For student 2, a similar pattern of response differentiation occurred, with all word sets showing differential acquisition effects except for word set 4. This means that for students 1 and 3, there were eight within-participant direct replications of the experimental effect, seven for student 2, and three for student 4. Given this high degree of within- and between-participant direct replication, it is judicious to say that experimental control using the repeated acquisition design was demonstrated.

A second example of a repeated acquisition design, from a study conducted by Danforth, Chase, Dolan, and Joyce (1990), is presented in Figure 12.2. The four participants, labeled subjects 1 through 4, were undergraduate university students. This laboratory study required students to learn a new sequence of arbitrary responses presented on a computer

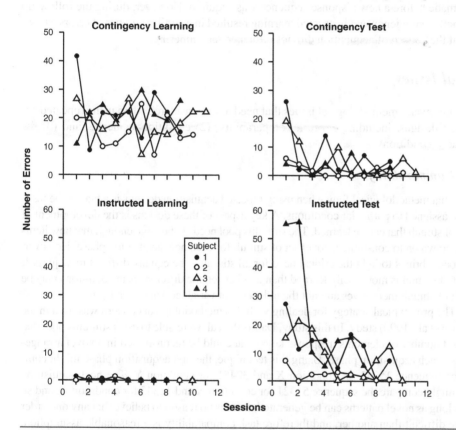

FIGURE 12.2 *Example of a repeated acquisition design.* Four participants (subjects 1 through 4) were undergraduate university students. Students learned a new sequence of arbitrary responses presented on a computer screen during each experimental session. Under one condition, participants were given trial-and-error feedback (labeled contingency learning), and under a second condition, they were verbally told what the sequence was (labeled instructed learning). The dependent measure for the study is the number of errors made until a response sequence was acquired. Which condition the participants were exposed to as they acquired the sequence varied from session to session (left-hand panel of graph). After four hours had elapsed, students were again tested to see if they remembered the sequence of responses (right-hand panel of graph).

Source: From J. S. Danforth, P. N. Chase, M. Dolan, and J. H. Joyce, "The Establishment of Stimulus Control by Instructions and by Differential Reinforcement," *Journal of the Experimental Analysis of Behavior,* 1990, *54,* fig. 2, p. 101. Copyright 1990 by the Society for the Experimental Analysis of Behavior. Reprinted by permission.

screen during each experimental session. Under one condition, participants were given trial-and-error feedback (labeled contingency learning), and under a second condition they were verbally told what the sequence was (labeled instructed learning). The dependent measure for the study was the number of errors made before a response sequence was learned. Which condition the participants were exposed to as they acquired the sequence varied from session to session (left-hand panel of graph). After four hours had elapsed, the students were again tested to see if they remembered the sequence of responses (right-hand panel of graph). The data show that instructed learning resulted in almost error-free response acquisition, whereas contingency learning resulted in approximately twenty errors being made before a new response sequence was acquired. However, during the follow-up tests, both contingency and instructed learning resulted in a similar number of errors, showing that the pattern of acquisition did not influence remembering.

Methodological Issues

There are several methodological issues that need to be considered when using repeated acquisition designs, including (1) task comparability, (2) condition sequence, and (3) the number of conditions.

Task Comparability

A potential methodological flaw when using repeated acquisition designs is a bias in the tasks that are assigned to particular conditions. A key aspect of these designs is the development of a pool of stimuli that can be learned. The stimulus pool needs to be large enough that new items can be drawn on to constitute a novel set of stimuli for each new acquisition phase. However, this process brings to light the critical need for all stimuli to be equally difficult to acquire. If one set of stimuli is more easily learned than another set, the differences in conditions may be a result of stimuli themselves and not the independent variable(s) under analysis.

The prototypical strategy for dealing with this methodological concern was used in the Danforth et al. (1990) study. In this study, Danforth et al. were able to use a stimulus pool that had a set number of elements (response keys) that could be reconstituted in a novel arrangement for each acquisition phase. Using this technique, the first acquisition phase might compare the sequence 15243 for condition X and 32451 for condition Y. The next acquisition phase might compare the sequence 54321 for condition X and 12345 for condition Y, and so on. As long as novel patterns can be generated, there is no reason to believe that any one order is more difficult than another, and therefore task comparability is a reasonable assumption.

An approach that can be used in educational research is to develop a large enough pool of stimuli so that the stimuli can be randomly assigned to conditions. For example, if the acquisition task is the successful reading of sight-words, then a stimulus pool can be established that contains items of equivalent difficulty. When task comparability is not a reasonable assumption, then stimuli need to be empirically demonstrated to be equivalent. One means of doing this is to establish a pool of stimuli and then test acquisition of the stimuli under equivalent conditions with a few participants. This "pretesting" of the stimuli can be used to show that the stimuli are of equal difficulty and, just as important, to show the investigator what items are outliers that need to be removed from the stimulus pool prior to conducting the study using a repeated acquisition design.

Condition Sequence

When using repeated acquisition design, a similar set of issues emerges regarding condition sequencing as was discussed for multielement designs (Chapter 10). It is possible that exposure to one condition may influence performance on a subsequent task. Two procedural possibilities exist for addressing this issue. One approach is to hold the sequence of conditions fixed so that influence cannot be randomly spread between or among conditions. If interaction effects are a concern, they can be experimentally analyzed by systematically altering the sequence of conditions and studying whether any particular condition sequence produces an altered pattern of acquisition. A second option is the randomization approach. That is, during each acquisition phase, the experimenter can randomly assign one condition or another as first, second, and so on. Again, as was noted in Box 10.2 (page 146), randomization of conditions does not control for anything in single-case designs; it only distributes variability evenly across conditions if a large enough sample is used.

Number of Conditions

How many distinct conditions can be included in a repeated acquisition design is an issue of tractability. In the examples presented so far, only two conditions were compared. Such a comparison between conditions is an easily executed experimental arrangement. In Figure 12.3 (page 168), a study by Higgins, Woodward, and Henningfield (1989) compared four conditions in a repeated acquisition design. Participants were seven adult males. The dependent variable shown in the figure is the number of errors made each time a new skill was learned. The independent variable was the parametric analysis of the drug atropine at various dosages (i.e., placebo, 1.5, 3, or 6 mg/kg). In addition, a time course analysis was conducted (*x*-axis) to analyze the temporal effect of the independent variable on behavior (i.e., prior to drug administration, 0.5, 1.5, 3, 5, 7, 9, or 24 hours post dosing). Higgins and colleagues' results show that the greater the drug dosage, the more errors participants made during acquisition; less effect was seen when the individuals were asked to repeat a previously learned response sequence.

The data in Figure 12.3 illustrate the use of multiple conditions in repeated acquisition designs. As with other experimental arrangements used to conduct comparative, component, or parametric analyses, the number of conditions included is a function of two issues: (1) the minimal number of conditions that need to be included, given a particular experimental question and (2) whether the number of conditions to be included in an experiment permit the successful completion of the study in a time frame consistent with available resources.

Strengths and Limitations

Although repeated acquisition designs have been used in basic research since the 1960s, their use in single-case educational research has been less frequent and delayed. This follows a well-known pattern of transfer of new experimental techniques from basic laboratory settings to applied settings. Interestingly, use of such designs in applied behavioral research seems to be increasing. This may be in part because of increasing attention on integrating basic and applied behavior analysis (Mace, 1994).

The use of repeated acquisition designs allows single-case researchers to study behaviors that cannot be reversed. This includes such educationally relevant behaviors as

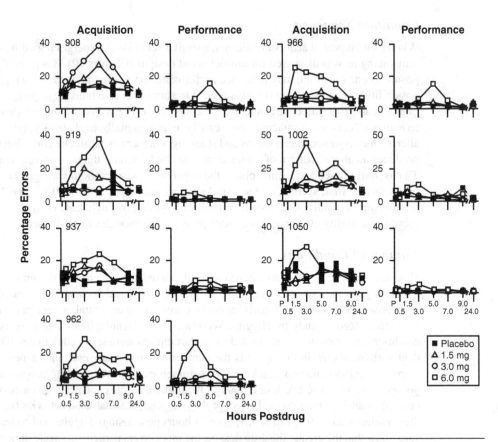

FIGURE 12.3 *Example of use of multiple conditions within a repeated acquisition design.*
Participants were seven adult males. The dependent variable shown is the number of errors made
each time a new skill was learned. The independent variable is the parametric analysis of the
drug atropine at various dosages (i.e., placebo, 1.5, 3, or 6 mg/kg). In addition, a time course
analysis was conducted (*x*-axis) to analyze the temporal effect of the independent variable on
behavior (i.e., prior to drug administration [P], 0.5, 1.5, 3, 5, 7, 9, or 24 hours post dosing).

Source: From S. T. Higgins, B. M. Woodward, and J. E. Henningfield, "Effects of Atropine on the Repeated
Acquisition and Performance of Response Sequences in Humans," *Journal of the Experimental Analysis of
Behavior,* 1989, *51,* fig. 2, p. 10. Copyright 1989 by the Society for the Experimental Analysis of Behavior.
Reprinted by permission.

spelling, addition and subtraction, reading comprehension, and motor skill development, to
name only a few. Repeated acquisition design is used to accomplish this analytical feat by
establishing a stimulus pool of equivalent items and studying their acquisition under different experimental conditions. A primary limitation of this design is the establishment and
demonstration of item substitutability (or equivalence) among the stimuli. If some type of
asymmetry in task difficulty is established in the original pool of items, it may serve as an
important threat to internal validity. However, if this challenge can be met, repeated acquisition designs are an efficient means of studying learning processes, both from a basic behavioral perspective and an applied teaching orientation.

13

Brief Experimental Designs

One concern with any type of experimental design used in educational settings is the amount of time required to complete the analysis. Schools are busy settings with a large number of logistical challenges, and the sooner that an analysis can be completed, the more likely the setting can tolerate the necessary manipulations. However, because single-case designs require repeated measures both prior to and following an intervention, the time/scope of analyses are often a challenge for researchers and educators alike. Educational settings are not the only environments with time restrictions. Outpatient clinics, related-service therapies, and standardized testing settings all require specific tasks be accomplished in a limited amount of time.

Because of these restrictions, researchers working in educational or related settings have developed an approach to experimental design referred to as brief experimental designs (Wacker, Berg, Harding, & Cooper, in press). First introduced by Cooper, Wacker, Sasso, Reimers, and Dunn (1990), brief experimental designs are variants of the A-B-A-B and multielement design types. They were explicitly developed for use in situations where internal validity is necessary to assess some behavioral outcome but the amount of time in which to accomplish this task is extremely limited. In the initial Cooper et al. study, parent-child interactions in an outpatient hospital setting were analyzed to establish the source of behavior problems engaged in by typically developing children. Because the researchers had only ninety minutes to complete their analysis and make treatment recommendations, they adapted currently existing single-case designs to the requirements of this setting. Since this initial demonstration, dozens of studies have been published using this relatively new approach to single-case design.

Brief Experimental Designs

Using brief experimental designs, a researcher conducts a single session under one set of conditions, conducts another type of session, and then reverses back to the initial condition if a change in behavior is observed. If no experimental influence is detected in the initial conditions, an additional condition might be tested. If an effect is observed, the researcher reverts to an earlier condition to reverse the observed effect on behavior. Typically, one session is conducted before switching to another condition, and each session lasts from five to fifteen minutes—hence, the term *brief experimental designs*. There are two primary variants of the brief experimental designs that integrate features of A-B-A-B or multielement designs.

A-B-A-B Variants

This approach to brief experimental designs follows the logic of withdrawal or reversal designs discussed in Chapter 9. An initial baseline session is conducted, and then a second condition is tested. If there is a change in the level of behavior, then the researcher returns to the initial condition. Such an arrangement constitutes a brief A-B-A design. If time permits, additional replications can be conducted within and/or between participants, increasing the believability of the results.

An example of an A-B-A-B brief experimental design is presented in Figure 13.1. In this study by Richman et al. (2001), children's ability to respond to adult demands of varying complexity was analyzed. The number of directives accurately completed by four children (Brad, Eric, Brandon, and Tabitha) constituted the dependent variable. At the top of each graph are labels for each demand condition tested: (1) one-step demand with modeling prompt (1-M), (2) one-step demand with verbal prompt (1-V), (3) three-step demand with verbal prompt (3-V), (4) three-step demand with verbal prompt plus an additional discrimination (3-V group discrim.), and (5) three-step demand with verbal prompt plus a conjunctive discrimination (3-V conj.). For example, Brad was able to respond to demands with the response modeled by the adult (1-M) but not to demands with verbal prompts from the adult (1-V). Each session contained five demand opportunities, and the effects of demand complexity were replicated in an A-B-A-B-A sequence. Similar analyses were conducted for the other three children, with sequences individualized based on each participant's response to the independent variables.

A more complex variant of the A-B-A-B brief experimental design is shown in Figure 13.2 (page 172). Boyajian, DuPaul, Handler, Eckert, and McGoey (2001) studied the aggression, engagement, and requests ("mands") of children with attention deficit hyperactivity disorder. Each session lasted ten minutes in length and tested different hypotheses about why the children might be aggressive. The initial experimental conditions that each child was exposed to included play (a control condition), attention for aggression, tangible objects for aggression, or reduction in demands for aggression. Figure 13.2 shows data for Terry. Aggression during the initial four sessions was only elevated in the tangible condition, suggesting that his aggression occurred to obtain preferred objects (e.g., toys). Two sessions were then conducted to replicate the initial finding (sessions 5 and 6). Again, aggression was reduced during the play condition but increased in the tangible condition. The authors then conducted a third phase of experimental manipulations. Having already demonstrated and replicated the effect of the tangible reinforcement condition, a reversal of the reinforcement contingency was conducted (sessions 7 through 9). During sessions 7 and 9, tangible objects were provided for the absence of aggression, and during session 8 tangible objects were provided contingent on aggression. Consistent with the previous effects on behavior, reversal of the reinforcement contingency decreased behavior.

The experimental tactic used in Figure 13.2 highlights the degree of flexibility possible when using brief experimental designs. Because the design permits rapid alternation between or among conditions, the possibility for conducting comparative, component, or

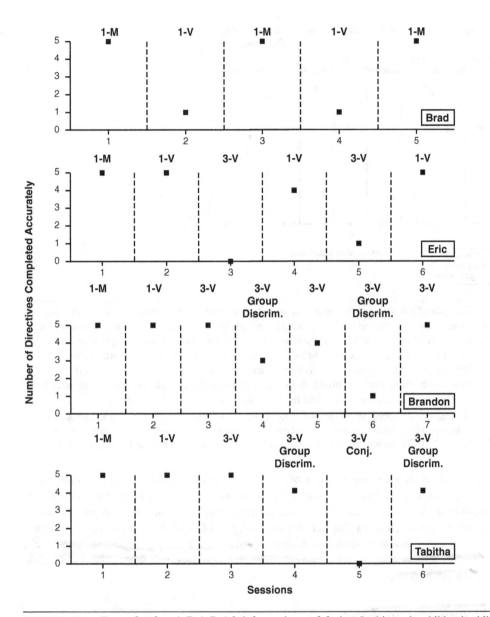

FIGURE 13.1 *Example of an A-B-A-B-A brief experimental design.* In this study, children's ability to respond to adult demands of varying in complexity was analyzed. The number of directives accurately completed by four children (Brad, Eric, Brandon, and Tabitha) constituted the dependent variable. Each session contained five demand opportunities. At the top of each graph are labels for each demand condition tested: (1) one-step demand with modeling prompt (1-M), (2) one-step demand with verbal prompt (1-V), (3) three-step demand with verbal prompt (3-V), (4) three-step demand with verbal prompt plus an additional discrimination (3-V group discrim.), and (5) three-step demand with verbal prompt plus a conjunctive discrimination (3-V conj.).

Source: From D. M. Richman, D. P. Wacker, L. J. C. Brown, K. Kayser, K. Crosland, T. J. Stephens, and J. Asmus, "Stimulus Characteristics within Directives: Effects on Accuracy of Task Completion," *Journal of Applied Behavior Analysis,* 2001, *34,* fig. 1, p. 298. Copyright 2001 by the Society for the Experimental Analysis of Behavior. Reprinted by permission.

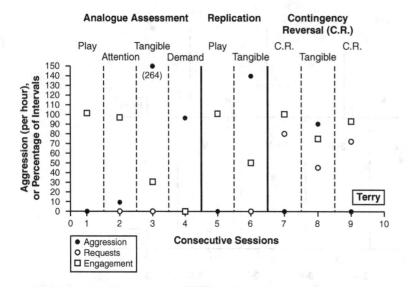

FIGURE 13.2   *Example of a brief experimental design with three phases of conditions.* The study analyzed the aggression, engagement, and requests of Terry, a child with attention deficit hyperactivity disorder. Each session lasted ten minutes and tested different hypotheses about why the child might be aggressive. The initial experimental conditions that Terry was exposed to included play (a control condition), attention for aggression, tangible objects for aggression, or reduction in demands for aggression. Play and tangible conditions were then replicated in a second phase. A final phase reversed the reinforcement contingency to conclusively show that access to tangible items functions as a positive reinforcer.

Source: From A. E. Boyajian, G. J. DuPaul, M. W. Handler, T. L. Eckert, and K. E. McGoey, "The Use of Classroom-Based Brief Functional Analyses with Preschoolers At-Risk for Attention Deficit Hyperactivity Disorder," *School Psychology Review,* 2001, *30,* fig. 2, p. 283. Copyright by the National Association of School Psychologists. Reprinted by permission.

parametric analyses across a variety of conditions is made possible. In the case of the Boyajian et al. (2001) analysis, individual conditions were embedded within three general experimental designs (see also Baer, Wolf, & Risley, 1987). Because this design type can be used very quickly, it allows for not only a high degree of flexibility but also for creating and altering experimental designs in real time. By doing this type of analysis, researchers can literally follow their data and create an experimental design as patterns in behavior unfold during observations.

Multielement Variants

A second general variant of brief experimental design uses a multielement orientation. In these designs, there is an emphasis on replicating each experimental condition once or twice. The rationale for this is to assess the effect each set of experimental procedures has on the behavior(s) of interest. In addition, the sequence of conditions is not based on the presence or absence of an experimental effect in the previous condition. Instead, as was discussed in Chapter 10, conditions are either block randomized or assigned a fixed sequence.

An example of a multielement brief design is shown in Figure 13.3. In this study by Eckert, Ardoin, Daly, and Martens (2002), the oral reading fluency of six elementary school

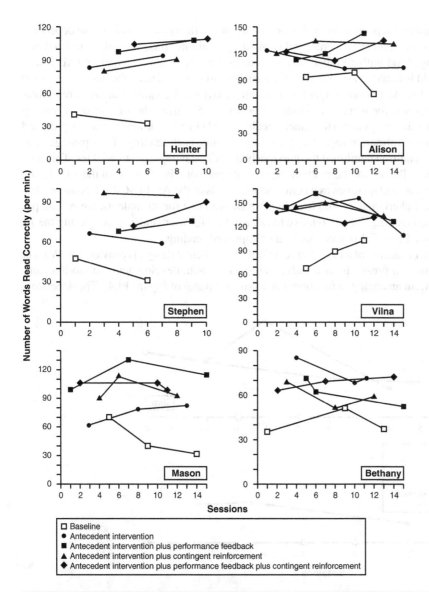

FIGURE 13.3 *Example of a multielement brief experimental design.* The study analyzed the oral reading fluency of six elementary school students. The dependent variable was the number of words read correctly per minute. Baseline consisted of a child reading aloud with no other intervention. The antecedent intervention (AI) condition had the child listen to an adult read the passage and then practice the passage for three repetitions. The AI plus contingent reinforcement (AI+CR) condition added a reinforcement contingency for increasing reading fluency by 5% from the first to third reading repetition. The AI plus performance feedback (AI+PF) condition had the adult provide the child with information regarding his or her performance after each reading of the passage. The AI+PF+CR condition combined the previously described independent variables.

Source: From T. L. Eckert, S. P. Ardoin, E. J. Daly III, and B. K. Martens, "Improving Oral Reading Fluency: A Brief Experimental Analysis of Combining an Antecedent Intervention with Consequences," *Journal of Applied Behavior Analysis,* 2002, *35,* fig. 1, p. 277. Copyright 2002 by the Society for the Experimental Analysis of Behavior. Reprinted by permission.

students (Hunter, Stephen, Mason, Alison, Vilna, and Bethany) was studied. The dependent variable was the number of words read correctly per minute. Baseline (BL) consisted of a child reading aloud with no other intervention. In the antecedent intervention (AI) condition, the child listened to an adult read the passage and then practiced the passage for three repetitions. The AI plus contingent reinforcement (AI+CR) condition added a reinforcement contingency for increasing reading fluency by 5% from the first to third reading repetition. In the AI plus performance feedback (AI+PF) condition, the adult provided the child with information regarding performance after each reading of the passage. The AI+PF+CR condition combined the previously described independent variables. This analytic approach allowed for the study of the separate and combined effects of the AI, PF, and CR interventions and qualifies as a component analysis of the AI+PF+CR intervention. The results of the Eckert et al. (2002) investigation showed that for all students, the AI component increased reading fluency relative to BL and that for four students, combining the AI with either the PF or CR procedures further improved reading.

Another example of a multielement brief experimental design is provided by Wacker and colleagues (in press). In this study, a child (Jim) with developmental disabilities initially underwent an analogue functional analysis (top panel of Figure 13.4). The dependent

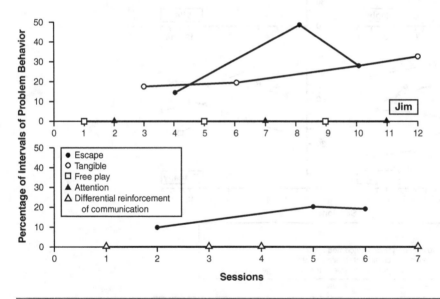

FIGURE 13.4 *Example of a multielement brief experimental design.* In this study, a child with developmental disabilities (Jim) initially underwent an analogue functional analysis (top panel). The dependent measure was the percentage of intervals of problem behavior. The experimental conditions lasted five minutes and were standard analogue functional analysis procedures: attention, escape, free play, and tangible (see Iwata, Dorsey, Slifer, Bauman, and Richman, 1982). A second analysis was then conducted under escape and differential reinforcement of communication (DRC) conditions (bottom panel). The dependent variable was the same as the previous analysis, as was the escape condition. The DRC intervention taught the child to use language rather than problem behavior to communicate his needs.

Source: From D. Wacker, W. Berg, J. Harding, and L. Cooper-Brown, "Use of Brief Experimental Analyses in Outpatient Clinic and Home Settings," *Journal of Behavioral Education,* in press. Copyright pending by Human Sciences Press. Reprinted by permission.

measure was the percentage of intervals of problem behavior. The experimental conditions lasted five minutes and used standard analogue functional analysis procedures: attention, escape, free play, and tangible (see Iwata, Dorsey, Slifer, Bauman, and Richman, 1982). The results showed that problem behaviors were multiply determined, occurring in the escape and tangible conditions. A second analysis was then conducted under escape and differential reinforcement of communication (DRC) conditions (bottom panel). The dependent variable was the same as the previous analysis, as was the escape condition. The DRC intervention taught the child to use language rather than problem behavior to communicate his needs. The DRC intervention was shown to be effective in reducing Jim's problem behavior in comparison to the escape condition.

 Both the Eckert et al. and Wacker et al. studies highlight how quickly and efficiently multielement brief designs can be used to establish a functional relation. Although the multielement strategy requires more sessions to be conducted than the A-B-A-B variant of the brief experimental design, it allows for replication of the effects of each condition. These additional data facilitate the estimation of patterns resulting from each experimental manipulation, if time and resources permit.

Strengths and Limitations

Brief experimental designs have emerged over the past decade in response to the requirements of educational and clinical settings. A perusal of the leading research journals publishing single-case design research suggests these designs are becoming increasingly common. The primary strength of brief experimental designs is that they can be used to demonstrate a functional relation in a limited time frame. This characteristic allows single-case designs to be used in situations where A-B or B-only approaches to intervention could be used. In addition, it allows behavior intervention plans or reading interventions, as an example, to be based on assessment data rather than teacher or therapist intuition.

Currently, brief experimental designs use procedures consistent with A-B-A-B and multielement designs. Such arrangements provide a great deal of efficiency as well as the requisite analytical power. That is, the A-B-A-B and multielement variants permit the demonstration of a functional relation but also allow for comparative, component, and parametric analyses. It is conceivable that multiple baseline, rapid acquisition, or combined designs could be integrated into a brief experimental design format, although this has yet to occur.

A primary limitation of brief experimental designs is the lack of within-condition replication. Or, said another way, because only individual data points are obtained within a particular condition, the assessment of trends or variability within a condition is often not possible. This raises the concern that the internal validity of a study might be compromised, resulting in false positive findings.

Figure 13.5 (page 176) shows a two-by-two matrix of possible outcomes from an experiment. A primary goal of an analysis is to arrive at a correct positive finding. That is, an effect is found and it is consistent with how the behavior-environment relations function. The inability to establish a functional relation should result in a correct negative finding. That is, no effect is found because the experimental conditions were not consistent with how the behavior-environment relations function. However, another possible outcome, a false positive finding, can occur. False positive findings occur when an experimental effect

Experimental Result

	Effect	No Effect
Effect	Correct positive finding	False negative result
No Effect	False positive result	Correct negative result

(Row axis label: Veridical Result)

FIGURE 13.5 *Two-by-two matrix of possible outcomes from an experiment.* Experimental results are the outcomes of an experimental analysis. Veridical results are what should have occurred if the analysis was accurate. A primary goal of an analysis is to arrive at a correct positive finding. That is, an effect is found and it is consistent with how the behavior-environment relations function. The inability to establish a functional relation should result in a correct negative finding. That is, no effect is found because the experimental conditions were not consistent with how the behavior-environment relations function. A false negative finding occurs when some type of behavioral phenomenon exists but the experimental procedures fail to identify it as a functional relation. False positive findings occur when an experimental effect is obtained but it is the result of some extraneous variable other than the independent variable (e.g., an interaction effect between two conditions).

is obtained but is the result of some extraneous variable other than the independent variable (e.g., an interaction effect between two conditions).

False positive findings are always a concern in any research domain. For example, setting the probability value of an inferential statistic in group comparison research at $p < 0.05$, by definition, guarantees that one in twenty positive findings is due to chance and is a false positive. Because single-case research follows an inductive approach, false positive findings resulting from chance are not an issue (see Chapter 3). However, false positive findings resulting from inadequate experimental procedures or the influence of extraneous variables are always a concern. Because brief experimental designs base the demonstration of experimental control on the minimal amount of information possible, they are probably more susceptible to producing false positive findings than extended experimental analyses. However, this differential sensitivity to producing false positives has yet to be empirically demonstrated and is therefore only an argument based on logic (see Chapter 1).

A second concern with brief experimental designs is that they may be more likely to produce false negative findings. A false negative finding occurs when some type of behavioral phenomenon exists but the experimental procedures fail to identify it as a functional relation. For example, a child's problem behavior may be due to an idiosyncratic event (e.g., the sound of an ambulance) that is not analyzed in a functional behavioral assessment; therefore, the researchers may not observe the behaviors of concern and may conclude that no problem exists (see Wacker et al., in press). The identification of false negative findings is a particularly difficult task because of the absence of a finding. Because brief experimental designs occur during a limited amount of time, they may not sample enough behavioral situations to identify variables that occur infrequently.

A related concern is the use of short session lengths. This concern is not limited to brief experimental designs but applies to any experimental analysis. However, because the use of brief experimental designs is primarily based on limited availability of research participants, this concern is probably most germane to this design tactic. As discussed in Chapter 7, the length of an observational session should be determined by criteria that focus on the adequacy of the time being sampled to represent accurately the activities of an educational context and the behavioral processes being studied. Research has shown that reducing session lengths can result in increased false positive and false negative findings (Wallace & Iwata, 1999). Therefore, the use of brief sessions may produce behavioral effects that are transient (i.e., false positive findings) or that do not allow the expression of behavioral processes that take longer to unfold (i.e., false negative findings). As with any experimental question, if researchers suspect that session length is influencing the results of a study, they should make a point of analyzing this effect to understand its influence on behavior.

14

Combined Designs

Previous chapters in this part discussed individual approaches to design tactics. Each approach has been treated within a single-case logic as if it were a separate approach to experimental design. This discussion of individual design tactics serves as an introduction to single-case designs. Many of the most exciting and innovative uses of these designs derive from a synthetic approach to experimental design—that is, the combining of individual single-case designs to explore behavioral processes that have yet to yield to experimental analysis. These designs are referred to as combined designs.

By merging two or more different single-case design tactics, combined designs provide the researcher with multiple ways of demonstrating a functional relation. There are several benefits to using combined designs. First, and perhaps most important, combined designs can be used to study more complex behavioral processes than an individual single-case design might permit. For example, a researcher may want to simultaneously compare two different conditions via a multielement design while also analyzing the effect of a third variable on each of the two conditions by using an A-B-A-B design. Second, if one aspect of a combined design (e.g., a multiple baseline design) fails to show a functional relation, another aspect of the design (e.g., an A-B-A-B design) may be used to demonstrate experimental control. Third, combined designs, because they can be used to demonstrate experimental control in multiple ways, provide stronger demonstrations of functional relations. That is, these designs can be used to show multiple replications within an experimental analysis. Given these positive attributes, it is not surprising that during the last ten years, there has been an increase in the use of combined designs by single-case researchers.

Combined Designs

Early methodology textbooks on single-case designs either did not mention combined designs (e.g., Barlow & Hersen, 1984) or mentioned them briefly (e.g., Kazdin, 1982). When combined designs were discussed, it was typically in the context of adding an additional design element to an experiment if initial attempts at demonstrating experimental control were unsuccessful. However, since the 1980s the field of behavior analysis has grown substantially in its ability to study behavioral processes in applied situations. Early in the use of single-case designs in educational research (see Chapter 2), $N = 1$ designs were used primarily to demonstrate that a particular intervention could effectively change behavior. Hence, designs like multiple baseline or A-B-A-B designs were adequate for the analytical task.

In the late 1980s and continuing today, researchers began asking more refined questions. Instead of asking whether an independent variable could change behavior, researchers began asking why a particular intervention changed behavior (see Mace, 1994). That is, researchers began exploring the behavioral processes responsible for the observed behavior change. Such questions, as noted by Baer, Wolf, and Risley (1987), often require more complex experimental designs. Therefore, combined designs have been used more frequently to meet the analytical needs of researchers seeking to explore the causes, not just the effects, of behavior change.

Table 14.1 shows possible combinations of two or more single-case designs in various configurations. As with many aspects of experimental design, the primary limitations on how different single-case designs are combined are tractability and parsimony. Combining too many designs may result in an intractable or impossible-to-implement experimental analysis, which, despite its elegance on paper or in verbal description, is essentially useless. Parsimony becomes an issue because, as a researcher, you want to demonstrate functional relations as simply as the phenomenon allows. Using an unnecessarily complex experimental design is wasteful and merely an exercise in fitting the experimental question to the experimental design, rather than vice versa (see Chapter 3).

Figure 14.1 shows an example of a design that combines multiple baseline and A-B-A-B design elements. The study, by Lee, McComas, and Jawor (2002), analyzed how schedules of reinforcement can alter the variability of behavior (see also Neuringer, 2002). Participants were three people (David, Charles, and Larry) of various ages with autism. The dependent variable was the number of varied and appropriate verbalizations made in response to questions. The baseline consisted of a schedule of differential reinforcement of appropriate (DRA) behaviors in which rewards were delivered contingent on appropriate utterances. The independent variable was a combined DRA plus a lagged reinforcement schedule in which the response needed to differ from a previous utterance and be appropriate (lag 1/DRA). The results shown in Figure 14.1 show that the DRA baseline produced

TABLE 14.1 *Various Combinations Used in Combined Designs*

Combining Two Single-Case Designs
A-B-A-B and multielement design
A-B-A-B and multiple baseline design
A-B-A-B and repeated acquisition design
Multielement and multiple baseline design
Multielement and repeated acquisition design
Multiple baseline and repeated acquisition design

Combining Three or More Single-Case Designs
A-B-A-B, multielement, and multiple baseline design
And so on.

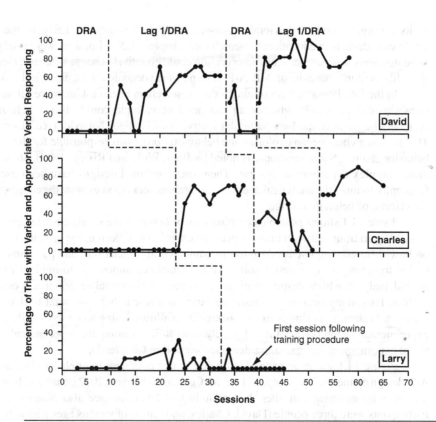

FIGURE 14.1 *Example of a multiple baseline and A-B-A-B combined design.* The study analyzed how schedules of reinforcement can alter the variability of behavior. Participants were three people of various ages with autism. The dependent variable was the number of varied and appropriate verbalizations made in response to questions. The baseline consisted of a differential reinforcement of appropriate (DRA) behaviors schedule in which rewards were delivered contingent on appropriate utterances. The independent variable was a combined DRA plus a lagged reinforcement schedule in which the response needed to differ from a previous utterance and be appropriate (lag 1/DRA).

Source: From R. Lee, J. J. McComas, and J. Jawor, "The Effects of Differential and Lag Reinforcement Schedules on Varied Verbal Responding by Individuals with Autism," *Journal of Applied Behavior Analysis,* 2002, *35,* fig. 1, p. 396. Copyright 2002 by the Society for the Experimental Analysis of Behavior. Reprinted by permission.

little variability in verbal behavior. However, when the lag 1/DRA schedule was introduced, response variability increased within the conversational context. Not only was the effect of the independent variable analyzed sequentially across participants, but for David and Charles an A-B-A-B design was added to the multiple baseline design. Thus, the experimental analysis showed the independent variable entering into a functional relation with behavior; this effect could be reversed by returning to baseline reinforcement contingencies.

A somewhat more complex combination of multiple baseline and A-B-A-B designs is shown in Figure 14.2. In this experiment by Kelley, Lerman, and Van Camp (2002), the problem behavior and alternative communicative responses of three children (Roger, Gary, and

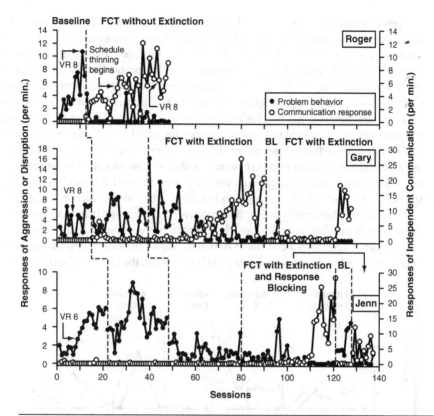

FIGURE 14.2 *Variation of the multiple baseline and A-B-A-B combined design.* This design was individualized according to each child's pattern of behavior. The experimental question focused on how competing reinforcement contingencies influence the acquisition of novel forms of communication that serve the same operant function as problem behavior (see Carr & Durand, 1985). The dependent measures were the occurrence per minute of problem behavior or alternative communication. Baseline consisted of a variable ratio (VR) reinforcement schedule for problem behavior and no programmed contingencies for communication responses. Two independent variables were studied. First, a functional communication training (FCT) procedure without extinction was analyzed. In this contingency arrangement, communication was reinforced as was problem behavior. In the second independent variable arrangement, the same FCT procedure was used for communication, but problem behavior was placed on extinction.

Source: From M. E. Kelley, D. C. Lerman, and C. M. Van Camp, "The Effects of Competing Reinforcement Schedules on the Acquisition of Functional Communication," *Journal of Applied Behavior Analysis,* 2002, *35,* fig. 2, p. 62. Copyright 2002 by the Society for the Experimental Analysis of Behavior. Reprinted by permission.

Jennifer) with developmental disabilities was analyzed. The experimental question focused on how competing reinforcement contingencies influence the acquisition of novel forms of communication serving the same operant function as problem behavior (see Carr & Durand, 1985). The dependent measures were the occurrence per minute of problem behavior or alternative communication. Baseline consisted of a variable ratio reinforcement schedule for problem behavior and no programmed contingencies for communication responses. Two independent variables were studied. First, a functional communication training (FCT) procedure without extinction was analyzed. In this contingency arrangement, communication was reinforced, as was problem behavior. In the second independent variable arrangement, the same FCT procedure was used for communication, but problem behavior was placed on extinction. Initially, the FCT-without-extinction procedure was sequentially introduced in a multiple-baseline-across-participants arrangement. This was followed by a change to the FCT-with-extinction procedure for two participants (Gary and Jennifer). For Gary, the procedures were then reversed to baseline and then back to the FCT-with-extinction procedure. For Jennifer, an additional procedure (FCT, extinction, and response blocking) was introduced, withdrawn (i.e., returned to baseline), and then reintroduced. It is important to note that this experimental arrangement could not have been planned a priori but instead was a response to how each child responded to the initial intervention. Hence, Kelley et al. used a combined design tailored to each child's behavior to explore the behavioral processes that influenced their problem behaviors and the possible interventions to reduce them.

Figure 14.3 shows a combined A-B-A-B and multielement design used by Ringdahl, Winborn, Andelman, and Kitsukawa (2002) to analyze the effects of various stimuli on be-

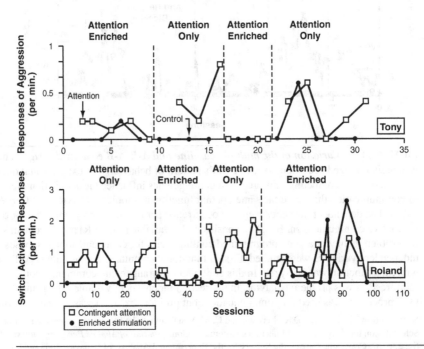

FIGURE 14.3   *Example of a combined A-B-A-B and multielement design used to analyze the effects of various stimuli on behavior.* The dependent variables were the frequency of aggression (Tony) or switch activation (Roland). The multielement component of the design was used to compare enriched stimulation (i.e., control) (closed circle) versus contingent attention (open square) for the behaviors of interest. The A-B-A-B component of the design compared enriched attention and attention only, with the former involving the addition of extra contingent stimuli along with attention.

Source: From J. E. Ringdahl, L. C. Winborn, M. S. Andelman, and K. Kitsukawa, "The Effects of Noncontingently Available Alternative Stimuli on Functional Analysis Outcomes," *Journal of Applied Behavior Analysis,* 2002, *35,* fig. 1, p. 409. Copyright 2002 by the Society for the Experimental Analysis of Behavior. Reprinted by permission.

havior. The dependent variables were the frequency of aggression (Tony) or switch activation (Roland). The multielement component of the design was used to compare enriched stimulation (i.e., control; closed circles) versus contingent attention (open squares) for the behaviors of interest. The A-B-A-B component of the design compared enriched attention and attention only with the former, involving the addition of extracontingent stimuli along with attention. The results of the Ringdahl et al. study showed that adding an additional form of stimulation enhanced the positively reinforcing effects of the attention intervention.

In a more elaborate design, Richman, Wacker, and Winborn (2001) analyzed the interaction between response effort and concurrent operants (see Box 14.1, page 184) on the aggression of a child with a disability (Mike). Mike's aggression (responses per minute) occurred to access positive reinforcement in the form of adult attention (see Figure 14.4). The experiment contained two phases. In the first phase, an A-B-A comparison was conducted in which Mike could either aggress or use a response card to access attention. When the card was available, he tended to use it at a rate of once per minute. In the second phase, a less effortful response (saying "Please") was introduced and compared against each of the previous response options. The results showed that Mike emitted the "please" response at a much higher rate than either the card or aggression, suggesting that the least effortful response was his preferred means of accessing attention. This design combined A-B-A-B and concurrent operant procedures to establish experimental control.

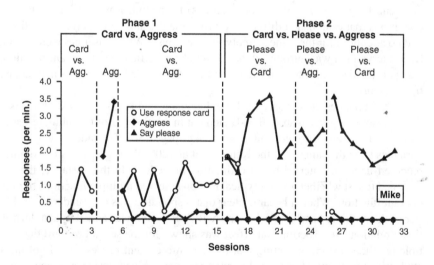

FIGURE 14.4 *Example of design combining A-B-A-B and concurrent operant procedures.*
The experiment contained two phases. In the first phase, an A-B-A comparison was conducted in which Mike could either aggress or use a response card to access attention. When the card was available, he tended to use it at a rate of once per minute. In the second phase, a less effortful response (saying "Please) was introduced and compared against each of the previous response options.

Source: From D. M. Richman, D. P. Wacker, and L. Winborn, "Response Efficiency during Functional Communication Training (FCT): Effects of Effort on Response Allocation," *Journal of Applied Behavior Analysis,* 2001, *34,* fig. 1, p. 75. Copyright 2001 by the Society for the Experimental Analysis of Behavior. Reprinted by permission.

BOX 14.1 • *Concurrent Operants as an Element in Combined Designs*

In the 1990s, applied researchers have began adopting procedures that were originally developed in the experimental analysis of behavior (see Chapter 2). One of the most prominent findings from the basic research literature is the study of choice, using concurrent schedules of reinforcement (see Herrnstein, 1970). Using concurrent schedules, two separate reinforcement contingencies are simultaneously available, and the allocation of behavior to each option is assessed. This schedule of reinforcement establishes concurrent operants. By varying some parameter of the reinforcement schedule (e.g.,

magnitude of reinforcement or response effort), the influence of that variable on choice responding can be analyzed. This procedure has been widely adopted in applied behavior analysis, particularly in the analyses of why people choose to engage in problem behaviors versus other more socially desirable alternatives (Fisher & Mazur, 1997). However, a concurrent operants procedure is not a "stand-alone" single-case design. Instead, the use of a concurrent operants procedure requires some other type of single-case design to establish a functional relation.

Another approach is to combine the concurrent operants design with a multiple baseline design. Such a design is shown in Figure 14.5. A study by Kennedy, Meyer, Knowles, and Shukla (2000) examined the stereotypical behaviors of students with autism. The dependent measures were the percentage of intervals with stereotypical behavior (closed circles) and frequency of signing (open circles) for a student named James. Baselines were conditions that established different reinforcement contingencies (i.e., attention, demand, and no attention) for the same stereotypical response. When baselines were established, an FCT intervention was introduced that targeted a specific type of operant function. The design permitted an analysis of the degree to which a single behavior was maintained by multiple functions.

A similar design was used by Tang, Patterson, and Kennedy (2003), but this combined design also incorporated an A-B-A-B element in the first tier of the multiple-baseline-plus-concurrent-operants arrangement (Figure 14.6, page 186). The independent and dependent variables were the same as in the Kennedy et al. (2000) study, except that signing was also recorded using an interval-based estimation procedure. In this instance, the design was arranged to test whether a stereotypical response served multiple functions or only a single operant function. When it became clear that responding was only under control in the first tier of the multiple baseline design, an A-B-A-B design was added to demonstrate a functional relation. No experimental effect was shown for the second or third tiers of the multiple baseline design, indicating that those reinforcement processes did not influence the student's stereotypy. Hence, in this example, a combined design was necessary to show some degree of experimental control over the behavior of interest.

A final example of a combined design is shown in Figure 14.7 (page 187). The figure shows the results of a study by Martens et al. (2002) that analyzed the effects of a probabilistic reward contingency on the academic performance of three students in an elementary school mathematics class. The dependent variable was the number of correct problems solved. Baseline was comprised of the typical classroom procedures the general educator used. The independent variable was the introduction of a lottery system that provided students with rewards for completing different easy-to-hard ratios of math problems. The de-

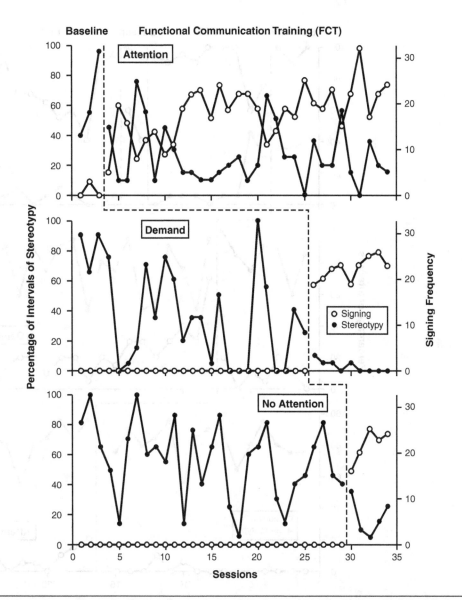

FIGURE 14.5 *Example of a concurrent operants design combined with a multiple baseline design.* This study analyzed the stereotypical behaviors of students with autism. The dependent measures were the percentage of intervals with stereotypical behavior and frequency of signing for a student named James. Baselines were conditions that established different reinforcement contingences (i.e., attention, demand, and no attention) for the same stereotypical response. When baselines were established, an FCT intervention was introduced that targeted a specific type of operant function and associated sign.

Source: From C. H. Kennedy, K. A. Meyer, T. Knowles, and S. Shukla, "Analyzing the Multiple Functions of Stereotypical Behavior for Students with Autism: Implications for Assessment and Treatment," *Journal of Applied Behavior Analysis,* 2000, *33,* fig. 2, p. 565. Copyright 2000 by the Society for the Experimental Analysis of Behavior. Reprinted by permission.

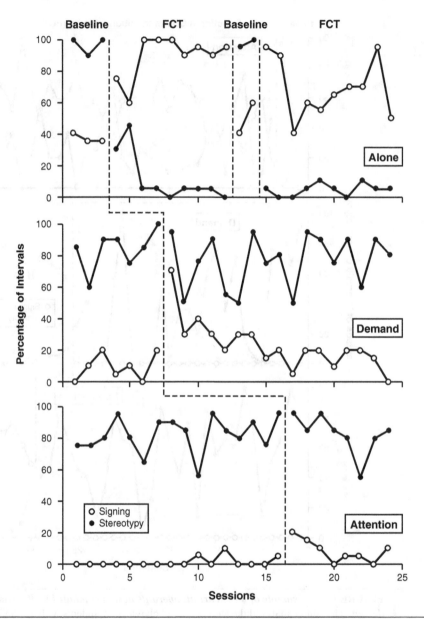

FIGURE 14.6 *Example of a combined multiple baseline across operant functions, concurrent operant, and A-B-A-B design.* The independent and dependent variables were the same as in Figure 14.5, except that signing was also recorded using an interval-based estimation procedure. In this instance the design was arranged to test whether a stereotypical response served multiple functions or only a single operant function.

Source: From J-C. Tang, T. G. Patterson, and C. H. Kennedy, "Identifying Specific Sensory Modalities Maintaining the Stereotypy of Students with Multiple Profound Disabilities," *Research in Developmental Disabilities,* 2003, *24,* fig. 6, p. 446. Copyright 2003 by Pergamon Press. Reprinted by permission.

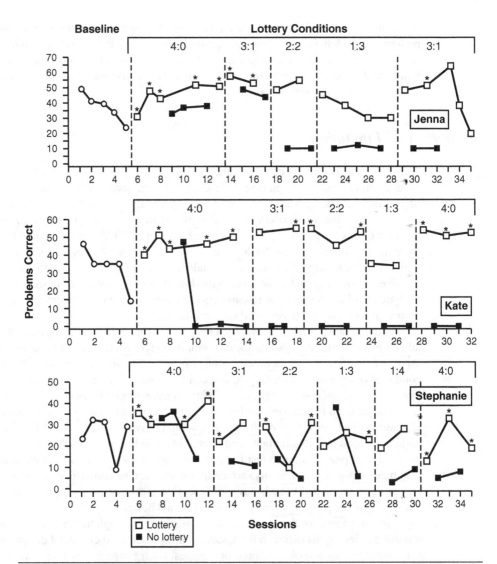

FIGURE 14.7 *Effects of a probabilistic reward contingency on academic performance.* Data are from three students in an elementary school mathematics class. The dependent variable was the number of correct problems solved individually on worksheets. Baseline was comprised of the typical classroom procedures. The independent variable was the introduction of a lottery system that provided students with rewards for completing different ratios of easy-to-hard problems. The design constitutes a combined multielement design because it alternated between baseline (i.e., no lottery) and lottery conditions and a parametric A-B-A-B analysis of different easy-to-hard ratios.

Source: From B. K. Martens, S. P. Ardoin, A. M. Hilt, A. L. Lannie, C. J. Panahon, and L. A. Wolfe, "Sensitivity of Children's Behavior to Probabilistic Reward: Effects of a Decreasing-Ratio Lottery System on Math Performance," *Journal of Applied Behavior Analysis,* 2002, *35,* fig. 1, p. 405. Copyright 2002 by the Society for the Experimental Analysis of Behavior. Reprinted by permission.

sign constituted a combined multielement design because it alternated between baseline (i.e., no lottery) and lottery conditions and a parametric A-B-A-B analysis of different easy-to-hard ratios. The results of the Martens et al. analysis showed that (1) in the absence of the lottery contingency, few problems were completed correctly; and (2) as the ratio emphasized harder questions, the lottery was less effective.

Strengths and Limitations

As noted in the beginning of this chapter, combined designs have emerged in recent years as an exciting means of exploring more complex behavioral processes in educational settings. Combined designs allow for a more in-depth analysis of the variables maintaining responding and have the flexibility to be changed as an experiment progresses. An excellent example of this flexibility is provided in the Kelley et al. (2002) data shown in Figure 14.2. By using a combined design, Kelley et al. were able to extend a design noted for its inflexibility (i.e., the multiple baseline across students) and individually tailor the analysis to the variables influencing each child's behavior. For this reason, combined designs are often the analytical tool of choice when researchers are interested in understanding the basic mechanisms influencing behaviors of educational interest.

Additional strengths of combined designs are the ability to demonstrate experimental control in multiple ways and the opportunity to show a functional relation even if one aspect of the design does not show control over responding. The primary limitations of combined designs are twofold. First, one can "overdesign" an experiment and build in too much experimental control at the cost of parsimony. Simplicity has its virtues and benefits. A second concern is that these designs require a fairly sophisticated understanding of single-case methodology. One of the chief benefits in favor of the multiple-baseline-across-participants design is its simplicity and tractability. It is hoped that such designs can be used by a range of practitioners to test the effectiveness of their own educational innovations. Combined designs, by necessity, are complex and require knowledge not only of single-case designs, but also of basic behavioral processes. However, as noted previously, this limitation is also the greatest strength of the combined design.

In many respects, this final chapter on single-case design tactics is not an ending but a starting point. By its nature, a book such as this presents experimental designs in a manner similar to how a cookbook presents recipes. Each recipe focuses on a single product, with a fixed sequence of steps necessary to successfully complete the task. However, like good recipes, single-case designs are often the most interesting when you synthesize different approaches and tailor the processes to producing unique outcomes. For this reason, this final chapter on combined designs is really an invitation to learn more about single-case designs. There is no single, correct way to analyze behavior. Thinking and problem solving need to be adapted to the task at hand rather than done in a rote and inflexible manner. This perspective on experimental designs is what led Baer, Wolf, and Risley (1987) to write, "A good design is one that answers the question convincingly, and as such needs to be constructed in reaction to the question" (p. 319).

Part V

Analyzing Data

15

Visual Data Analysis

In behavior analysis, as data are collected, information is graphed and analyzed on a continuous basis until the experiment is completed. Information from each session is plotted in a graphic display, and patterns in the data are studied to decide what the next step in the experiment will be. An example will help illustrate this process. After selecting the initial procedures for an experiment and deciding on a design tactic (e.g., an A-B-A-B design), data collection begins. After the first observational session, the data are scored, summarized, and charted in graphic form. The research team then visually inspects the data. After the first day, there are no trends or patterns in the data apart from the specific levels obtained for each variable. However, as this process is repeated, visually analyzing the data begins to yield more interesting patterns. For instance, the occurrence of problem behavior and on-task behavior may occur at consistent levels day after day. If this pattern is replicated within a participant, decisions need to be made about the introduction of an independent variable. If the pattern in the data makes this a logical decision, then the intervention could be introduced. Or, if the pattern in the data had downward or upward trends or was highly variable, the research team may choose to continue baseline until a stable pattern is obtained. As the study unfolds, decisions are made on a daily basis whether to continue, change, or end a particular set of procedures. These decisions are ongoing during a study and always made in reference to the data. This process is summarized by the expression, often heard among behavior analysts, "Follow your data."

This is a dynamic process and roughly analogous to a chess match. The first observation is made (you move a chess piece), data are collected (your opponent makes a move), the results analyzed (your next step is planned), and the next move executed, the data collected, and so on. In chess, when errors are made or unexpected moves from an opponent occur, the tactical plan is changed accordingly and as often as needed to be successful. In single-case research, plans are changed as patterns in the data unfold, with the goal of revealing some type of behavioral process in the form of a functional relation. The use of graphic displays to visualize quantitative information is central to this process. The data, in graphic format, can act as a road map for conducting a study, since the course cannot be predicted in an a priori manner (Latour, 1990).

This process can be contrasted with group comparison designs in which an experimental design (e.g., a pre/postcontrol group design; cf. Campbell & Stanley, 1966) is selected before the start of the study, data are then collected prior to and after intervention, the data are summarized, and the appropriate inferential statistics are used to test for an experimental effect (see Box 15.1). In such a case, the analysis occurs after the data are collected, and no change in the experimental design can be made without limiting internal validity. Unlike group comparison designs, single-case designs are highly dynamic, and often the most exciting analyses unfold over time as patterns in the data emerge and the experimental tactic is adjusted in reaction to the data (e.g., see Chapter 14).

The process of inspecting graphic data is a very powerful way of revealing functional relations (Hacking, 1983; Smith, Best, Stubbs, Archibald, & Roberson-Nay, 2002). In behavior analysis, the use of graphs to analyze data is as old as the field itself. In B. F. Skinner's seminal work, *The Behavior of Organisms* (1938), which led to the development of behavior analysis, visual displays of data were prominently featured as the primary means of data analysis. Figure 15.1 shows the first graph from Skinner (1938). In this figure, the cumulative number of responses by a rat is shown during the initial shaping of a lever press. The data show that three lever presses occurred during the first 120 minutes of the session, with large temporal gaps between responses. However, approximately 130 minutes into the conditioning session, the fourth response was emitted, and lever pressing began to occur at a rapid and regular rate for the remainder of the session. At this point, lever pressing had been brought under the control of a positive reinforcer. Figure 15.1 reveals this process in a manner that is easily accessed by other researchers. It is the most revealing way of analyzing the data and provides the most information to the viewer.

BOX 15.1 • *Use of Inferential Statistics in Single-Case Designs*

The use of inferential statistics in single-case research has an intellectually interesting, but fractious, history. Some researchers who use single-case designs have written eloquently about the potential that inferential statistics possess for this experimental methodology (e.g., Kratochwill, 1978; Thompson et al., 1999). Other behavior analysts have written equally eloquent expositions on why inferential statistics are not useful for researchers using single-case designs (Baer, 1977; Michael, 1974). However, these arguments—for and against—are largely moot points.

The practical problem with using inferential statistics in single-case designs is that the currently existing statistics either violate fundamental statistical assumptions or are intractable in the large majority of applied research (e.g., time-series analysis, randomization tests, or R_n test of ranks;

see Hartmann et al., 1980; Kazdin, 1982, app. B). This former concern centers around issues such as normalcy of distributions and serial dependency. The latter is largely an issue of the statistical test placing severe constraints on an experimental design, either in terms of the number of data points needed or the requirement of randomizing conditions.

Therefore, the use of inferential statistics in single-case designs is largely an academic debate and not a practical issue for researchers looking for new analytical tools. If, in the future, inferential statistics can be developed that fit the design requirements of single-case research, then the issue will require renewed debate. Until that time arrives, however, single-case researchers will continue to use the visual analysis of data as a primary means of examining their data.

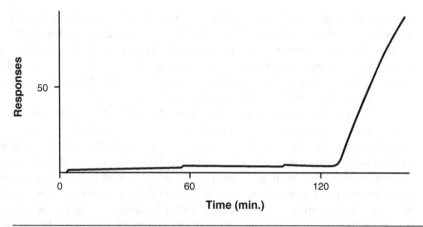

FIGURE 15.1   *The first data set presented in B. F. Skinner's* **The Behavior of Organisms** *(see Catania, 1988).* The *y*-axis displays the occurrence of individual responses as a cumulative function. The *x*-axis represents the passage of time.

Source: From B. F. Skinner (1938). *The behavior of organisms: An experimental analysis,* fig. 2, p. 67. Acton, MA: Copley. Copyright 1991 by the B. F. Skinner Society. Reprinted by permission.

The use of graphic displays by Skinner was no accident. He was using the tools of experimental biology to analyze psychological phenomena (see Chapter 2). Graphic displays—because of their flexibility, ease of use, and aid in visualizing functional relations—quickly became a mainstay in the experimental analysis of behavior, a practice that continues today. Not surprisingly, when researchers began to apply the behavioral processes discovered in the laboratory to natural settings, such as public schools, the use of graphs was continued, along with many other scientific practices. In fact, one of the most powerful interventions that allows educators to be more effective in teaching is the graphing of student performance and the visual analysis of the data on a regular basis, with appropriate adjustments to teaching procedures as indicated by the data (Alper & White, 1971; Lindsley, 1991).

This chapter explores how to use graphs in single-case research. First, the elements comprising a graph are reviewed. The discussion then explores how to visually inspect data so that a conclusion can be reached about patterns in the data and whether experimental control was demonstrated. Examples of how to use graphs to explore and analyze different facets of the data collected in an experiment follow. Finally, the topic of how to teach people to visually inspect data so that there is a high level of consistency among those inspecting data is examined.

Elements of a Graph

Although there are a multitude of graphic formats that can be used to visually display data, there are some elements that most graphs share in common (see Parsonson & Baer, 1978, for an extensive treatment of this topic). An excellent source for how to create graphs for publication purposes is contained in the January issues (2000 through 2003) of the *Journal of the Experimental Analysis of Behavior.* Figure 15.2 shows an example of a graph from a study conducted by Smith and Churchill (2002). This graph is reviewed here, not for its content, but for its structure and composition. This particular figure presents four panels in a two-by-two matrix configuration. The elements of the matrix are composed of two different independent variable manipulations labeled at the top of the graph and two different dependent variables labeled on the left-hand side of the figure.

The first place to start is with the *y*-axis, also referred to as the vertical axis or ordinate. The vertical line on the left-hand side of the graph demarks the *y*-axis of the graph and is marked according to some metric, in this case an equal-interval metric that is labeled 0 to 3 in units of one along the top panel and 0 to 10 in units of two along the bottom panel. Placement of the zero point of a graph varies among researchers, with some preferring to have the zero point raised above the *x*-axis, and others preferring the zero point to rest on the *x*-axis. These metrics are then labeled with individual descriptors that provide information regarding the measurement unit and topography of behaviors. In this instance, the upper panel is labeled "Responses per Minute (SIB)," and the lower panel is labeled "Responses per Minute (precursors)." The information arrayed along the vertical axis of this

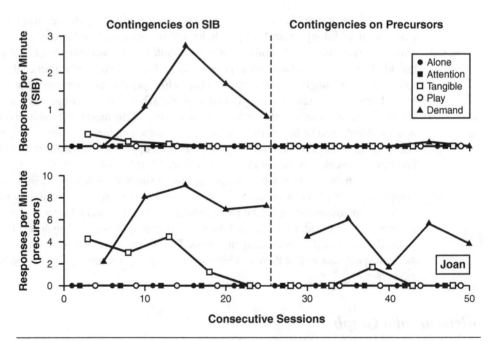

FIGURE 15.2   *Example of a graph from a study used to illustrate the elements in a graph.*

Source: From R. G. Smith and R. M. Churchill, "Identification of Environmental Determinants of Behavior Disorders through Functional Analysis of Precursor Behaviors," *Journal of Applied Behavior Analysis,* 2002, *35,* fig. 1, p. 130. Copyright 2002 by the Society for the Experimental Analysis of Behavior. Reprinted by permission.

graph informs the reader of what types of behaviors were measured, what measurement system was used to quantify responding, and what metric is being used to display the data.

The bottom of the graph is referred to as the *x*-axis, horizontal axis, or abscissa. The horizontal line running along the lower end of Figure 15.2 displays an equal-interval metric that ranges from 0 to 50 in units of ten. The metric label is presented below the numeric demarcations along the *x*-axis and identifies this part of the graph as "Consecutive Sessions." This part of the figure informs the reader, in this instance, that data are plotted on a session-by-session basis.

In this particular study, Smith and Churchill used a combined multielement and A-B design. The A-B components of the design are labeled with descriptors at the top of the graph, in this instance "Contingencies on SIB" (left side) and "Contingencies on Precursors" (right side). The phase change line—that is, the point in the experiment when conditions were changed from A to B—is designated as a dashed line running vertically through the graph at midpoint. Some researchers prefer to use solid lines, and others prefer to use broken lines to denote phase changes.

Within Figure 15.2 are the data. In this example, five different experimental conditions were analyzed: alone, attention, tangible, play, and demand. The experimental conditions are labeled in a legend contained within the graph and presented adjacent to the specific symbol (closed circle, closed square, open square, open circle, and closed triangle, respectively) that represents each condition. The quantitative outcomes from individual sessions are presented as individual data points connected by lines. Note that the data points are not connected across phase changes. Finally, the pseudonym or other identifier for the individual whose behavior is being analyzed in the study is placed in a box within the graph (in this case "Joan"). Some researchers use boxes for the names and legends in a graph to clearly set them apart from the data, but others do not.

One last component of a graph is the figure caption, which is placed below or next to the figure if the study is published. The figure caption provides a written description of the information contained in the actual figure. Ideally, the reader should be able to look at the graph and read the figure caption and understand what the data represent without having to refer to the Method section or other text in the published paper. This information can include a general description of what the graph represents, a description of the *y*- and *x*-axes, and the phases and experimental conditions used in the study.

The components just reviewed comprise the basic elements of a graphic display. However, what specific form a graph takes depends on the nature of the data and what aspect of the experiment the investigators are trying to visualize (Tufte, 1997; Ware, 2000). One stylistic issue to be considered when constructing graphs is Tufte's (1983) concept of data ink and nondata ink. Data ink are those elements in a graph that are drawn to display information that is critical for the visual analysis of the data. Nondata ink are those parts of the graph that could be erased without removing any information critical to the visual analysis. In general, data ink should be maximized within a graphic display, and nondata ink should be eliminated whenever possible. An example of this concept is displayed in Figure 15.3 (page 196). In this figure, a histogram that might appear in a journal article is shown in the left-hand panel, which contains both data and nondata ink. In the center panel is are the nondata ink. In the right-hand panel is the remaining drawing, which presents only the data ink necessary for analyzing the figure. Although the right-hand panel may be

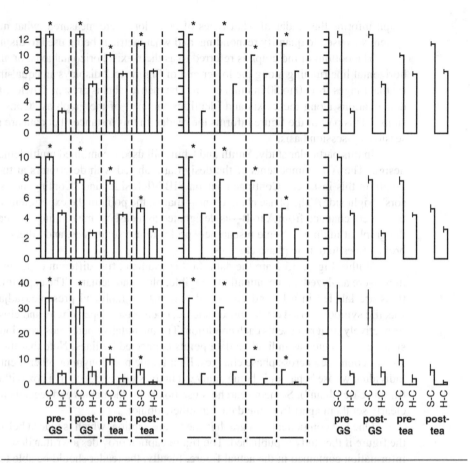

FIGURE 15.3 *A histogram that might be seen in a scientific journal article.* The histogram is shown in the left-hand panel, containing both data and nondata ink. In the center panel are only the nondata ink. In the right-hand panel is the remaining drawing that presents only the essential data ink necessary for analyzing the figure.

Source: From E. R. Tufte, *The visual display of quantitative information,* p. 102. Cheshire, CT: Graphics Press. Copyright 1983 by Graphics Press. Reprinted by permission.

considered an extreme case of minimizing nondata ink, it nicely illustrates the point that graphs should be kept as simple and uncluttered as possible so the eye is drawn to the data.

Visual Inspection of Graphs

The evaluation of quantitative information via visual inspection is accomplished by analyzing specific types of patterns in the data display. It may not seem obvious at first, but when researchers look at a graph, they look for a series of patterns that allow them to draw conclusions regarding what the data represent. These dimensions are familiar to someone who has been trained in their use, but for someone who is unfamiliar with them, their use is nonintuitive. In this section, we will review various dimensions of data that are visualized in graphs and used for analysis.

Within-Phase Patterns

The first dimension used in visual analysis is the level of the data. Level refers to the average of the data within a condition and is typically calculated as the mean or median. The left-hand panel in Figure 15.4 shows a baseline data set, with the level drawn over the data. There are six data points in the panel, with a mean of 4.7. Attending to the level of data within a phase allows for the estimation of the central tendency of the data during a particular part of an experiment. It also allows for comparison of patterns between phases (see below). Although the absolute level within a phase is important, it should be noted, particularly in applied research, that the last few data points contain the most essential information regarding the level of behavior before a phase change. The pattern of data shown in the right-hand panel of Figure 15.4 illustrates this point. Although the mean level of the data is 6.7, the last three data points deviate from this level enough to warrant special emphasis.

A second dimension used to visually inspect graphs is the trend of the data. Trend refers to the best-fit straight line that can be placed over the data within a phase. Trend has two distinct elements that must be simultaneously evaluated: slope and magnitude. Slope is the upward or downward slant or inclination of the data within a phase. Slopes are generally positive (upward), flat, or negative (downward). A positive slope is one in which the data points are increasing in value within a phase (see the upper left-hand panel of Figure 15.5, page 198). A negative slope is just the opposite, a downward pattern in the data within a phase (see the lower right-hand panel of Figure 15.5). The second element of a trend is magnitude, which is the size or extent of the slope. The magnitude of a trend is

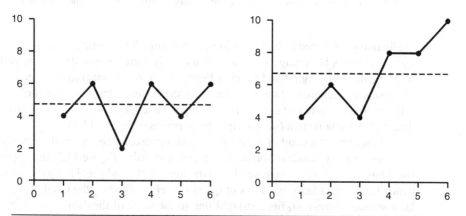

FIGURE 15.4 *An example of level used to visually inspect data.* The left-hand panel in the figure shows a baseline data set, with the level drawn over the data. There are six data points in the panel, with a mean of 4.7. The right-hand panel in the figure shows a data set in which the most essential information is within the last three data points, rather than the overall average.

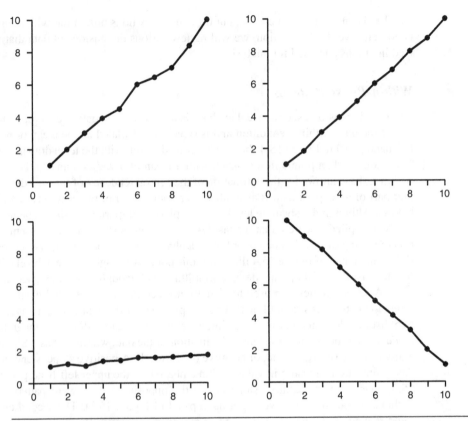

FIGURE 15.5   *Examples of slope and magnitude used to estimate trend.* Slope is the upward or downward slant or inclination of the data within a phase. Slopes are generally positive, flat, or negative. The magnitude of a trend is qualitatively estimated as high, medium, or low.

qualitatively estimated as high, medium, or low (much the same as a correlation or effect-size statistic). A high-magnitude slope is a rapidly increasing or decreasing pattern in the data (see the upper right-hand panel of Figure 15.5). A low-magnitude slope is a gradually increasing or decreasing pattern in the data (see the lower left-hand panel of Figure 15.5). It is important to note that the greater the slope, the less meaningful level is as a general estimate of the data pattern (see the right-hand panels of Figure 15.5).

In judging the trend of a data set within a phase, a person simultaneously estimates the slope and magnitude of the data. For example, using Figure 15.5, the upper left-hand panel has a moderate positive trend, and the lower left-hand panel has a moderate negative trend. There are at least two ways of quantitatively estimating the trend of data. The first, least-squares regression, fits a straight line to the slope of the data set by minimizing the sum of squared deviations of the observed data from the line. Figure 15.6 shows a diagram of how to calculate a least-squares regression line (from Parsonson & Baer, 1978, p. 131). Table 15.1 (page 200) describes how to calculate the same data shown in Figure 15.6. The

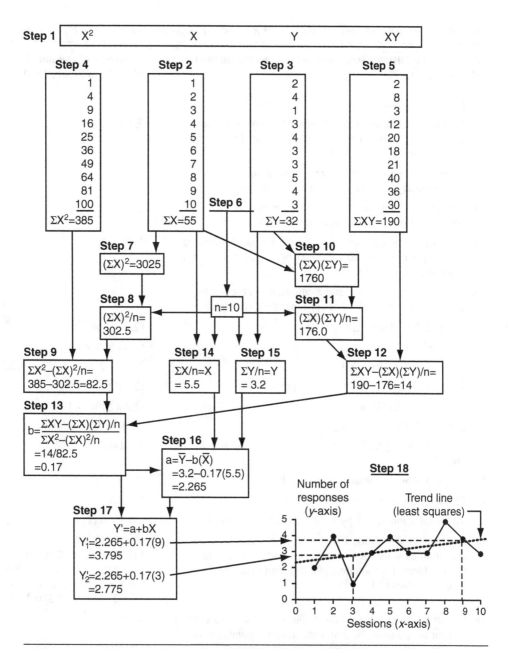

FIGURE 15.6 *Diagram outlining the process for calculating a least-squares regression coefficient.* See also Table 15.1 for a textual description of the process.

Source: From B. S. Parsonson and D. M. Baer, "The Analysis and Presentation of Graphic Data, 1978 (fig. 2.21, p. 131). In T. R. Kratochwill (Ed.), *Single subject research: Strategies for evaluating change* (pp. 101–166). New York: Academic Press. Copyright 1978 by Academic Press. Reprinted by permission.

TABLE 15.1 *How to Calculate a Least-Squares Regression Line for the Data Shown in Figure 15.6*

Procedure for fitting a straight-line trend by the method of least squares	Examples of computation (data from Figure 15.6)
1. Head four columns as follows: X^2, X, Y, XY.	
2. Fill out the X column with the number of days, sessions, or trials—in ascending numerical order—in the phase being analyzed, and their sum (ΣX).	$\Sigma X = 55$
3. In the Y column, enter the scores obtained on each successive day, session, etc., and their sum (ΣY).	$\Sigma Y = 32$
4. Fill out the X^2 column with the square of each of the corresponding X entries, and their sum (ΣX^2).	$\Sigma X^2 = 385$
5. The XY column is composed of the cross products obtained by multiplying each Y column entry by its paired X column entry, and their sum (ΣXY).	$\Sigma XY = 190$
6. The number of pairs of X and Y entries, n, is obtained by counting the number of entries in either the X or Y columns.	$n = 10$
7. Square ΣX to obtain $(\Sigma X)^2$.	$(\Sigma X)^2 = 3025$
8. Divide $(\Sigma X)^2$ by n.	$(\Sigma X)^2/n = 302.5$
9. Subtract $(\Sigma X)^2/n$ from ΣX^2.	$\Sigma X^2 - (\Sigma X)^2/n = 385 - 302.5 = 82.5$
10. Multiply ΣX and ΣY to obtain $(\Sigma X)(\Sigma Y)$.	$(\Sigma X)(\Sigma Y) = 1760$
11. Divide $(\Sigma X)(\Sigma Y)$ by n.	$(\Sigma X)(\Sigma Y)/n = 176.0$
12. Subtract $(\Sigma X)(\Sigma Y)/n$ from ΣXY.	$\Sigma XY - (\Sigma X)(\Sigma Y)/n = 190 - 176 = 14$
13. Divide $\Sigma XY - (\Sigma X)(\Sigma Y)/n$ by $\Sigma X^2 - (\Sigma X)^2/n$ (step 9) to obtain b.	$b = 14/82.5 = 0.17$
14. Divide ΣX by n to obtain mean of X, $\bar{X}$.	$\bar{X} = 5.5$
15. Divide ΣY by n to obtain mean of Y, $\bar{Y}$.	$\bar{Y} = 3.2$
16. To obtain a, multiply $\bar{X}$ by b and subtract $b\,(\bar{X})$ from $\bar{y}$.	$a = \bar{Y} - b\,(\bar{x}) = 3.2 - 0.17(5.5) = 2.265$
17. The regression equation $Y' = a + bX$ is solved by substituting the values of a and b, and values of X from the X column. Two solutions, for different values of X, give two values of Y'.	$Y_1' = 2.265 + 0.17(X)$ Let $X = 9$ (ninth X entry); $Y_1' = 2.265 + 0.17(9) = 3.795$ Let $X = 3$ (third X entry): $Y_2' = 2.265 + 0.17(3) = 2.775$
18. Locate Y_1' on the y-axis of the graph and the selected value of X on the x-axis of the graph and mark the point at which they intersect. Similarly, locate Y_2' on the y-axis and mark their point of intersection. A straight line drawn through the two points is the line of best fit and describes the trend in the data.	

Source: From B. S. Parsonson and D. M. Baer, "The Analysis and Presentation of Graphic Data, 1978, in T. R. Kratochwill (Ed.), *Single subject research: Strategies for evaluating change* (pp. 101–166). New York: Academic Press. Copyright 1978 by Academic Press. Reprinted by permission.

second method for quantitatively estimating trend is the split-middle technique (White, 1971). Using the split-middle technique requires seven or more data points within a phase and splits the data set in half, establishes a median for each half, and then plots a line that intersects the two medians (see Figure 15.7, from Kazdin, 1982, p. 313). A procedure for calculating the trend of a data set using the split-middle technique is presented in Table 15.2 (page 202).

A third dimension used to judge within-phase data patterns is variability. Variability can be defined as the degree to which individual data points deviate from the overall trend. Or, stated another way, variability is the degree to which the data points are dispersed relative to the best-fit straight line. Like the magnitude of a trend line, the terminology used to refer to variability is largely qualitative. Variability is typically referred to as being high, medium, or low. Figure 15.8 (page 202) shows two examples of variability. The left-hand panel shows a graph with low variability. That is, the data points are very close to the

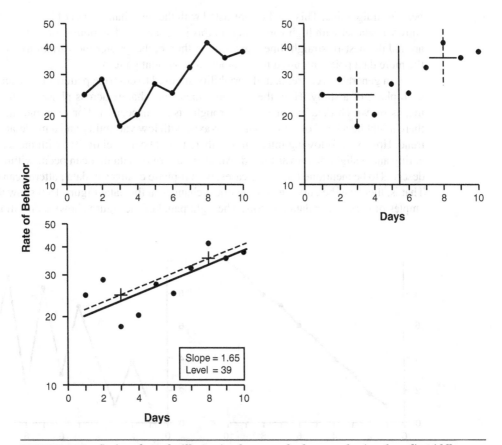

FIGURE 15.7 *Series of graphs illustrating how to calculate trend using the split-middle technique described in Table 15.2.*

Source: From A. E. Kazdin, *Single-case research designs.* New York: Oxford University Press. Copyright 1982 by Oxford University Press. Reprinted by permission.

TABLE 15.2 *How to Calculate a Split-Middle Trend Estimation Line*

1. Count the number of data points in the phase that is being used for trend estimation.
2. Draw a line on the graph at the median data point to divide the graph into two halves.
3. Divide each of the halves in half using the technique described in step 2.
4. Identify the median level of the data in each half of the split graph.
5. Mark the point at which the median number of sessions (*x*-axis) and median data level (*y*-axis) intersect for each half of the split graph.
6. Plot a straight line that intersects the two marks made in step 5.
7. Adjust the straight line plotted in step 6 so that 50% of the data points are above and below the line, making sure not to alter the slope of the line.

Note: Example uses data from Figure 15.7.

best-fit straight line. This can be contrasted with the right-hand panel of Figure 15.8, which shows a data set with high variability. In this instance, the data points are scattered widely around the best-fit straight line. As a rule of thumb, the greater the variability in the data, the more data points required to document a consistent pattern.

In general, level, trend, and variability are used to describe patterns that occur within each phase of a study. How these three dimensions change across phases is the primary means by which data are analyzed through visual inspection. For example, in baseline there might be a level of 50% along the *y*-axis, with low variability and a moderate upward trend. However, following intervention, there might be a level of 5%, with moderate variability and a slight downward trend. Another pattern of data that can occur within a phase deserves to be mentioned. In some cases, within-phase changes in data patterns can emerge. That is, there can be curvilinear or cyclical changes in the data. Figure 15.9 show three examples of curvilinear data patterns. The right panel of the figure shows a curvilinear data

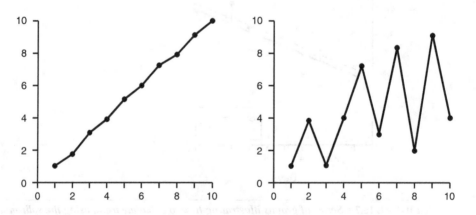

FIGURE 15.8 *Examples of two different degrees of variability in data.* The left-hand panel shows a graph with low variability. This can be contrasted with the right-hand panel, which shows a data set with high variability.

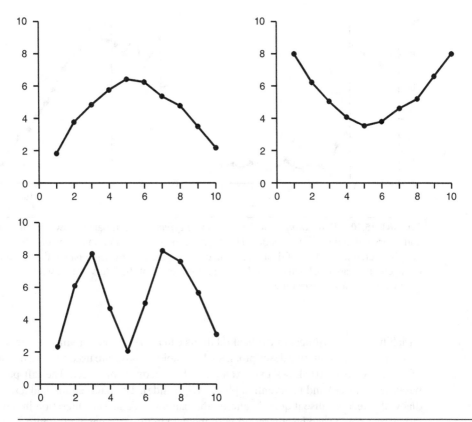

FIGURE 15.9   *Three examples of curvilinear and cyclical data patterns.* The upper left panel shows an inverse curvilinear data pattern (also referred to as an inverted U) in which the data trend increases and then decreases during a particular phase. The right panel shows a curvilinear data pattern (also referred to as a U pattern). At the bottom of the figure is a cyclical data pattern, where data increase and decrease in phasic manner.

pattern (also referred to as a U pattern). The upper left panel of Figure 15.9 shows an inverse curvilinear data pattern (also referred to as an inverted U) in which the data trend increases and then decreases during a particular phase. The bottom panel of the figure shows a cyclical data pattern in which data increase and decrease in a phasic manner.

Between-Phase Patterns

Along with level, trend, variability, and curvilinear or cyclical patterns within a phase, patterns occurring between phases are also used to visually inspect data. The first such pattern is referred to as immediacy of effect (or rapidity of change). This dimension of data display can be defined as how quickly a change in the data pattern is produced after the phase change. This is typically expressed as changes in the level and trend of the data, although

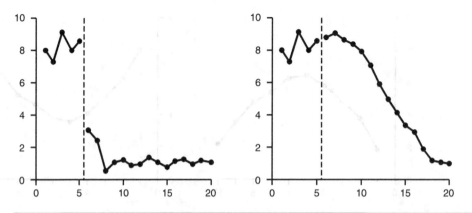

FIGURE 15.10   *Two examples of immediacy of effect.* The left panel shows baseline (left side) and intervention phases (right side). The intervention had a rapid immediacy of effect, because it clearly altered the pattern of data represented in the graph. In the right panel, there is no initial change in the pattern of behavior following introduction of the intervention, with the data then gradually decreasing over time.

variability and curvilinear or cyclical relations can also contribute to the change. Like slope and variability, qualitative descriptors, such as rapid or slow, are used to describe this aspect of data. Figure 15.10 shows two examples of immediacy of effect. The left panel shows baseline (left side) and intervention phases (right side). The intervention had a rapid immediacy of effect because it quickly altered the pattern of data. This alteration in the data pattern across phases can be contrasted with the data in the right panel of Figure 15.10. In this data set, there is no initial change in the pattern of behavior following introduction of the intervention, but then the data gradually decrease over time. Such a pattern would be referred to as having a slow immediacy of effect. In general, the greater the immediacy of effect, the briefer a phase can be and the more convincing is the functional relation.

A second between-phase pattern is referred to as overlap. Overlap can be defined as the percentage or degree to which data in adjacent phases share similar quantitative values. Figure 15.11 shows three distinct patterns of overlap between baseline (left side) and intervention phases (right side). In the upper left panel of the figure, there is no overlap (i.e., 0%) between baseline and intervention phases. This is because there are no overlapping data values between the two phases. The right panel of Figure 15.11 shows an example of complete (i.e., 100%) overlap between baseline and intervention phases. In this case, the intervention data completely overlap with the baseline data (although the converse is not true, so specifying the directionality of overlap is important). The final data set in Figure 15.11 (bottom panel) presents a common data pattern that leads to misinterpretation. Although there is no overlap between the data in adjacent phases, there is a trend that is continuous across phases. In such cases, trend overrides the importance of overlap in evaluating whether a functional relation has been established.

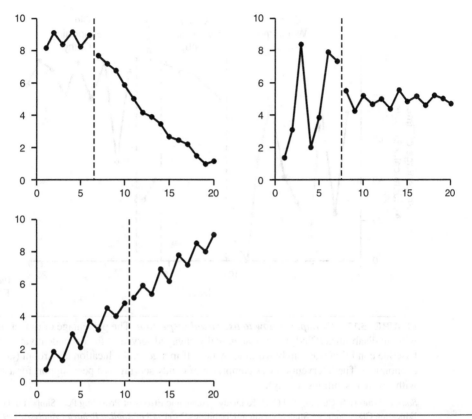

FIGURE 15.11 *Three examples of overlap in data between phases.* In the upper left panel, there is no overlap (i.e., 0%) between baseline and intervention phases. The right panel shows an example of complete (i.e., 100%) overlap between baseline and intervention phases. The final data set (bottom panel) presents a common data pattern that often leads to misinterpretation.

An Example

An illustration of how to use visual inspection to characterize a data set and arrive at a judgment regarding whether a functional relation has been established can be done using Figure 15.12 (page 206). In this study by Cushing and Kennedy (1997) the percentage of time a student without disabilities (Cindy) was academically engaged served as the dependent variable. The baseline condition was Cindy working by herself in a general education classroom. During the initial baseline, there was a high degree of variability, with a mean of 42 (range, 0 to 76%) and a moderate downward trend. The intervention was comprised of Cindy serving as a peer support for a student with severe disabilities (Cathy). Following intervention, there was an immediate increase in the level of the dependent variable ($M = 91$) with a small upward trend, little variability, and no overlap with the previous baseline.

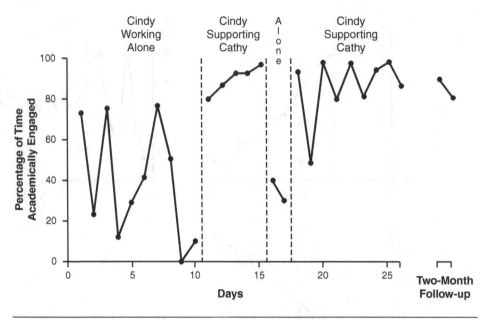

FIGURE 15.12   *Example of how to use visual inspection.* The percentage of time a student without disabilities (Cindy) was academically engaged served as the dependent variable. The baseline condition was Cindy working by herself in a general education classroom (i.e., home economics). The intervention was comprised of Cindy serving as a peer support for a student with severe disabilities (Cathy).

Source: From L. S. Cushing and C. H. Kennedy, "Academic Effects of Providing Peer Support in General Education Classrooms on Students without Disabilities," *Journal of Applied Behavior Analysis,* 1997, *30,* fig. 1, p. 145. Copyright 1997 by the Society for the Experimental Analysis of Behavior. Reproduced by permission.

withdrawal of the intervention coincided with a reversal to baseline levels of performance ($M = 38\%$). Reintroducing the intervention resulted in an increase in academic engagement ($M = 85\%$), which after several sessions returned to levels similar to the previous intervention phase. Using the A-B-A-B withdrawal design, Cushing and Kennedy were able to demonstrate that Cindy was more academically engaged when she assisted Cathy than when she worked alone.

aphs to Analyze Data

ollowing this review of the elements of line graphs and the basic issues in visual analysis, focus will now shift to how to use graphs to explore various aspects of a data set. Data are often multifaceted and lend themselves to a variety of analyses. Depending on the ach taken, different aspects of the nature of the data will be revealed. Therefore, visual analysis of data is much more than simply putting data into a graphic template and deg the information. Instead, visual analysis is a process of using graphs to explore and visualize different aspects of the data so that researchers can arrive at a better understanding of the nature of their findings.

An example of how graphs can be used to focus on various aspects of a data set in educational research is provided by Haring and Kennedy (1988). These authors analyzed a task analysis data set, using various graphic strategies. Task analysis is a process of breaking complex sequences of behavior into component parts. This procedure has proven effective at teaching people complex skills (Gold, 1976). In this instance, a leisure activity was taught to a young man with severe disabilities. Table 15.3 shows the task analysis of the leisure activity and notes the steps that were critical for independently completing the skill, as compared to the steps that were based on social convention.

Figure 15.13 (page 208) shows five different approaches to visualizing the task analysis data, each showing different properties of the original data. Graph A is a standard line graph that presents the percentage of correct steps for each baseline and training session. This graphic approach shows day-to-day variation in the dataset but does not provide information regarding when the skill was independently performed (i.e., all critical steps) and does not show the types of errors that occurred. Graph B shows the number of sessions (in blocks of five) that were independently completed. This second approach to visualizing the data allows for an analysis of independent performances but does not show day-to-day variability or the types of errors that were made. Graph C displays the data as the number of sessions to criterion for each step in the task analysis (i.e., correctly performed three days in a row for a single step). This graphic approach shows the errors that were made in a summative fashion but does not display day-to-day variation or when competent performances occurred. A fourth approach to visually displaying the data is shown in Graph D. This graph shows the cumulative number of times that the skill was performed independently. This approach allows analysis of whether a session was independently performed and on what day (preserving day-to-day variation at a certain level) but provides no information regarding what types of errors were made. Graph E combines elements of Graphs A and D to display the percentage of steps correct and the occurrence of independent performances. By doing this, the graph shows all of the characteristics of the data previously described, with the ex-

---

TABLE 15.3 *Task Analysis of a Leisure Skill*

Steps in Task Analysis
1. Gets radio and magazine[a]
2. Sits down in leisure area[a]
3. Turns radio on[a]
4. Selects radio station[a]
5. Puts headphones on appropriately
6. Looks at magazine[a]
7. Stops activity when signaled that break is finished[a]
8. Takes headphones off[a]
9. Turns radio off[a]
10. Puts magazine and radio away

---

[a]Critical steps.

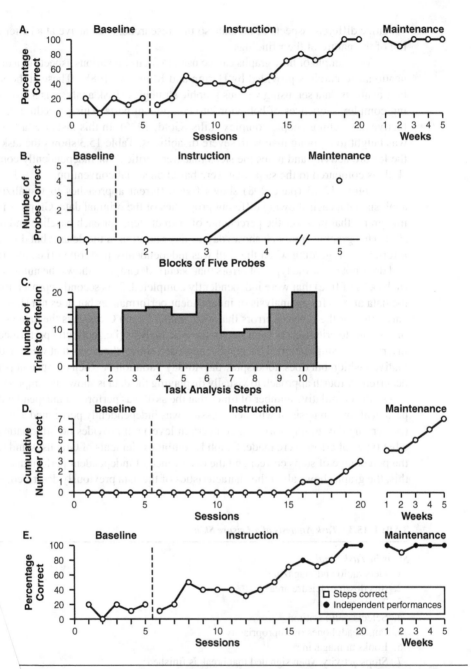

FIGURE 15.13 *Example of how graphs can be used to focus on various aspects of a data set in educational research.* Each graph reveals a different aspect of the original data.

From T. G. Haring and C. H. Kennedy, "Units of Analysis in Task-Analytic Research," *Journal of Behavior Analysis,* 1988, *21,* fig. 1, p. 209. Copyright 1988 by the Society for the Experimental of Behavior. Reproduced by permission.

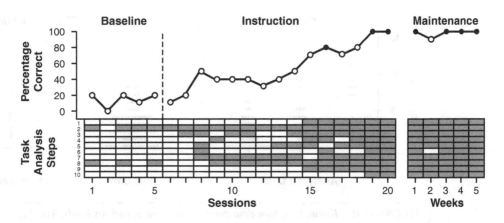

FIGURE 15.14 *This graph allows for a comprehensive visual analysis of the original data displayed in various ways in Figure 15.13.*

Source: From T. G. Haring and C. H. Kennedy, "Units of Analysis in Task-Analytic Research," *Journal of Applied Behavior Analysis,* 1988, *21,* fig. 2, p. 213. Copyright 1988 by the Society for the Experimental Analysis of Behavior. Reproduced by permission.

ception of an error pattern analysis. A final graph was constructed by Haring and Kennedy that met each of the criteria previously discussed (see Figure 15.14). This final graph allows for a comprehensive visual analysis of the original data.

The previous examples illustrate how using various approaches to graphically display data can allow for the visualization of different aspects of a data set. The variety of means for visualizing data is enormous, and researchers need to select those graphic approaches that best represent salient aspects of their data. An issue that needs to be addressed when graphing data is the level at which the information will be summarized. In some instances, it may be more desirable to summarize data as averages (e.g., percentage of intervals), while at other times it may be best to graph data at a more fine-grained level (e.g., cumulative occurrences in real time). The former approach is sometimes referred as a molar approach, and the latter as a molecular approach.

Figure 15.15 (page 210) illustrates how the same data set can be visualized at various levels (Iversen, 1988). The data are from a laboratory experiment that analzyed the number of times a response was emitted following the delivery of a response-independent positive reinforcer. The y-axis displays this as the number of responses that occurred within thirty seconds of each reinforcing event. In the center panel of the graph are the raw data. It show that on one occurrence, twelve responses were emitted; on four occurrences, eleven responses were emitted; on one occurrence ten responses were emitted; and so on. If the data were summarized at a molar level, such as the mean and standard deviation of the raw data it would look like the graph in the right-hand panel of Figure 15.15. If the data were analyzed at a more molecular level, one approach would be to adopt the strategy shown in the hand panel. In this instance, the data were further analyzed in terms of the contiguity tween reinforcer delivery and the last response prior to the reinforcer delivery. The da

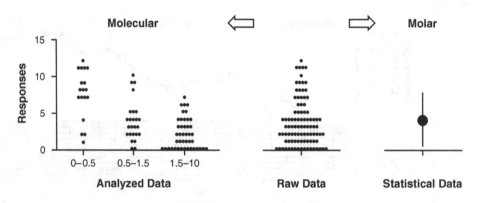

FIGURE 15.15 *Example of how data can be visualized at various levels.* The data are from a laboratory experiment that measured the number of times a response was emitted following the delivery of a response-independent positive reinforcer. The vertical axis displays this as the number of responses that occurred within thirty seconds of each reinforcing event. Each of the panels aggregates the data at a different level of refinement.

Source: From I. H. Iversen, "Tactics of Graphic Design: A Review of Tufte's *The Visual Display of Quantitative Information*," *Journal of the Experimental Analysis of Behavior*, 1988, *49*, fig. 6, p. 179. Copyright 1988 by the Society for the Experimental Analysis of Behavior. Reproduced by permission.

the left-hand panel clearly show that the greater the contiguity (e.g., 0 to 0.5 s) between prior responses and reinforcer delivery, the greater the number of postreinforcement responses.

The data displays in Figure 15.15 show how information can be summarized at different levels of aggregation and disaggregation. The raw data show the general distribution of events, the statistical data show central tendency and dispersion at the most coarse level, and the disaggregated data show specific patterns in the data. The information shown in the left-hand panel also illustrates the power of graphic displays to more completely analyze data. With the addition of a second variable along the horizontal axis, the author was able to account for variability in the behavior unexplained in the other panels. In this sense, graphs can be used to explore, visualize, and explain variability in behavior.

Another approach to visualizing information that is becoming increasingly common is to conduct within-session analyses. The information in Figures 15.2 through 15.15 show data-summarizing events occurring during an entire session. That is, the data represent the average level of events within the experimental session. However, in some instances, information regarding the pattern of events within a session can aid in the understanding of variables influencing behavior. One assumption that is implicit in summarizing whole-session data as individual data points is that the pattern of behavior observed in an experimental session was uniform throughout that session. For instances in which there are changes in responding during a session, within-session data analysis can reveal potentially important patterns that otherwise might not be discovered.

One of the first applied examples of within-session analysis was provided by Carr, on, and Binkoff (1980). Carr and colleagues were interested in understanding why aggression occurred in two boys with developmental disabilities. The analysis shown in

Figure 15.16 indicates that the behavior was related to instructional demands. When demands were made, high levels of aggression occurred; under no-demand conditions, aggression rarely occurred. An important aspect of the experimental procedures was that the length of each session was fixed. Once the session was over, the demands stopped. Technically, if the children's behavior was reinforced by escape from instruction, termination of a session could constitute a fixed-interval (FI) schedule of negative reinforcement (see Catania, 1999). An important characteristic of FI schedules is that they produce a scalloped pattern of behavior in which responding is less frequent early on but increases in probability as the end of the interval nears (i.e., reinforcement is more proximal). To see if the data they were obtaining fit this well-known pattern of behavior, Carr et al. conducted a within-session analysis that contrasted two conditions: the presence of a "safety signal" indicating

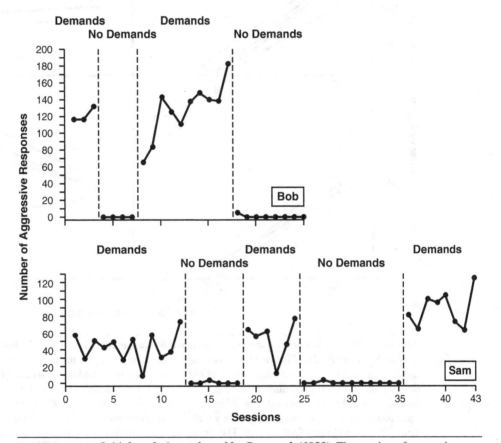

FIGURE 15.16 *Initial analysis conducted by Carr et al. (1980).* The number of aggressive responses for Sam and Bob (two boys with developmental disabilities) served as the dependent variable. The independent variable was the presence or absence of instructional demands.

Source: From E. G. Carr, C. D. Newsom, and J. A. Binkoff, "Escape as a Factor in the Aggressive Behavior of Two Retarded Children," *Journal of Applied Behavior Analysis,* 1980, *13,* fig. 1, p. 105. Copyright 1980 by the Society for the Experimental Analysis of Behavior. Reproduced by permission.

no more demands would be made versus a "no-safety-signal" condition in which demands were continued (see Figure 15.17). In the absence of the safety signal, aggression increased as the sessions continued; when the safety signal was presented, aggression decreased. This within-session analysis helped provide additional evidence that the aggression was

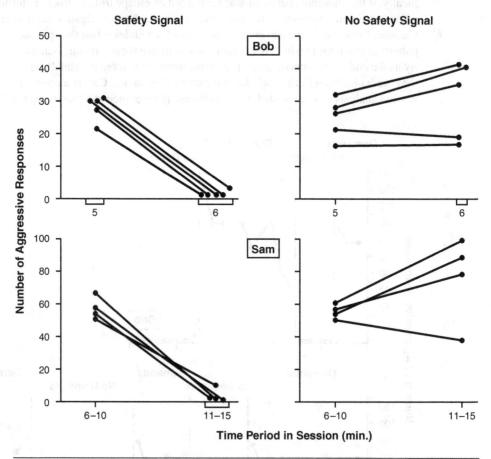

FIGURE 15.17 *Within-session analysis conducted by Carr et al. (1980) from the between-session data displayed in Figure 15.16.* As described by Carr et al., "Number of aggressive responses during the fifth and sixth minute of each session in the second demands condition for Bob (top half of figure) and during the sixth to tenth minute and eleventh to fifteenth minute of each session in the third demands condition for Sam (bottom half of figure). The left panels show data taken during safety signal sessions in which the experimenter signaled to each child that demands were no longer forthcoming. The signal was given to Bob at the start of the sixth minute and to Sam at the start of the eleventh minute. The right panels show data taken during no-safety-signal sessions in which neither child received any cue that demands had ended. Some of the data points have been slightly displaced horizontally to enhance presentation clarity" (p. 106).

Source: From E. G. Carr, C. D. Newsom, and J. A. Binkoff, "Escape as a Factor in the Aggressive Behavior of Two Retarded Children," *Journal of Applied Behavior Analysis,* 1980, *13,* fig. 2, p. 106. Copyright 1980 by the Society for the Experimental Analysis of Behavior. Reproduced by permission.

negatively reinforced (see Carr, 1977) and followed principles of behavior that were well established in basic research (see Sidman, 1960b).

Another example of within-session analysis is provided by Vollmer, Ringdahl, Roane, and Marcus (1997) in an analysis of adventitious positive reinforcement using non-contingent reinforcement (NCR) procedures to treat behavior problems. The top panel of Figure 15.18 shows an analysis of NCR to treat the behavior problem of an adolescent with developmental disabilities. During the second NCR phase (sessions 14 through 20),

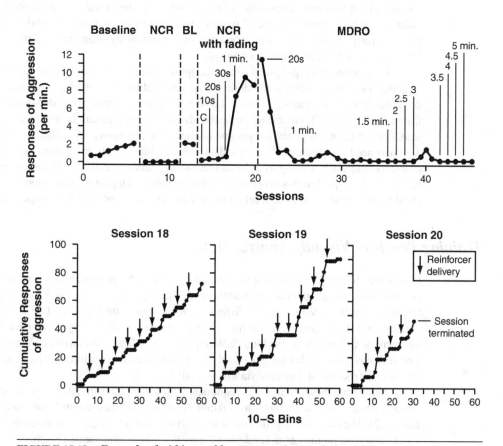

FIGURE 15.18 *Example of within- and between-session analysis of data.* Vollmer et al. (1997) describe this figure: "The upper panel shows aggression rates during baseline, continuous NCR, NCR with fading, and MDRO conditions (values for MDRO are shown in minutes). The fading steps are indicated by the lines and reinforcer delivery schedule values. The lower panel shows cumulative records of aggression during sessions 18 through 20. Arrows indicate when reinforcers were presented" (p. 163).

Source: From T. R. Vollmer, J. E. Ringdahl, H. S. Roane, and B. A. Marcus, "Negative Side-Effects of Noncontingent Reinforcement," *Journal of Applied Behavior Analysis,* 1997, *30,* fig. 1, p. 163. Copyright 1997 by the Society for the Experimental Analysis of Behavior. Reproduced by permission.

problem behavior began to rapidly increase in frequency. Vollmer et al. conducted within-session analyses of these sessions, which are displayed in the lower panels of the figure. Using the NCR procedure, a reinforcer was delivered on a response-independent fixed-time (FT) schedule. The pattern of responding and stimulus delivery on the NCR FT schedule showed a pattern of responding very similar to that previously discussed for FI schedules of reinforcement. That is, the authors had inadvertently (i.e., adventitiously) established a positive reinforcement contingency for the problem behavior, thus making it increase over time. Given the results of the within-session analysis, Vollmer et al. were able to arrange a momentary-differential-reinforcement-of-other (MDRO) schedule of reinforcement to counteract the adventitious positive reinforcement schedule established via the NCR procedure. In this example, the use of within-session analysis provided the ability to analyze the contiguity of events that were occurring on a moment-by-moment level that would not have otherwise been available for analysis.

This section has highlighted a few examples of how graphs can be used to explore data. This type of process is frequently done in experimental biology and the experimental analysis of behavior (see Chapter 2) but is far more rare in psychology or educational research (Smith et al., 2002). There are no prescribed limits to how data can be explored and visualized, nor are there templates for graphic analysis that are universally effective. Instead, researchers need to look carefully at their data and at multiple levels, in conjunction with a range of events potentially serving as independent and dependent variables. The use of graphs can be extremely helpful in this process of exploring data and trying to more thoroughly understand what type(s) of functional relations may have been established in an experiment.

Training People to Visually Analyze Data

One of the chief criticisms of the visual analysis of data by proponents of inferential statistics has been that judgments are inconsistent. That is, if two or three different researchers inspect a graph, they may reach different conclusions. The basis for this concern were studies showing interrater variability when conducting visual analyses of data (e.g., DeProspero & Cohen, 1979; Furlong & Wampold, 1982; Jones, Weinrott, & Vaught, 1978). The findings showed that judges could differ under certain conditions when categorizing the size of experimental effects via visual analysis.

At the time these studies were conducted, they were interpreted by researchers not familiar with single-case methods as a damning critique of this research methodology (see Box 15.2). The criticism was that the data analysis methods of this new discipline were invalid, or at least inconsistent, rendering the methodology inadequate (Fisch, 2001; Shavelson & Towne, 2002). The logic was that if researchers varied in their visual interpretation of graphs, the data analysis methods used in behavior analysis were flawed. On the surface this criticism seems to have merit. However, the logic seems inconsistent with certain aspects of the scientific process. First, the judgment of raters differed primarily under conditions of small level changes between conditions and high variability within phases. Few, if any, single-case researchers would attempt to claim functional relations under such circumstances. If they did, their claims would likely be challenged by other single-case researchers on the bases that (1) any assertion regarding a functional relation needs to be

BOX 15.2 • *Applied Psychology's Disfavor with Visual Data Analysis*

Considerable attention was given to the emergence of applied behavior analysis in the 1960s and 1970s. Part of that attention was from applied psychologists, who criticized the nascent field's primary approach to data analysis—graphic displays. This approach to data analysis contradicted the predominant approach in psychology, which was the use of inferential statistics. Applied psychologists have criticized researchers using single-case designs for not following proper scientific method (Shavelson & Towne, 2002).

One of the underlying issues of this debate was two fundamentally different approaches to designing experiments and analyzing data. Using group comparison methods, subjects are randomly assigned to prescribed conditions; after the data are collected, the results are analyzed to estimate the degree to which a particular finding is due to chance. If that probability is low enough, the results are accepted as due to experimental effects and not extraneous variables. In behavior analysis, experiments are designed to reveal how behavioral processes operate, and data analysis is focused on demonstrating functional relations via repeated experimental manipulations. The designs are inductive and changed as the data require. The two approaches have distinct epistemological assumptions, meaning that they are not reconcilable (Catania, 1973). Rather, they exist as distinct approaches to conducting experiments. Criticizing one approach by using the experimental criteria of the other is logically unsatisfactory.

There is a long-standing truism among researchers that the appropriate analytical technique is not tied to a specific research methodology but to the success of researchers in answering their experimental questions. Whether single-case designs are an adequate approach to answering experimental questions should not be judged by a particular person's aesthetic sense of what a research method should be but by how useful that method is in answering the experimental questions being posed. Given that research in the behavior-analytic tradition has thrived for most of the twentieth century, from laboratory to school settings, and is only showing signs of increasing in prevalence across a range of academic disciplines, this approach to experimental design must be producing useful results. Otherwise, it would have ceased to be used as a tool for understanding human nature long ago.

Perhaps what is fundamentally at issue with applied psychology's disfavor of various methods used in single-case research is not the inadequacy of those methods but the critics' lack of familiarity with single-case methods and their underlying assumptions. To dismiss a functional relation derived from a single-case design as not adequate because inferential statistics were not used is no more substantive than behavior analysts complaining that group comparison designs hide variability or are inefficient because they require too many participants to demonstrate experimental control. Ultimately, the adequacy of any particular experimental method will rest on researchers' ability to produce findings and solve problems by using that particular method.

highly qualified and (2) the finding would require direct replication with additional participants before it was publishable. Hence, the criticism that visual inspection may lead to increased Type I errors (i.e., claims of an effect when none exists) ignores the larger social context of how data are evaluated in science (see Smith et al., 2002). Rarely, in single-case research, do claims of an experimental effect rest on a single ambiguous A-B analysis. Such a claim would not survive the peer review process, which serves as the primary quality control system for introducing new findings into the research literature (see Chapter 1). Given that multiple individuals (i.e., researchers, reviewers, and editors) visually analyze each data set prior to publication, the odds of every person making a Type I error following this type of training is extremely small.

A second flaw in criticisms leveled against visual inspection is that they ignore the self-corrective nature of the research process. If researchers were to claim a functional relation from a limited data set with small effects, those findings would still need to be independently replicated. If researchers did make a Type I error by overinterpreting their data, they and others would be unable to replicate the original findings. The result would be that the original finding would be viewed as an anomaly and disregarded as a valid claim. It is important to remember that at the heart of the scientific method is a "quality control system" called replication (see Chapter 4).

A final limitation of critiques of visual analysis is that this approach to data analysis is demonstrably effective as a scientific technique. Ignoring for the moment the findings of experimental biology and medicine over the last two centuries (which often rely on visual analysis of data; see Latour & Woolgar, 1986), the single-case literature in educational research has repeatedly produced important findings over the last forty years. Those findings, as noted in Chapter 2, have been repeatedly replicated, extended, and refined over time and have led to important insights into behavioral processes and innovative new teaching techniques. If the basis for data analysis in single-case research were fundamentally flawed, it is unclear how a continuous stream of important discoveries could be made (and repeatedly replicated).

A more adequate solution to concerns about interrater variability using visual analysis is one very familiar to educators and behavior analysts: teach people how to analyze graphed data. In every research team, such a process is done informally (or at least without an explicit curriculum) using visual analysis methods and is a standard component of university courses in behavior analysis. Recent data have shown that untrained observers can interpret graphed data (as indexed by a consensus of experts) with approximately 55% accuracy. However, following training, those same raters improve their performances to approximately 95% (Fisher et al., 2003).

Fisher et al.'s (2003) recently validated approach to training visual analysis skills will be used as an example. First, a set of A-B graphs are developed that show a range of effects relating to trend, level, variability, immediacy of effect, and overlap. The graphs are then categorized into varying degrees of change between conditions as an index against which trainees' judgments can be indexed. Trainees are then exposed to the concepts of visual inspection (reviewed in the previous sections of this chapter). The A-B graphs are then presented individually to the trainees, who are asked to record whether an effect is present or not, and they are then provided with feedback regarding the accuracy of their performances. This relatively simple method can be used to train consistent visual inspectors in less than an hour, according to Fisher et al. (2003).

This type of formal training scenario, combined with regular reading and discussion of published research, seems to be the best approach to teaching people how to visually analyze data. Combine these approaches with the daily and weekly decisions that are required when engaging in either research or practice, and a rigorous training regimen is established. Twenty-five years after the debate over whether visual data analysis is an acceptable method, the focus has changed from whether the approach works to how to effectively teach people to use this demonstrably effective data analysis technique. In other words, with the vantage gained by hindsight, the issues regarding the use of visual data analysis are not if, but how.

Conclusion

The visual inspection of graphed data has proven to be one of the most powerful analytical techniques in science. By visualizing different aspects of a data set, the results of a study can be explored and described in a variety of ways. Such a process allows researchers to delve into various aspects and patterns of their data to gain a deeper understanding of the nature of their findings. The use of visual analysis techniques match the inductive nature of single-case designs by facilitating data exploration and the provision of readily developed and updated data analysis formats. That is, as an experiment unfolds, the data can be tracked on a daily basis for decision-making purposes and the experimental procedures adjusted accordingly.

Because of these properties, graphed data have been the central means of data analysis for the experimental analysis of behavior since its inception in the 1930s. As basic laboratory findings were extended to socially relevant issues, the data analysis techniques of basic researchers were adopted by applied investigators. Although the use of graphs instead of inferential statistics as a primary means of data analysis is contrary to traditional approaches to psychology, this technique has proven useful in the biological and medical sciences. This chapter has provided an introduction to the visual analysis of data as well as a few examples of how graphic displays can be used to better understand the nature of functional relations that result from single-case research. However, like all aspects of research methodology, there is no single "correct way" of graphing data. Instead, researchers need to adapt the techniques available to them to the analytical task at hand and use, or develop, the most appropriate means to reveal what patterns exist in their data.

16

Social Validity

If this book were strictly about behavioral processes analyzed in laboratory settings, then this final chapter would not be necessary. However, this book is not about basic research. Instead, it has explicitly focused on how to analyze behavioral processes in educational settings. Such a focus requires researchers to work directly with people, many of whom are in some type of need and require help from others. This makes applied behavior analysis different from the experimental analysis of behavior. Although both disciplines seek to understand the underlying nature of human behavior through the analysis of behavioral processes, applied research does so within a highly public context.

Typically, in educational settings, researchers are working to ameliorate some type of problematic situation, whether it be increasing the acquisition of reading skills, improving a child's articulation, or intervening to reduce aggressive behavior. In addition, because schools are public settings, other students, teachers, paraprofessionals, school administrators, and related services personnel are likely to be involved. Most directly affected are the students and their families. Such a research context, by definition, occurs within a social milieu in which multiple individuals may be affected by the behavior change intervention, even if that intervention is focused on a single student.

Because of the applied nature of educational research, additional analytical activities are necessary to evaluate the effects of interventions on a range of consumers. If researchers want to understand the impact of their intervention on a classroom, more may be needed than to graph a functional relation between the intervention and improvements in math performances. Additional information may be gained from the following questions: Did the teacher find the intervention easy or hard to implement? How did the students react to the new procedure? Did the teacher use the intervention after the study was completed? Were there any positive or negative side-effects associated with the intervention? Did the recipients of the intervention perform at levels typical of other students their age? Did the principal view the results as worth replicating in other classrooms? Such information helps investigators understand the larger context of effects their intervention may produce. Such an understanding can help in interpreting functional relations within the social contexts in which they occur and potentially can improve the effectiveness, or at least the acceptability, of educational interventions. In order to understand the social context within which single-case research is conducted, researchers have developed a concept referred to as social validity.

Social Validity

Social validity is the estimation of the importance, effectiveness, appropriateness, and/or satisfaction various people experience in relation to a particular intervention. If, after fifteen chapters focusing on the scientific virtues of being precise, objective, and analytical, this seems somewhat subjective, that is because it is subjective. And this is the reason why social validity is so integral to understanding the effects produced in applied settings. Because educational research occurs in applied contexts, knowing how people in those settings react to an intervention is an important component in understanding the effects of a behavioral intervention.

The concept of social validity was introduced to the field of applied behavior analysis by Kazdin (1977) and Wolf (1978). However, there were antecedents to this concept in other disciplines. In the 1930s, the business sector became interested in whether the employees making products and the consumers using those products were satisfied (e.g., Rothlisberger & Dickson, 1939). In psychotherapy, psychologists and psychiatrists were interested in the expectations their clients had toward what they would experience and whether they believed they benefited from therapy (e.g., Rogers, 1942). Finally, in medicine, researchers and clinicians became interested in measuring whether patients were satisfied with the medical treatments they received (e.g., Makeover, 1950). Each of these lines of inquiry focused on establishing what people expected, experienced, and perceived were the effects of a particular endeavor.

When Kazdin (1977) and Wolf (1978) developed the concept of social validity, it was during the initial, rapid growth of applied behavior analysis. As was noted in Chapter 2, applied behavior analysis had emerged from earlier laboratory research and by the early 1970s was a well-established discipline, but one that was controversial (Kazdin, 1978). Much of the controversy was due to public concerns about researchers "controlling" the behavior of other people. These concerns, in part, were due to the effectiveness of behavioral interventions and their explicit, operationally defined procedures focusing on the consequences of responding (Goldiamond, 1976). Whatever the actual basis for concern, there was a great deal of public debate about whether "behavior modification" was ethical or desirable.

Unfortunately, when behavior analysts tried to address these public concerns, there were scant data from their own studies to buttress their arguments about the acceptability of their work. Because behavior analysts tended to focus on carefully defined behaviors that are directly relevant to a particular experimental question, there were little available data about how people "felt" about a particular experiment. This left behavior analysts in the uncomfortable situation of having very little data on which to argue in favor of their interventions, other than the changes in behavior they typically documented. This historical context set the occasion for Kazdin (1977) and Wolf (1978) to suggest measuring the social impact of behavioral interventions using the construct of social validity.

In Wolf's (1978) original description of social validity, he focused on the use of subjective judgments regarding the adequacy and desirability of behavioral interventions. He suggested that by understanding the subjective nature of interventions, applied behavior analysts could gain a better understanding of the social importance of their work. Specifically, he outlined three general domains for subjective analysis: goals, procedures, and outcomes. Goals refer to the targets of an intervention, including individuals, settings, and specific behaviors. Procedures are the techniques used in a study to change behavior—that is, what the experimenter did to increase or decrease the probability of specific behaviors. Outcomes are the behavioral changes produced by an intervention, both direct and indirect.

These three domains were a framework to begin the study of social validity in applied behavior analysis. Such a system allowed for the systematic study of subjective data. However, these suggestions ran contrary to decades of research in behavior analysis in which only objectively defined variables were permitted into a behavioral analysis. In a sense, the empirical approach championed in behavior analysis required that these researchers incorporate subjective data into their studies in order to better understand the effects being produced. This was, and still is, somewhat ironic, but it was a necessary condition for understanding the effects of behavioral interventions in applied settings (see Box 16.1).

This historical context led Wolf (1978) to write the following:

> Earlier in our history, Watson and Skinner argued forcefully against subjective measurement because they were concerned about the inappropriate causal roles that hypothetical internal variables, subjectively reported, were playing in social science. As a result, many of us concluded that all subjective measurement was inappropriate. A new consensus seems to be de-

---

BOX 16.1 • *Applying Social Validity*

Given the value of understanding the social impact of an experiment, should all studies in applied behavior analysis use social validity assessments? One could argue that any study seeking to change a person's behavior in an applied context should have the social validity of that endeavor assessed. However, the appropriateness of using social validity assessments depends on what one means by "applied context." In many respects, the "applied" versus "basic" distinction is a false dichotomy. Rather than being a binary distinction, these concepts actually span a continuum from basic to applied research. That is, some researchers may use humans and even study a behavior of clear social importance (e.g., self-injurious behavior) but be focused on how basic behavioral processes produce these behaviors.

Such studies have been referred to as "bridge studies" because they fall between applied and basic research (Mace, 1994). In such instances,

the use of social validity data may not meaningfully contribute to the interpretation of the experimental results. However, the rationale for such investigations is gaining a better understanding of behavioral processes impacting socially important situations so that more effective interventions can be developed (Lerman, 2003). If this is the case, and bridge studies are successful at identifying new behavior-environment mechanisms, then such findings necessarily need to be translated into practical interventions.

Because such a translation has a clear therapeutic intent, those studies would clearly need to assess the social validity of their goals, procedures, and/or outcomes. However, at this point in time, given the complex range of research occurring within the field of behavior analysis, the use of social validity assessments should probably be reserved for studies in which some type of intervention effect is being studied.

veloping. It seems that if we aspire to social importance, then we must develop systems that allow our consumers to provide us feedback about how our applications relate to their values, to their reinforcers. This is not a rejection of our heritage. Our use of subjective measures does not relate to internal causal variables. Instead, it is an attempt to assess the dimensions of complex reinforcers in socially acceptable and practical ways. It is an evolutionary event that is occurring as a function of the contingencies of the applied research environment; contingencies that our founders would probably say they appreciate, if we had the nerve to ask them for such subjective feedback on our behavior. (p. 213)

Approaches to Social Validity

Over the last twenty-five years, three approaches have been introduced to estimate social validity (see Box 16.2). Each approach focuses on a different aspect of the construct of social importance. As one might deduce, each has its strengths and limitations, and no single approach to assessing social validity can be referred as "the gold standard." Therefore, this section reviews the different approaches to social validity estimation, explains the purpose of each approach, provides examples of their use, and critiques the strategies.

Subjective Evaluation

The original conceptualization of social validity focused around what Kazdin (1977) and Wolf (1978) referred to as subjective evaluation. This approach is used to gather information regarding people's perceptions of some dimension of the goals, procedures, and/or outcomes of an experiment. The purpose is to estimate how people view some dimension of the experimental situation. Which aspect of the experimental situation is assessed is largely

---

BOX 16.2 • *Language Use and Social Validity*

Unlike most aspects of behavior-analytic research, which deal with explicit events, social validity presents researchers with a different type of analytical situation. Behavior analyses, by definition, focus on physical events that can be operationalized and directly measured. This rigorous approach to experimental methodology has been one of the key aspects of the success of behavior analysis over the past century. With the introduction of social validity, however, this situation was altered in some respects.

The essence of the argument for social validity, particularly in the use of subjective evaluation, is to allow verbal constructs such as "like," "acceptable," and "inappropriate" into experimental analyses. While this is entirely appropriate within

the framework of studying the social validity of behavior analyses, it has led to some confusion in the language used to describe social validity.

Because social validity is a social construction, that is it is based on social conventions and poorly defined concepts, it is not a thing. Therefore, its use as a noun, as in "We need to show that this intervention has social validity," is inaccurate and misleading. Rather, social validity is an adjective that describes some characteristics of the goals, procedures, and/or outcomes of an experiment in light of some defined social context. Because of this aspect of language use (see Hineline, 1990), it is more accurate to refer to estimating or assessing social validity.

a function of the experimental question and what the researcher wants to learn about. For example, if the investigators are working on a novel applied problem, then they might gather social validity data on whether this topic is viewed as important and whether their goals for reducing these behaviors are desirable. However, if the investigators are focusing on the use of a novel intervention, then they might want to assess whether people view their new technique as acceptable. Or if the experimenters want to demonstrate the desirable qualitative outcomes of their techniques, they might have people subjectively evaluate the behavior of interest before and after intervention. Depending on what the experimenters want to learn, any or all of these approaches to subjective evaluation can be used.

Conducting Subjective Evaluations.   The first step in using subjective evaluation is to identify whether the aim is to receive feedback about the goals, procedures, or outcomes or some combination of these. Once this has been decided, researchers need to identify who they will solicit information from. Schwartz and Baer (1991) identified four types of consumers: (1) direct consumers, (2) indirect consumers, (3) members of the immediate community, and (4) members of the extended community. Direct consumers are the immediate recipients of the intervention—for example, the student whose spelling is being improved or the teacher who is receiving technical assistance to improve recommended research practices. Indirect consumers are people involved in the situation being studied. These individuals can include the parents of a child who is receiving the spelling intervention or the principal in charge of supervising the teacher who is learning to use new instructional techniques. Members of the immediate community are those who are indirectly impacted by the study but who have some type of contact with the direct and indirect consumers. These individuals can include other children and their parents, other teachers in the school, or school board members. Members of the extended community are individuals who do not have direct contact with consumers but who may be interested in the potential beneficial or detrimental effects of a study. Examples could include taxpayers, legislators, media reports, content experts, or anyone else who might be interested in the researchers' efforts (see Kennedy, 2002a).

Again, which group(s) is the focus on the social validity assessment is a function of the question being posed. At one of end of the continuum, a researcher may want to understand how children and teachers react to a particular type of educational intervention. For example, researchers might compare lecture-based instruction with cooperative learning groups and ask the direct consumers which approach they prefer and why. At the other end of the continuum, researchers might be interested in polling a regionally representative group of home owners (i.e., people who pay the property taxes that finance local school systems) about whether they view school violence as an important enough issue that they would endorse cuts in other school programs (e.g., extramural sports) to increase services to reduce violence.

Once the consumer group(s) is identified, researchers need to select the assessment strategy to be used. In general, there are four approaches to collecting subjective evaluation information: (1) questionnaires, (2) forced-choice procedures, (3) structured interviews, and (4) open-ended interviews. Questionnaires are the most frequently used method (Kennedy, 1992). Questionnaires typically present a series of questions to which a particular person responds in writing or some other medium. The questions focus on some aspect of the investigation the experimenter wants to learn about. For example, the questionnaire might ask a series of questions regarding the acceptability of the intervention procedures given certain circumstances (see Kazdin, 1980). Forced-choice procedures require informants to make choices among possible goals, procedures, and/or outcomes. For example, individuals might be asked to sort in order of acceptability a variety of interventions used to reduce behavior problems. In some instances, these choices are abstractions sampling a person's opinion; in other instances, individuals may be asked to actually choose among possible goals or procedures they will be the recipients of (see Schwartz & Baer, 1991).

Using structured interviews requires the development of a series of questions that are read to the respondent followed by the opportunity for the individual to answer. Typically, these questions have a fixed number of response options to choose from. For example, the interviewer may ask the informant a series of questions, to which they respond "yes," "no," or "maybe." Open-ended interviews pose predetermined questions to a respondent that allow the individual to provide an extended and unstructured answer. For example, an experimenter may ask questions such as "What did you think of the cooperative learning intervention?" or "How did the students respond to whole-class instruction?" The answers are then recorded using some medium for later summarization.

The final step in conducting a subjective evaluation assessment is data analysis. This step in the process is the least clearly defined in the research literature. If the data are based on discrete, quantifiable elements (e.g., Likert-type scales or yes/no responses), then the use of descriptive statistics specifying the average and variation in responses would be appropriate. For example, in response to the statement "This treatment is one that I would agree to use with my child," parental reports could be summarized as a mean of 4.3 (range, 2 to 5) on a five-point Likert-type scale (with 1 being "strongly disagree" and 5 being "strongly agree"). Another option is summarizing the number of response options that were selected for each question. Table 16.1 (page 224) shows the results of a treatment acceptability analysis for students with severe disabilities and behavior problems, with respondents being special educators (Kennedy, 1994).

If the data are qualitative in nature (i.e., verbal responses), being most likely derived from structured or open-ended questions, then a qualitative analysis of the data may be required. A review of the research literature using social validity assessments suggests that content analysis is the most frequently published form of qualitative data analysis conducted on this type of data (see Miles & Huberman, 1984). In content analysis, the responses to each question are copied onto response cards or some other medium. Members of the research team then individually read and thematically sort them into self-constructed categories. Once two or more members have done this, then the research team meets and discusses their categorization schemes. Then the group revises the categorization scheme, as appropriate, and agrees as a group on how to sort each response item to a particular question. A similar process is undertaken for each question asked of respondents. These data can be summarized in at least two ways. A study by Cox and Kennedy (2003) will be used to illustrate both types of data summarization. The data reflect parental responses to open-ended questions about the hospitalization and subsequent recovery of their child who had a multiple disability. Table 16.2 (page 225) shows a content analysis that specified general response categories to each question and summarized the percentage of answers from respondents included in each category. Another technique for presenting these same data

TABLE 16.1 *Results from the Treatment Evaluation Inventory Assessment*

1. How acceptable do you find this treatment to be for the student's problem behavior?

					1	2	5
not at all acceptable			moderately acceptable				very acceptable

2. How willing would you be to carry out this procedure yourself if you had to change the student's problem behavior?

						3	5
not at all willing			moderately willing				very willing

3. How cruel or unfair do you find the treatment?

							8
very cruel			moderately cruel				not cruel at all

4. To what extent does this procedure treat the student humanely?

							8
does not treat humanely at all			treats them moderately humanely				treats them very humanely

5. How much do you like the procedures used in this treatment?

						1	7
do not like them at all			moderately like them				like them very much

6. How likely is this treatment to make permanent improvements in the student?

					5		3
unlikely			moderately				very likely

7. To what extent are <u>un</u>desirable side effects likely to result from this treatment?

					1	6	1
many undesirable side effects likely			some undesirable side effects likely				no undesirable side effects likely

8. Overall, what is your general reaction to this form of treatment?

							8
very negative			ambivalent				very positive

Note: N = 8

would be to present subcategories of answers to questions and exemplars of the actual responses that were received. Table 16.3 (page 226) shows the data from question 1 of Table 16.2 in this more detailed format. As with the visual analysis of data, what is most important in analyzing this type of data is that the process and presentation reveal the character of the data that are obtained in as clear and concise a manner as possible.

TABLE 16.2 *Parent Responses to Open-Ended Questions*

What did your child's school do that was helpful?
> Nothing (14.3%)
> Offered support (85.7%)

What could the school have done to be more helpful?
> More communication and coordination (35%)
> Nothing (50%)
> School not responsible (15%)

What did the hospital do that was helpful?
> Nothing (20%)
> Provided health services to child (24%)
> Provided support services to parents (8%)
> Supportive staff (48%)

What could the hospital have done to be more helpful?
> Improve support for parents (13.3%)
> Improved care (26.7%)
> Increase continuity and collaboration (13.3%)
> More staff education (26.7%)
> Nothing (20%)

How successful was home-school-hospital communication?
> Communication not an issue (10.5%)
> No communication among entities (47.4%)
> Parent assumed lead (26.3%)
> Satisfactory (15.8%)

What could have been done to improve home-school-hospital communication?
> Improved communication (26%)
> Not sure what to recommend (8.7%)
> School and hospital separate issues (65.3%)

What was the effect of the hospitalization on your child's education?
> Improved performance (15.8%)
> No or little effect (42.1%)
> Small negative effect (21%)
> Substantial negative effect (21.1%)

TABLE 16.3   *Examples of Responses to Types of Support Provided in Question 1 of Table 16.2*

Provided general support
  "PT and teachers called and came to hospital."
  "Teacher called and brought homework."

Offered general support
  "Called once they heard child was in the hospital."
  "School offered homebound services but we declined."

Homebound services
  "Homebound teacher was already part of IEP. The teacher just came to the hospital."
  "Homebound teacher provided laptop at the hospital."

Source: From J. A. Cox and C. H. Kennedy, "Transitions between School and Hospital for Students with Multiple Disabilities: A Survey of Causes, Educational Continuity, and Parental Perceptions," *Research and Practice for People with Severe Disabilities* (formerly *JASH*), 2003, *28,* 1–6. Copyright 2003 by TASH. Reproduced by permission.

Strengths and Limitations.   There are several strengths and limitations to using subjective evaluation as a technique for estimating social validity. An important strength, and one championed by Kazdin (1977) and Wolf (1978), is that subjective evaluation allows qualitative information to be added to data gathered through an experimental analysis of behavior. A second strength of subjective evaluation is that its use broadens the range of dependent variables used in a study. Both of these strengths are based on including people's perceptions and opinions into the interpretation of what was done and what resulted from an experiment designed to have beneficial outcomes to particular individuals. An important limitation of subjective evaluation is that the questions posed are often biased toward receiving a positive outcome. That is, researchers often develop questions or present them in ways in which the situation predisposes respondents toward favorable answers. A second limitation of this technique is that people's perceptions of situations may not meaningfully reflect changes in a participant's behavior. A third limitation is that most instruments developed for subjective evaluation studies have unknown psychometric properties. That is, the reliability and validity of the instruments are typically unknown (see Sax, 1996). Overall, the use of subjective evaluation can be an important tool if a particular experimental question is developed in which this information would be useful.

Normative Comparison

A second approach to estimating social validity was developed largely in response to concerns about the highly qualitative nature of the data derived from subjective evaluations. The approach, referred to as normative comparison, was outlined by Van Houten (1979) shortly after the Kazdin (1977) and Wolf (1978) papers were published. In normative comparison, a particular behavior(s) engaged by a participant is compared to some reference sample of individuals. Typically, the reference group is chosen because it can serve as an exemplar of desirable levels or topographies of the behavior(s) of interest. The focus is to reference the behavior change goals and outcomes for the participants in a study against some normative group whose behavior is considered typical or desirable.

An early example of the use of normative comparisons is provided by Walker and Hops (1976). These authors focused on improving the behavior of students considered to have conduct problems in general education classrooms. As a reference regarding the treatment goals and as an index of intervention outcomes, Walker and Hops sampled levels of appropriate and inappropriate behaviors among classroom peers identified by teachers as behaving appropriately. The children with conduct problems were then given an intervention in a separate setting until their behavior approximated that of their peers in the general education classrooms (see Figure 16.1). The children with conduct problems were then reintroduced into the general education classroom and maintained similar behavioral levels to those of their peers. Such a demonstration shows quantitatively that the appropriate behavior of the students who originally had conduct problems was similar to that of their peers without behavior problems following intervention.

Conducting Normative Comparisons. To conduct normative comparisons, researchers need to begin by identifying the behaviors of interest in the group of students whose behavior will receive intervention. Then, a decision is made whether to base the goals, outcomes, or both aspects of intervention on a normative sample. If goals alone are chosen for comparison, then researchers will have an intervention target to reach but no information

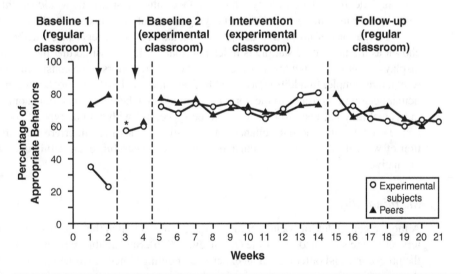

FIGURE 16.1 *Example of the use of normative comparison.* The data show the percentage of appropriate behaviors along the vertical axis and weeks of school along the horizontal axis. The variables were the behavior of children with conduct problems and the behavior of peers in the classroom deemed to behave appropriately by teachers.

Source: From H. M. Walker and H. Hops, "Use of Normative Peer Data as a Standard for Evaluating Classroom Treatment Effects," *Journal of Applied Behavior Analysis,* 1976, *9,* fig. 1, p. 164. Copyright 1976 by the Society for the Experimental Analysis of Behavior. Reproduced by permission.

on normative outcomes. If only outcomes are the focus of comparison, then researchers will have a metric of the normative outcomes of their intervention effects but no quantitative goals to guide their efforts. For these reasons, it is probably best to use normative comparison both to identify the goals to be achieved and then further demonstrate that after those goals have been met, they are still normative values.

Once these decisions are made, researchers will need to identify an appropriate reference group to sample data from. Often, the choice is made to sample from a group of individuals who already show desirable levels of the behavior of interest. Then, levels of those behaviors need to be measured in the environments in which they would naturally occur. These data, when summarized, provide the basis for comparing the goals and outcomes of the intervention that will then be experimentally analyzed.

Strengths and Limitations.   Benefits of this approach to social validity assessment are primarily that there is a clear and defendable basis for setting the goals of an intervention. It is likely that in educational research when a child is identified as deviant in some aspect, the subsequent expectations for change in the child's behavior are higher than for their peers, who are not viewed as needing intervention. Collecting normative data may help with this concern. An additional strength of this approach is that it provides a reference, after interventions have been implemented, regarding whether the person's behavior is within the range of the peers, whose behavior has been deemed acceptable. A final strength of this approach is the logical foundation for basing treatment gains, which gives this strategy a high degree of face validity. That is, at face value most experts would say this is a reasonable and rationale approach to identifying intervention goals and evaluating outcomes.

Limitations of normative comparison include concerns regarding whether the group chosen as the normative sample is indeed normative. It is possible that the group sampled displays either too high a level or too low a level of behaviors to be considered a truly representative sample. In addition, as noted by Van Houten (1979), the goals chosen for a particular person in reference to the normative sample may be unobtainable. In some cases, an individual may not need to be average to be successful within some type of social or academic context, and the overreliance on normative values may interfere with the evaluation of what it takes for a particular person to be successful, even if this does not mean normative.

Sustainability

A more recent index of social validity is the degree to which the effects of a particular intervention are sustained over time (Kennedy, 2002b). Sustainability is an index of whether the procedures and outcomes of an experiment continue once the research is completed and the researchers are no longer involved. If the consumers present in a particular context consider the procedures being used and the behavioral changes that resulted from them as desirable, then they are likely to work at maintaining the program. The use of sustainability as an index of social validity comes from the observation that "if an intervention is socially invalid, it can hardly be effective, even if it changes its target behaviors thoroughly and with an otherwise excellent cost-benefit ratio; social validity is not sufficient for effectiveness but is necessary to effectiveness" (p. 323; Baer, Wolf, & Risley, 1987). Therefore, if an intervention is sustained over time, it must have some qualities that are consistent with what is meant by social validity.

An example of sustainability is provided by Altus, Welsh, Miller, and Merrill (1993). Altus et al. studied a program used to educate members of a university student housing cooperative regarding their responsibilities for managing their housing unit. As is shown in Figure 16.2, when credits and fines were established as contingencies, the program was effective in having new members complete the training materials. During the first fourteen weeks of the intervention, researchers managed the contingencies. After this, the research team turned over the program to the housing cooperative members. Nine years later, when the researcher again sampled the behavior of new members regarding training activities, the program had maintained at levels similar to the earlier analysis. Such a result suggests that this intervention was useful and acceptable to those using it.

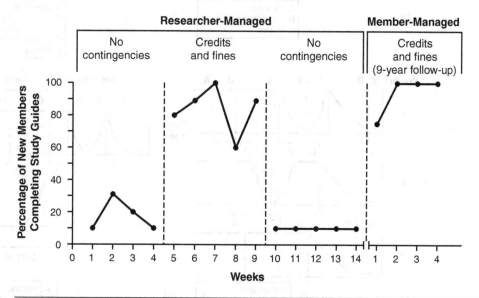

FIGURE 16.2 *Example of sustainability.* The authors studied a program used to educate members of a university student housing cooperative regarding their responsibilities for managing their housing unit. When credits and fines were established as contingencies, the program was effective in having new members complete the training materials. During the first fourteen weeks of the intervention, researchers managed the contingencies. After this, the research team turned over the program to the housing cooperative members. Nine years later, when the researcher again sampled the behavior of new members regarding training activities, the program had maintained at levels similar to the earlier analysis.

Source: From D. E. Altus, T. M. Welsh, L. K. Miller, and M. H. Merrill, "Efficacy and Maintenance of an Education Program for a Consumer Cooperative," *Journal of Applied Behavior Analysis,* 1993, *26,* fig. 1, p. 404. Copyright 1993 by the Society for the Experimental Analysis of Behavior. Reproduced by permission.

The study of maintenance was first proposed by Rusch and Kazdin (1981) within the context of experimentally analyzing the factors involved in treatment success over time. These authors suggested that the use of withdrawal designs over extended time periods can be used to analyze the maintenance of interventions and their effects on behavior. Figure 16.3 shows several hypothetical examples of withdrawal designs proposed to experimen-

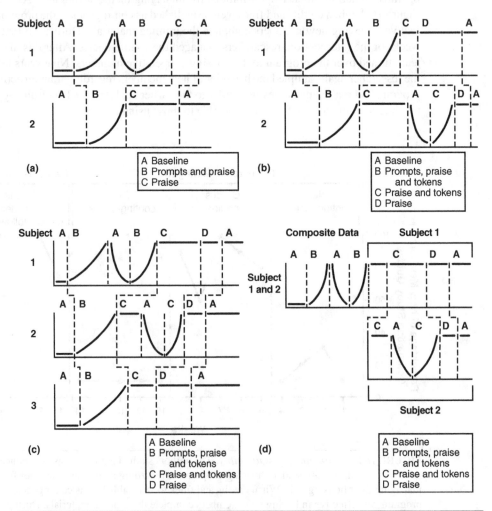

FIGURE 16.3 *Hypothetical examples of withdrawal designs.* A systematic withdrawal of a two-component treatment across two subjects is represented in the upper left graph (a). Withdrawal of a three-component treatment across two subjects is indicated in the upper right graph (b). A systematic withdrawal of a three-component treatment across three subjects is shown in the lower left portion of the figure (c). Finally, withdrawal of a three-component treatment across two subjects within an A-B-A-B reversal is depicted in the lower right portion (d).

Source: From F. R. Rusch and A. E. Kazdin, "Toward a Methodology of Withdrawal Designs for the Assessment of Response Maintenance," *Journal of Applied Behavior Analysis,* 1981, *14,* fig. 2, p. 137. Copyright 1981 by the Society for the Experimental Analysis of Behavior. Reproduced by permission.

tally study maintenance. If we put Rusch and Kazdin's suggestions within the framework put forward in Chapter 5 regarding experimental questions, such an analytical scheme sets the occasion for conducting component and parametric analyses (Kennedy, 2002). Component analyses allow investigators to remove one or more aspects of an independent variable, assess its effects on behavior, and then return to the previous conditions. Such analyses could be used to identify those components of an intervention that are necessary for it to be sustained by consumers. Conducting parametric analyses would permit a cost-benefit analysis of differing levels of intervention, the effects on behavior, and whether consumers choose to sustain the intervention. Such experiments could produce important information, not only of how interventions are sustained over time but why they are, or are not, sustained over time.

Strengths and Limitations.   The primary strength of sustainability as an index of social validity is its face validity. If a group of consumers maintain an intervention over extended periods of time, there must be something about the intervention and its effects that are reinforcing to those consumers. This, perhaps, is an empirical test of what subjective evaluation seeks to assess. However, there are several limits to the concept of sustainability. First, it requires an extended period of time to conduct the analysis, something that might not be logistically feasible. Second, other variables not known to the experimenters may influence the adoption and maintenance of an intervention (e.g., federal laws or court rulings), even if its use is noxious to those involved. Finally, sustainability is an indirect index of the degree to which the procedures and outcomes of an investigation have some degree of social validity.

Trends in the Use of Social Validity

Following the logic just outlined for the sustainability of interventions, if researchers find social validity assessments a useful analytical tool, then their use should be prevalent in the extant literature. If the data derived from such assessments are useful to investigators, they are likely to draw on such information when they conduct their studies. Conversely, if social validity data are not useful or are too cumbersome to make their collection experimentally reinforcing, these procedures might be employed less frequently.

Such archival data are available, and they are not encouraging. Kennedy (1992) and Carr, Austin, Britton, Kellum, and Bailey (1999) have documented the degree to which social validity assessments are incorporated into applied behavior-analytic research. The results of the Carr et al. analysis are presented in Figure 16.4 (page 232). Arrayed along the vertical axis is the percentage of research articles published in the *Journal of Applied Behavior Analysis* that report data related to social validity. The horizontal axis represents the year of publication. The top panel shows data for outcomes, the center panel for procedures, and the bottom panel for either or both types of social validity assessment. Not surprisingly, few studies used social validity assessments prior to the Kazdin (1977) and Wolf (1978) articles, but an increase occurred following their publication. A gradual decline in the use of social validity assessments occurred during the 1980s, with their use stabilizing at approximately 20% in the subsequent decade. Kennedy noted a similar pattern of reporting social validity assessments for papers in a second journal, *Behavior Modification*. In addition, Kennedy noted that less than 5% of published studies used normative comparison methods.

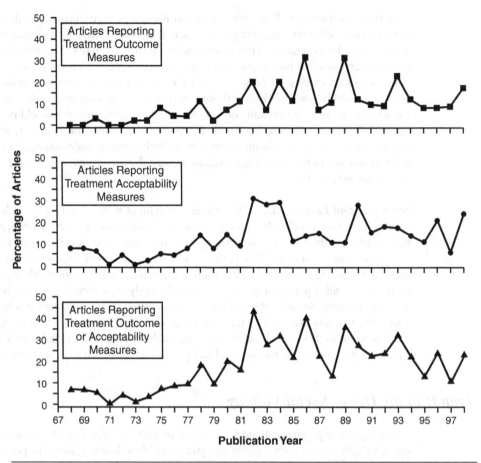

FIGURE 16.4   *Example of use of social validity assessments in applied behavior analysis.*
Arrayed along the *y*-axis is the percentage of research articles published in the *Journal of Applied Behavior Analysis* reporting data relating to social validity. The *x*-axis represents the year of publication. The top panel shows data for outcomes, the center panel for procedures, and the bottom panel for either or both types of social validity assessment.

Source: From J. E. Carr, J. L. Austin, L. N. Britton, K. K. Kellum, and J. S. Bailey, "An Assessment of Social Validity Trends in Applied Behavior Analysis," *Behavioral Interventions,* 1999, *14,* fig. 1, p. 227. Copyright 1999 by John Wiley and Sons. Reproduced by permission.

These data seem to suggest that researchers are only occasionally incorporating social validity assessments into their experimental methods. Two possible explanations have been put forward for this pattern. First, as noted in Box 16.1, not all studies in applied behavior analysis are directly focused on improving a person's quality of life via intervention. Many experiments, referred to as bridge studies, focus on analyzing the underlying mechanisms of behavior and fall between basic and applied research (Mace, 1994). This could account for some percentage of applied studies not using social validity assessments. However, a perusal of the literature over the past several decades reveals that a number of studies that are explicitly focused on interventions to improve behavior do not incorporate social validity assessments into their data collection protocols.

A second possible explanation for the underutilization of social validity assessments is that the procedures may not be yielding data that researchers find useful in interpreting the outcomes of their research. It might be that the nature of the data collected in many social validity assessments is not as beneficial as the cost of collecting the data. Part of this might relate to the rigor used in gathering social validity data. For example, Fawcett (1991) has suggested increasing the psychometric rigor of social validity assessments so that the reliability and validity of assessments are established prior to their being used in a research study. Schwartz and Baer (1991) have argued that the incorporation of consumer input should be central to social validity analyses, rather than something that is conducted as a secondary experimental effort. Finally, Hawkins (1991) has suggested that social validity should not only be assessed but should be subjected to experimental analyses that yield functional relations relating to the social importance of research findings rather than descriptive data. Each of these suggestions, if incorporated into studies of social validity, would improve the quality of the information obtained and potentially increase researchers' efforts to incorporate this important construct into their applied studies.

Conclusion

An interest in studying social validity emerged during the 1970s in applied behavior analysis. The impetus for this development was public concern that behavior-analytic methods might be effective but might not be socially acceptable. In order to better understand whether these concerns were warranted, Kazdin (1977) and Wolf (1978) introduced the construct of social validity. These methods have come to incorporate subjective evaluation, normative comparison, and sustainability as procedures for collecting social validity information.

If used as intended, social validity assessments allow the study of how behavioral interventions impact a range of individuals directly and indirectly involved in the investigation. Subjective evaluations allow the collection of data relating to personal perceptions of the appropriateness of the goals, procedures, and outcomes of a study. Normative comparisons provide a method for indexing the goals and outcomes of a study against some social standard or reference. Finally, sustainability permits an assessment of the extent to which the procedures and outcomes of an experiment are adopted and maintained by a group of individuals. Each approach to social validity assessment can provide important information about the effects of an intervention above and beyond what is typically reported in terms of dependent variables in applied research.

References

Agras, W. S., Leitenberg, H., Barlow, D. H., & Thomson, L. E. (1969). Instructions and reinforcement in the modification of neurotic behavior. *American Journal of Psychiatry, 125,* 1435–1439.

Alper, T. G., & White, O. R. (1971). Precision teaching: A tool for the school psychologist and teacher. *Journal of School Psychology, 9,* 445–454.

Altus, D. E., Welsh, T. M., Miller, L. K., & Merrill, M. H. (1993). Efficacy and maintenance of an education program for a consumer cooperative. *Journal of Applied Behavior Analysis, 26,* 403–404.

American Psychological Association. (2001). *Publication manual* (5th ed.). Washington, DC: Author.

Anger, D. (1956). The dependence of interresponse times upon the relative reinforcement of different interresponse times. *Journal of Experimental Psychology, 52,* 145–161.

Ayllon, T., & Michael, J. (1959). The psychiatric nurse as a behavioral engineer. *Journal of the Experimental Analysis of Behavior, 2,* 323–334.

Azrin, N., Jones, R. J., & Flye, B. (1968). A synchronization effect and its application to stuttering by a portable apparatus. *Journal of Applied Behavior Analysis, 1,* 283–295.

Bacon, F. (1620/2000). *The new organon* (L. Jardine & M. Silverthorne, trans.). New York: Cambridge University Press.

Baer, D. M. (1962). Laboratory control of thumbsucking by withdrawal and re-presentation of reinforcement. *Journal of the Experimental Analysis of Behavior, 5,* 525–528.

Baer, D. M. (1977). Perhaps it would be better not to know everything. *Journal of Applied Behavior Analysis, 10,* 167–172.

Baer, D. M. (1986). In application, frequency is not the only estimate of the probability of behavioral units. In T. Thompson & M. D. Zeiler (Eds.), *Analysis and integration of behavioral units* (pp. 117–136). Hillsdale, NJ: Erlbaum.

Baer, D. M., & LeBlanc, J. M. (1977). *New developments in behavioral research: Theory, method, and application: In honor of Sidney W. Bijou.* Hillsdale, NJ: Erlbaum.

Baer, D. M., Wolf, M. M., & Risley, T. R. (1968). Some current dimensions of applied behavior analysis. *Journal of Applied Behavior Analysis, 1,* 91–97.

Baer, D. M., Wolf, M. M., & Risley, T. R. (1987). Some still-current dimensions of applied behavior analysis. *Journal of Applied Behavior Analysis, 20,* 313–327.

Bakeman, R., & Gottman, J. M. (1997). *Observing interaction: An introduction to sequential analysis* (2nd ed.). England: Cambridge University Press.

Baldwin, J. D. (1987). *George Herbert Mead: A unifying theory for sociology.* Beverly Hills, CA: Sage.

Barbetta, P. M., Heward, W. L., Bradley, D. M., & Miller, A. D. (1994). Effects of immediate and delayed error correction on the acquisition and maintenance of sight words by students with developmental disabilities. *Journal of Applied Behavior Analysis, 27,* 177–178.

Barlow, D. H., & Hayes, S. C. (1979). Alternating treatments design: One strategy for comparing the effects of two treatments in a single subject. *Journal of Applied Behavior Analysis, 12,* 199–210.

Barlow, D. H., & Hersen, M. (1984). *Single case experimental designs: Strategies for studying behavior change* (2nd ed.). New York: Pergamon Press.

Barlow, D. H., Hayes, S. C., & Nelson, R. O. (1984). *The scientist practitioner: Research and accountability in clinical and educational settings.* New York: Pergamon Press.

Barrish, H. H., Saunders, M., & Wolf, M. M. (1969). Good behavior game: Effects of individual contingencies for group consequences on disruptive behavior in a classroom. *Journal of Applied Behavior Analysis, 2,* 119–124.

Baum, W. M. (2002). The Harvard Pigeon Lab under Herrnstein. *Journal of the Experimental Analysis of Behavior, 77,* 347–355.

Bellamy, G. T., Horner, R. H., & Inman, D. P. (1979). *Vocational habilitation of severely retarded adults: A direct service technology.* Austin, TX: ProEd.

Berg, W. K., Peck, S., Wacker, D. P., Harding, J., McComas, J., Richman, D., & Brown, K. (2000). The effects of presession exposure to attention on the results of assessments of attention as a reinforcer. *Journal of Applied Behavior Analysis, 33,* 463–477.

Bernard, C. (1865/1927). *An introduction to the study of experimental medicine* (H. Copley & A. M. Greene, trans.). New York: Macmillan.

Bijou, S. W. (1963). Theory and research in mental (developmental) retardation. *Psychological Record, 13,* 95–110.

Bijou, S. W. (1968). Ages, stages, and the naturalization of human development. *American Psychologist, 23,* 419–427.

Bijou, S. W. (1995). *Behavior analysis of child development* (2nd ed.). Reno, NV: Context Press.

Bijou, S. W., Peterson, R. F., & Ault, M. H. (1968). A method to integrate descriptive and experimental field studies at the level of data and empirical concepts. *Journal of Applied Behavior Analysis, 1,* 175–191.

Birnbrauer, J. S. (1981). External validity and experimental investigation of individual behavior. *Analysis and Intervention in Developmental Disabilities, 1,* 117–132.

Bjork, D. W. (1993). *B. F. Skinner: A life.* New York: Basic Books.

Boakes, R. A. (1984). *From Darwin to behaviorism: Psychology and the minds of animals.* Cambridge: Cambridge University Press.

Boren, J. J. (1963). The repeated acquisition of new behavioral chains. *American Psychologist, 18,* 421.

Boren, J. J., & Devine, D. D. (1968). The repeated acquisition of behavioral chains. *Journal of the Experimental Analysis of Behavior, 11,* 651–660.

Boring, E. G. (1950). *A history of experimental psychology* (2nd ed.). New York: Appleton-Century-Crofts.

Boyajian, A. E., DuPaul, G. J., Handler, M. W., Eckert, T. L., & McGoey, K. E. (2001). The use of classroom-based brief functional analyses with preschoolers at-risk for attention deficit hyperactivity disorder. *School Psychology Review, 30,* 278–293.

Browning, R. M. (1967). A same-subject design for simultaneous comparison of three reinforcement contingencies. *Behavior Research and Therapy, 5,* 237–243.

Campbell, D. T., & Stanley, J. C. (1966). *Experimental and quasi-experimental designs for research.* Chicago: Rand McNally.

Carr, E. G. (1977). The motivation of self-injurious behavior: A review of some hypotheses. *Psychological Bulletin, 84,* 800–816.

Carr, E. G., & Durand, V. M. (1985). Reducing behavior problems through functional communication training. *Journal of Applied Behavior Analysis, 18,* 111–126.

Carr, E. G., Newsom, C. D., & Binkoff, J. A. (1980). Escape as a factor in the aggressive behavior of two retarded children. *Journal of Applied Behavior Analysis, 13,* 101–117.

Carr, J. E., Austin, J. L., Britton, L. N., Kellum, K. K., & Bailey, J. S. (1999). An assessment of social validity trends in applied behavior analysis. *Behavioral Interventions, 14,* 223–231.

Catania, A. C. (1973). The psychologies of structure, function, and development. *American Psychologist, 28,* 434–443.

Catania, A. C. (1988). *The Behavior of Organisms* as work in progress. *Journal of the Experimental Analysis of Behavior, 50,* 277–281.

Catania, A. C. (1998). *Learning* (4th ed.). Upper Saddle River, NJ: Prentice Hall.

Catania, A. C., Matthews, T. J., Silverman, P. J., & Yohalem, R. (1977). Yoked variable-ratio and variable-interval responding in pigeons. *Journal of the Experimental Analysis of Behavior, 28,* 155–162.

Chiesa, M. (1994). *Radical behaviorism: The philosophy and the science.* Boston: Authors Cooperative.

Christle, C. A., & Schuster, J. W. (2003). The effects of using response cards on student participation, academic achievement, and on-task behavior during whole-class, math instruction. *Journal of Behavioral Education, 12,* 147–165.

Clark, N. M., Cushing, L. S., & Kennedy, C. H. (2003). *An intensive on-site technical assistance model to promote inclusive practices for students with severe disabilities.* Manuscript submitted for publication.

Cohen, J. A. (1960). A coefficient of agreement for nominal scales. *Educational and Psychological Measurement, 20,* 37–46.

Cohen, M. R., & Nagel, E. (1962). *An introduction to logic.* Indianapolis, IN: Hackett.

Collins, F. S., Green, E. D., Guttmacher, A. E., & Guyer, M. S. (2003). A vision for the future of genomics research: A blueprint for the genomic era. *Nature, 422,* 835–847.

Cooper, L. J., Wacker, D. P., Sasso, G. M., Reimers, T. M., & Donn, L. K. (1990). Using parents as therapists to evaluate appropriate behavior of their children: Application to a tertiary diagnostic clinic. *Journal of Applied Behavior Analysis, 23,* 285–296.

Cooter, R., & Pickston, J. (2000). *Medicine in the twentieth century.* Amsterdam: Harwood Academic Publishers.

Cox, J. A., & Kennedy, C. H. (2003). Transitions between school and hospital for students with multiple disabilities: A survey of causes, educational continuity, and parental perceptions. *Research and Practice for*

People with Severe Disabilities (formerly *JASH*), *28*, 1–6.

Critchfield, T. S., & Vargas, E. A. (1991). Self-recording, instructions, and public self-graphing: Effects on swimming in the absence of coach verbal interaction. *Behavior Modification, 15,* 95–112.

Cushing, L. S., & Kennedy, C. H. (1997). Academic effects of providing peer support in general education classrooms on students without disabilities. *Journal of Applied Behavior Analysis, 30,* 139–150.

Danforth, J. S., Chase, P. N., Dolan, M., & Joyce, J. H. (1990). The establishment of stimulus control by instructions and by differential reinforcement. *Journal of the Experimental Analysis of Behavior, 54,* 97–112.

Daniels, A. C. (1989). *Performance management.* Tucker, GA: Performance Management Publications.

Darwin, C. (1859). *On the origin of species by means of natural selection, or the preservation of favoured races in the struggle for life.* London: Murray.

Davison, M., & McCarthy, D. (1987). *The matching law: A research review.* Hillsdale, NJ: Erlbaum.

De Prey, R. L., & Sugai, G. (2002). The effect of active supervision and pre-correction on minor behavioral incidents in a sixth grade general education classroom. *Journal of Behavioral Education, 11,* 255–262.

Deitz, S. M. (1988). Another's view of observer agreement and observer accuracy. *Journal of Applied Behavior Analysis, 21,* 113.

Deno, S. L., Fuchs, L. S., Marston, D., & Shin, J. (2001). Using curriculum-based measurement to establish growth standards for students with learning disabilities. *School Psychology Review, 30,* 507–524.

DeProspero, A., & Cohen, S. (1979). Inconsistent visual analyses of intrasubject data. *Journal of Applied Behavior Analysis, 12,* 573–579.

Dewey, J. (1958). *Experience and nature.* New York: Dover.

Dews, P. B. (1987). An outsider on the inside. *Journal of the Experimental Analysis of Behavior, 48,* 459–462.

Dinsmoor, J. A. (1990). Academic roots: Columbia University, 1943–1951. *Journal of the Experimental Analysis of Behavior, 54,* 129–150.

Dugan, E., Kamps, D., Leonard, B., Watkins, N., Rheinberger, A., & Stackhaus, J. (1995). Effects of cooperative learning groups during social studies for students with autism and fourth-grade peers. *Journal of Applied Behavior Analysis, 28,* 175–188.

Eckert, T. L., Ardoin, S. P., Daly, E. J., III, & Martens, B. K. (2002). Improving oral reading fluency: A brief experimental analysis of combining an antecedent intervention with consequences. *Journal of Applied Behavior Analysis, 35,* 271–281.

Fawcett, S. B. (1991). Social validity: A note on methodology. *Journal of Applied Behavior Analysis, 24,* 235–239.

Ferster, C. B., & DeMyer, M. K. (1961). The development of performances in autistic children in an automatically controlled environment. *Journal of Chronic Diseases, 13,* 312–345.

Ferster, C. B., & Skinner, B. F. (1957). *Schedules of reinforcement.* New York: Appleton-Century-Crofts.

Fisch, G. S. (2001). Evaluating data from behavioral analysis: Visual inspection or statistical models? *Behavioural Processes, 54,* 137–154.

Fisher, W. W., & Mazur, J. E. (1997). Basic and applied research on choice responding. *Journal of Applied Behavior Analysis, 30,* 387–410.

Fisher, W. W., Kelley, M. E., & Lomas, J. E. (2003). Visual aids and structured criteria for improving visual inspection and interpretation of single-case designs. *Journal of Applied Behavior Analysis, 36,* 387–406.

Fisher, W. W., Piazza, C. C., & Roane, H. S. (2002). Sleep and cyclical variables related to self-injurious and other destructive behaviors. In S. Schroeder, M. L. Oster-Granite, & T. Thompson (Eds.), *Self-injurious behavior: Gene-brain-behavior relationships* (pp. 205–202). Washington, DC: American Psychological Association.

Flood, W. A., Wilder, D. A., Flood, A. L., & Masuda, A. (2002). Peer-mediated reinforcement plus prompting as treatment for off-task behavior in children with attention deficit hyperactivity disorder. *Journal of Applied Behavior Analysis, 35,* 199–204.

Fuchs, L. S., & Fuchs, D. (1996). Combining performance assessment and curriculum-based measurement to strengthen instructional planning. *Learning Disabilities Research and Practice, 11,* 183–192.

Fuller, P. R. (1949). Operant conditioning of a vegetative human organism. *American Journal of Psychology, 62,* 587–590.

Furlong, M. J., & Wampold, B. E. (1982). Intervention effects and relative variation as dimensions in experts' use of visual inference. *Journal of Applied Behavior Analysis, 15,* 415–421.

Garfinkle, A., & Kaiser, A. P. (in press). Communication. In C. H. Kennedy & E. Horn (Eds.), *Inclusion of students with severe disabilities.* Boston: Allyn and Bacon.

Gillat, A., & Sulzer-Azaroff, B. (1994). Promoting principals' managerial involvement in instructional improvement. *Journal of Applied Behavior Analysis, 27,* 115–129.

Gold, M. W. (1976). Task analysis of a complex assembly task by retarded children. *Exceptional Children, 43,* 78–85.

Goldiamond, I. (1965). Stuttering and fluency as manipulatable operant response classes. In L. Krasner & L. P. Ullmann (Eds.), *Research in behavior modification: New developments and implications* (pp. 231–259). New York: Holt, Rinehart, & Winston.

Goldiamond, I. (1976). Protection of human subjects and patients. *Behaviorism, 4,* 1–42.

Goldstein, H., & Cisar, C. L. (1992). Promoting interaction during sociodramatic play: Teaching scripts to typical preschoolers and classmates with disabilities. *Journal of Applied Behavior Analysis, 25,* 265–280.

Gould, S. J. (1981). *The mismeasure of man.* New York: Norton & Company.

Gould, S. J. (2002). *The structure of evolutionary theory.* Cambridge, MA: Harvard University Press.

Gresham, F. M., Gansle, K. A., & Noell, G. H. (1993). Treatment integrity in applied behavior analysis with children. *Journal of Applied Behavior Analysis, 26,* 257–263.

Guess, D., Sailor, W., Rutherford, G., & Baer, D. M. (1968). An experimental analysis of linguistic development: The productive use of the plural morpheme. *Journal of Applied Behavior Analysis, 1,* 297–306.

Hacking, I. (1983). *Representing and intervening.* Cambridge, England: Cambridge University Press.

Hagopian, L. P., Rush, K. S., Lewin, A. B., & Long, E. S. (2001). Evaluating the predictive validity of a single stimulus engagement preference assessment. *Journal of Applied Behavior Analysis, 34,* 475–485.

Hains, A. H., & Baer, D. M. (1989). Interaction effects in multielement designs: Inevitable, desirable, and ignorable. *Journal of Applied Behavior Analysis, 22,* 57–69.

Hake, D. F. (1982). The basic-applied continuum and the possible evolution of human operant behavior social and verbal research. *The Behavior Analyst, 5,* 21–28.

Hall, R. V., Lund, D., & Jackson, D. (1968). Effects of teacher attention on study behavior. *Journal of Applied Behavior Analysis, 1,* 1–12.

Halle, J. W., Marshall, A. M., & Spradlin, J. E. (1979). Time display: A technique to increase language use and facilitate generalization in retarded children. *Journal of Applied Behavior Analysis, 12,* 431–439.

Haring, N. G., & Phillips, E. L. (1972). *Analysis and modification of classroom behavior.* Englewood Cliffs, NJ: Prentice Hall.

Haring, T. G., & Kennedy, C. H. (1988). Units of analysis in task-analytic research. *Journal of Applied Behavior Analysis, 21,* 207–216.

Harrop, A., & Daniels, M. (1986). Methods of time sampling: A reappraisal of momentary time sampling and partial interval recording. *Journal of Applied Behavior Analysis, 19,* 73–77.

Hartmann, D. (1977). Considerations in the choice of inter-observer reliability estimates. *Journal of Applied Behavior Analysis, 10,* 103–116.

Hartmann, D. P., Gottman, J. M., Jones, R. R., Gardner, W., Kazdin, A. E., & Vaught, R. S. (1980). Interrupted time-series analysis and its application to behavioral data. *Journal of Applied Behavior Analysis, 13,* 543-559.

Harvey, M. T., May, M. E., & Kennedy, C. H. (in press). Nonconcurrent $N = 1$ experimental designs for educational program evaluation. *Journal of Behavioral Education.*

Hawkins, R. P. (1991). Is social validity what we are interested in? Argument for a functional approach. *Journal of Applied Behavior Analysis, 24,* 205–213.

Hawkins, R. P., & Dotson, V. A. (1975). Reliability scores that delude: An Alice in Wonderland trip through misleading characteristics of interobserver agreement scores in interval recording. In E. Ramp & G. Semb (Eds.), *Behavior analysis: Areas of research and application* (pp. 359–376). Englewood Cliffs, NJ: Prentice Hall.

Hayes, S. C., Rincover, A., & Solnick, J. V. (1980). The technical drift of applied behavior analysis. *Journal of Applied Behavior Analysis, 13,* 275–285.

Hayes, S. C., Rosenfarb, I., Wulfert, E., Munt, E. D., Korn, Z., & Zettle, R. D. (1985). Self-reinforcement effects: An artifact of social standard setting? *Journal of Applied Behavior Analysis, 18,* 201–214.

Healy, A. F., Kosslyn, S. M., & Shiffrin, R. M. (1992). *Essays in honor of William K. Estes,* Vol. 1: *From learning theory to connectionist theory;* Vol. 2: *From learning processes to cognitive processes.* Hillsdale, NJ: Erlbaum.

Heckaman, K. A., Alber, S., Hooper, S., & Heward, W. L. (1998). A comparison of least-to-most prompts and progressive time delay on the disruptive behavior of students with autism. *Journal of Behavioral Education, 8,* 171–201.

Herrnstein, R. J. (1970). On the law of effect. *Journal of the Experimental Analysis of Behavior, 13,* 243–266.

Herrnstein, R. J. (1990). Rational choice theory: Necessary but not sufficient. *American Psychologist, 45,* 356–367.

Hersen, M., & Barlow, D. H. (1976). *Single-case experimental designs: Strategies for studying behavior change.* New York: Pergamon Press.

Higgins, S. T., Woodward, B. M., & Henningfield, J. E. (1989). Effects of atropine on the repeated acquisition and performance of response sequences in humans. *Journal of the Experimental Analysis of Behavior, 51,* 5–15.

Hineline, P. N. (1990). The origins of environment-based psychological theory. *Journal of the Experimental Analysis of Behavior, 53,* 305–320.

Hineline, P. N. (1991). Modesty, yes; humility, no. *The Behavior Analyst, 14,* 25–28.

Hodos, W., & Ator, N. A. (1994). A festschrift in honor of Joseph V. Brady in his 70th year. *Journal of the Experimental Analysis of Behavior, 61,* 131–134.

Holz, W. C., Azrin, N. H., & Ayllon, T. (1963). Elimination of behavior of mental patients by response-produced extinction. *Journal of the Experimental Analysis of Behavior, 6,* 407–412.

Horner, R. D., & Baer, D. M. (1978). Multiple-probe technique: A variation of the multiple baseline. *Journal of Applied Behavior Analysis, 11,* 189–196.

Horner, R. H., Day, H. M., & Day, J. R. (1997). Using neutralizing routines to reduce problem behaviors. *Journal of Applied Behavior Analysis, 30,* 601–614.

Horner, R. H., Dunlap, G., & Koegel, R. L. (1988). *Generalization and maintenance: Life-style changes in applied settings.* Baltimore: Brookes.

Individuals with Disabilities Education Act Amendments of 1997, *P. L. 105-17, 1400, 37 stat. 111.*

Iversen, I. H. (1988). Tactics of graphic design: A review of Tufte's *The Visual Display of Quantitative Information. Journal of the Experimental Analysis of Behavior, 49,* 171–189.

Iwata, B. A., Dorsey, M. F., Slifer, K. J., Bauman, K. E., & Richman, G. S. (1994). Toward a functional analysis of self-injury. *Journal of Applied Behavior Analysis, 27,* 197–209. Reprinted from *Analysis and Intervention in Developmental Disabilities,* 1982, vol. 2, pp. 3–20.

Johnson, K. R., & Layng, T. V. J. (1996). On terms and procedures: Fluency. *The Behavior Analyst, 19,* 281–288.

Johnson, S. M., & Bolstad, O. D. (1973). Methodological issues in naturalistic observation: Some problems and solutions for field research. In L. A. Hamerlynck, L. C. Handy, & E. J. Mash (Eds.), *Behavior change: Methodology, concepts, and practice* (pp. 7–67). Champaign, IL: Research Press.

Johnston, J. M., & Hodge, C. (1989). Describing behavior with ratios of count and time. *The Behavior Analyst, 12,* 177–185.

Johnston, J. M., & Pennypacker, H. S. (1993). *Strategies and tactics of behavioral research* (2nd ed.). Hillsdale, NJ: Erlbaum.

Joncich, G. (1968). *The sane positivist: A biography of Edward L. Thorndike.* Middletown, CN: Wesleyan University Press.

Jones, R. R., Weinrott, M. R., & Vaught, R. S. (1978). Effects of serial dependency on the agreement between visual and statistical inference. *Journal of Applied Behavior Analysis, 11,* 277–283.

Journal of Applied Behavior Analysis (1968–present). Bloomington, IN: Society for the Experimental Analysis of Behavior. Online at http://www.envmed.rochester.edu/wwwrap/behavior/jaba/.

Journal of the Experimental Analysis of Behavior (1958–present). Bloomington, IN: Society for the Experimental Analysis of Behavior. Online at http://www.envmed.rochester.edu/wwwrap/behavior/jeab/jeabhome.htm.

Kahng, S., & Iwata, B. A. (1998). Computerized systems for collecting real-time observational data. *Journal of Applied Behavior Analysis, 31,* 253–261.

Kantor, J. R. (1963). *The scientific evolution of psychology* (vol. 1). Chicago: Principia Press.

Kazdin, A. E. (1977). Artifact, bias, and complexity of assessment: The ABCs of reliability. *Journal of Applied Behavior Analysis, 10,* 141–150.

Kazdin, A. E. (1977). Assessing the clinical or applied significance of behavior change through social validation. *Behavior Modification, 1,* 427–452.

Kazdin, A. E. (1978). *History of behavior modification.* Baltimore: University Park Press.

Kazdin, A. E. (1980). Acceptability of alternative treatments for deviant child behavior. *Journal of Applied Behavior Analysis, 13,* 259–273.

Kazdin, A. E. (1982). *Single-case research designs: Methods for clinical and applied settings.* New York: Oxford University Press.

Kazdin, A. E., & Geesey, S. (1977). Simultaneous-treatment design comparisons of the effects of earning reinforcers for one's peers versus oneself. *Behavior Therapy, 8,* 682–693.

Keller, E. F. (2002). *Making sense of life: Explaining biological development with models, metaphors, and machines.* Cambridge, MA: Harvard University Press.

Keller, F. S. (1968). Good-bye, teacher . . . *Journal of Applied Behavior Analysis, 1,* 79–89.

Keller, F. S., & Schoenfeld, W. N. (1950). *Principles of psychology: A systematic text in the science of behavior.* New York: Appleton-Century-Crofts.

Kelley, M. E., Lerman, D. C., & Van Camp, C. M. (2002). The effects of competing reinforcement schedules on the acquisition of functional communication. *Journal of Applied Behavior Analysis, 35,* 59–63.

Kelly, M. B. (1977). A review of the observational data-collection and reliability procedures reported in the *Journal of Applied Behavior Analysis. Journal of Applied Behavior Analysis, 10,* 97–101.

Kennedy, C. H. (1992). Trends in the measurement of social validity. *The Behavior Analyst, 15,* 147–156.

Kennedy, C. H. (1994). Manipulating antecedent conditions to alter the stimulus control of problem behavior. *Journal of Applied Behavior Analysis, 27,* 161–170.

Kennedy, C. H. (2002). The maintenance of behavior as an indicator of social validity. *Behavior Modification, 26,* 594–606.

Kennedy, C. H. (in press). Facts, interpretations, and explanations: A review of Evelyn Fox Keller's *Making Sense of Life. Journal of Applied Behavior Analysis.*

Kennedy, C. H., & Itkonen, T. (1993). Effects of setting events on the problem behavior of students with severe disabilities. *Journal of Applied Behavior Analysis, 26,* 321–328.

Kennedy, C. H., & Meyer, K. A. (1996). Sleep deprivation, allergy symptoms, and negatively reinforced problem behavior. *Journal of Applied Behavior Analysis, 29,* 133–135.

Kennedy, C. H., & Souza, G. (1995). Functional analysis and treatment of eye poking. *Journal of Applied Behavior Analysis, 28,* 27–37.

Kennedy, C. H., Caruso, M., & Thompson, T. (2001). Experimental analyses of gene-brain-behavior relations: Some notes on their application. *Journal of Applied Behavior Analysis, 34,* 539–549.

Kennedy, C. H., Cushing, L., & Itkonen, T. (1997). General education participation increases the social contacts and friendship networks of students with severe disabilities. *Journal of Behavioral Education, 7,* 167–189.

Kennedy, C. H., Meyer, K. A., Knowles, T., & Shukla, S. (2000). Analyzing the multiple functions of stereotypical behavior for students with autism: Implications for assessment and treatment. *Journal of Applied Behavior Analysis, 33,* 559–571.

Kennedy, C. H., Meyer, K. A., Werts, M. G., & Cushing, L. S. (2000). Effects of sleep deprivation on free-operant avoidance. *Journal of the Experimental Analysis of Behavior, 73,* 333–345.

Kern, L., Childs, K. E., Dunlap, G., Clarke, S., & Falk, G. D. (1994). Using assessment-based curricular intervention to improve the classroom behavior of a student with emotional and behavioral challenges. *Journal of Applied Behavior Analysis, 27,* 7–19.

Kipfer, B. A. (1998). *The order of things: How everything in the world is organized into hierarchies, structures, and pecking orders.* New York: Random House.

Kirby, M., & Kennedy, C. H. (in press). Effects of variable-interval length on behavioral tolerance to REM sleep deprivation. *Journal of the Experimental Analysis of Behavior.*

Kostewicz, D. E., Kubina, R. M., & Cooper, J. O. (2000). Managing aggressive thoughts and feelings with daily counts of non-aggressive thoughts and feelings: A self-experiment. *Journal of Behavior Therapy and Experimental Psychiatry, 31,* 177–187.

Kracotchwill, T. R. (1978). *Single subject research: Strategies for evaluating change.* New York: Academic Press.

Kuhn, T. S. (1957). *The Copernican revolution: Planetary astronomy in the development of western thought.* Cambridge, MA: Harvard University Press.

Lagemann, E. C. (2002). *An elusive science: The troubling history of education research.* Chicago: University of Chicago Press.

Lamarck, J-B. (1809/1984). *Philosophical zoology: An exposition with regard to the natural history of animals.* Chicago: University of Chicago Press.

Lancioni, G. E., Singh, N. N., O'Reilly, M. F., Oliva, D., Baccani, S., & Canevaro, A. (2002). Using simple hand-movement responses with optic microswitches with two persons with multiple disabilities. *Research and Practice for Persons with Severe Disabilities, 27,* 276–279.

Lane, H. (1963). The autophonic scale of voice level for congenitally deaf subjects. *Journal of Experimental Psychology, 66,* 328–331.

Laraway, S., Snycerski, S., Michael, J., & Poling, A. (2003). Motivating operations and terms to describe them: Some further refinements. *Journal of Applied Behavior Analysis, 36,* 407–414.

Latour, B. (1990). Drawing things together. In M. Lynch & S. Woolgar (Eds.), *Representation in scientific practice* (pp. 19–68). Cambridge, MA: MIT Press.

Latour, B., & Woolgar, S. (1986). *Laboratory life: The construction of scientific facts.* Princeton, NJ: Princeton University Press.

Lee, R., McComas, J. J., & Jawor, J. (2002). The effects of differential and lag reinforcement schedules on varied verbal responding by individuals with autism. *Journal of Applied Behavior Analysis, 35,* 391–402.

Leicester, J., Sidman, M., Stoddard, L. T., & Mohr, J. P. (1971). The nature of aphasic responses. *Neuropsychologia, 9,* 141–155.

Leitenberg, H. (1973). The use of single-case methodology in psychotherapy research. *Journal of Abnormal Psychology, 82,* 87–101.

Lerman, D. C. (2003). From the laboratory to community application: Translational research in behavior analysis. *Journal of Applied Behavior Analysis, 36,* 415–419.

Lindsley, O. R. (1956). Operant conditioning methods applied to research in chronic schizophrenia. *Psychiatric Research Reports, 5,* 118–139.

Lindsley, O. R. (1991). Precision teaching's unique legacy from B. F. Skinner. *Journal of Behavioral Education, 1,* 253–266.

Lippman, L. G., & Tragesser, S. L. (2003). Contingent magnitude of reward in modified human-operant DRL-LH and CRF schedules. *The Psychological Record, 53,* 429–442.

Logan, K. R., Jacobs, H. A., Gast, D. L., Murray, A. S., Daino, K., & Skala, C. (1998). The impact of typical peers on the perceived happiness of students with profound multiple disabilities. *Journal of the Association for Persons with Severe Handicaps, 23,* 309–318.

Lovaas, O. I., Freitag, G., Gold, V. J., & Kassorla, I. C. (1965). Experimental studies in childhood schizophrenia: Analysis of self-destructive behavior. *Journal of Experimental Child Psychology, 2,* 67–84.

Lovaas, O. I., Schreibman, L., Koegel, R. L., Rehm, R. (1971). Selective responding by autistic children to multiple sensory input. *Journal of Abnormal Psychology, 77,* 211–222.

Lovitt, T. C., & Curtiss, K. A. (1969). Academic response rate as a function of teacher- and self-imposed contingencies. *Journal of Applied Behavior Analysis, 2,* 49–53.

MacCorquodale, K., & Meehl, P. E. (1948). On a distinction between hypothetical constructs and intervening variables. *Psychological Review, 55,* 95–107.

Mace, F. C. (1994). Basic research needed for stimulating the development of behavioral technologies. *Journal of the Experimental Analysis of Behavior, 61,* 529–550.

Mager, R. F. (1962). *Preparing instructional objectives.* Palo Alto, CA: Fearon.

Makeover, H. B. (1950). The quality of medical care. *American Journal of Public Health, 41,* 824–832.

Malouf, D. B., & Schiller, E. P. (1995). Practice and research in special education. *Exceptional Children, 61,* 414–424.

March, R. E., & Horner, R. H. (2002). Feasibility and contributions of functional behavioral assessment in schools. *Journal of Emotional and Behavioral Disorders, 10,* 158–170.

Marr, M. J. (1986). Mathematics and verbal behavior. In T. Thompson & M. D. Zeiler (Eds.), *Analysis and integration of behavioral units* (pp. 161–183). Hillsdale, NJ: Erlbaum.

Martens, B. K., Ardoin, S. P., Hilt, A. M., Lannie, A. L., Panahon, C. J., & Wolfe, L. A. (2002). Sensitivity of children's behavior to probabilistic reward: Effects of a decreasing-ratio lottery system on math performance. *Journal of Applied Behavior Analysis, 35,* 403–406.

McDowell, E. (1817). Three cases of extirpation of diseased ovaria. *Eclectic Repertory, and Analytical Review, Medical and Philosophical, 7,* 242–244.

McGill, P. (1999). Establishing operations: Implications for the assessment, treatment, and prevention of problem behavior. *Journal of Applied Behavior Analysis, 32,* 393–418.

McGonigle, J. J., Rojahn, J., Dixon, J., & Strain, P. S. (1987). Multiple treatment interference in the alternating treatments design as a function of the intercomponent interval length. *Journal of Applied Behavior Analysis, 20,* 171–178.

McKenzie, T. L., & Rushall, B. S. (1974). Effects of self-recording on attendance and performance in a competitive swimming training environment. *Journal of Applied Behavior, 7,* 199–206.

Medland, M. B., & Stachnik, T. J. (1972). Good-behavior game: A replication and systematic analysis. *Journal of Applied Behavior Analysis, 5,* 45–51.

Michael, J. (1974). Statistical inference for individual organism research: Mixed blessing or curse? *Journal of Applied Behavior Analysis, 7,* 647–653.

Miles, M. B., & Huberman, A. M. (1984). *Qualitative data analysis: A sourcebook of new methods.* Beverly Hills, CA: Sage.

Miltenberger, R. G., Rapp, J. T. & Long, E. S. (1999). A low-tech method for conducting real-time recording. *Journal of Applied Behavior Analysis, 32,* 119–120.

Moore, J. (1984). On privacy, causes, and contingencies. *The Behavior Analyst, 7,* 3–16.

Murray, L. K., & Kollins, S. H. (2000). Effects of methylphenidate on sensitivity to reinforcement in children diagnosed with attention deficit hyperactivity disorder: An application of the matching law. *Journal of Applied Behavior Analysis, 33,* 573–592.

Neuringer, A. (1991). Humble behaviorism. *The Behavior Analyst, 14,* 1–14.

Neuringer, A. (2002). Operant variability: Evidence, functions, and theory. *Psychonomic Bulletin and Review 9,* 672–705.

Nevin, J. A. (1991). Beyond pride and humility. *The Behavior Analyst, 14,* 35–36.

Nevin, J. A. (1996). The momentum of compliance. *Journal of Applied Behavior Analysis, 29,* 535–547.

Nevin, J. A., Milo, J., Odum, A. L., & Shahan, T. A. (2003). Accuracy of discrimination, rate of responding, and resistance to change. *Journal of the Experimental Analysis of Behavior, 79,* 307–321.

Newman, D. L., & Brown, R. D. (1993). School board member role expectations in making decisions about educational programs. *Urban Education, 28,* 267–280.

Nunes, E. V., Carroll, K. M., & Bickel, W. K. (2002). Clinical and translational research: Introduction to the special issue. *Experimental and Clinical Psychopharmacology, 10,* 155–158.

O'Reilly, M. F. (1995). Functional analysis and treatment of escape-maintained aggression correlated with sleep deprivation. *Journal of Applied Behavior Analysis, 28,* 225–226.

Pace, G. M., & Toyer, E. A. (2000). The effects of a vitamin supplement on the pica of a child with severe mental retardation. *Journal of Applied Behavior Analysis, 33,* 619–622.

Page, T. J., & Iwata, B. A. (1986). Interobserver agreement: History, theory, and current methods. In A. Poling, R. W. Fuqua, & R. Ulrich (Eds.), *Research methods in applied behavior analysis: Issues and advances* (pp. 99–126). New York: Plenum.

Parsons, M. B., Reid, D. H., Green, C. W., & Browning, L. B. (1999). Reducing individualized job coach assistance provided to persons with multiple severe disabilities in work settings. *Journal of the Association for Persons with Severe Handicaps, 24,* 292–297.

Parsonson, B. S., & Baer, D. M. (1978). The analysis and presentation of graphic data. In T. R. Kratochwill

(Ed.), *Single subject research: Strategies for evaluating change* (pp. 101–166). New York: Academic Press.

Parsonson, B. S., & Baer, D. M. (1992). The visual analysis of data, and current research into the stimuli controlling it. In T. R. Kratochwill & J. R. Levin (Eds.), *Single-case research design and analysis: New directions for psychology and education* (pp. 15–40). Hillsdale, NJ: Erlbaum.

Pavlov, I. P. (1960). *Conditioned reflexes: An investigation of the physiological activity of the cerebral cortex* (G. V. Anrep, trans.). New York: Dover.

Peterson, L., Homer, A. L., & Wonderlich, S. A. (1982). The integrity of independent variables in behavior analysis. *Journal of Applied Behavior Analysis, 15,* 477–492.

Piazza, C. C., Fisher, W. W., Hanley, G. P., LeBlanc, L. A., Worsdell, A. S., Lindauer, S. E., & Keeney, K. M. (1998). Treatment of pica through multiple analyses of its reinforcing functions. *Journal of Applied Behavior Analysis, 313,* 165–190.

Powell, J., Martindale, A., & Kulp, S. (1975). An evaluation of time-sample measures of behavior. *Journal of Applied Behavior Analysis, 8,* 463–469.

Reese, H. W. (1997). Counterbalancing and other uses of repeated-measures Latin-square designs: Analyses and interpretations. *Journal of Experimental Child Psychology, 64,* 137–158.

Repp, A. C., Deitz, D. E. D., Boles, S. M., Deitz, S. M., & Repp, C. F. (1976). Differences among common methods for calculating interobserver agreement. *Journal of Applied Behavior Analysis, 9,* 109–113.

Repp, A. C., Roberts, D. M., Slack, D. J., Repp, C. F., & Berkler, M. S. (1976). A comparison of frequency, interval, and time-sampling methods of data collection. *Journal of Applied Behavior Analysis, 9,* 501–508.

Richman, D. M., Wacker, D. P., & Winborn, L. (2001). Response efficiency during functional communication training: Effects of effort on response allocation. *Journal of Applied Behavior Analysis, 34,* 73–76.

Richman, D. M., Wacker, D. P., Brown, L. J. C., Kayser, K., Crosland, K., Stephens, T. J., & Asmus, J. (2001). Stimulus characteristics within directives: Effects on accuracy of task completion. *Journal of Applied Behavior Analysis, 34,* 289–312.

Ringdahl, J. E., Winborn, L. C., Andelman, M. S., & Kitsukawa, K. (2002). The effects of noncontingently available alternative stimuli on functional analysis outcomes. *Journal of Applied Behavior Analysis, 35,* 407–410.

Robinson, P. W., Newby, T. J., & Ganzell, S. L. (1981). A token system for a class of underachieving hyperactive children. *Journal of Applied Behavior Analysis, 14,* 307–315.

Roethlisberger, F. J., & Dickson, W. J. (1939). *Management and the worker.* Cambridge, MA: Harvard University Press.

Rogers, C. R. (1942). *Counseling and psychotherapy: New concepts in practice.* New York: Houghton Mifflin.

Ross, D. F., Read, J. D., & Toglia, M. P. (2003). *Adult eyewitness testimony: Current trends and developments.* Cambridge, UK: Cambridge University Press.

Rusch, F. R., & Kazdin, A. E. (1981). Toward a methodology of withdrawal designs for the assessment of response maintenance. *Journal of Applied Behavior Analysis, 14,* 131–140.

Sagan, C. (1995). *The demon-haunted world: Science as a candle in the dark.* New York: Random House.

Sax, G. (1996). *Principles of educational and psychological measurement and evaluation.* New York: Wadsworth.

Schepis, M. M., Reid, D. H., Behrmann, M. M., & Sutton, K. A. (1998). Increasing communicative interactions of young children with autism using a voice output communication aid and naturalistic teaching. *Journal of Applied Behavior Analysis, 31,* 561–578.

Schoenfeld, W. N. (1995). "Reinforcement" in behavior theory. *The Behavior Analyst, 18,* 173–185.

Schwartz, I. S., & Baer, D. M. (1991). Social validity assessments: Is current practice state of the art? *Journal of Applied Behavior Analysis, 24,* 189–204.

Sechenov, I. M. (1965). *Reflexes of the brain: An attempt to establish the physiological basis of psychological processes* (S. Belsky, trans.). Cambridge, MA: MIT Press.

Shapiro, E. S., Kazdin, A. E., & McGonigle, J. J. (1982). Multiple-treatment interference in the simultaneous- or alternating-treatments design. *Behavioral Assessment, 4,* 105–115.

Shavelson, R. J., & Towne, L. (2002). *Scientific research in education.* Washington, DC: National Academy Press.

Sherman, J. A. (1965). Use of reinforcement and imitation to reinstate verbal behavior in mute psychotics. *Journal of Abnormal Psychology, 70,* 155–164.

Sherrington, C. E. (1975). Charles Scott Sherrington (1857–1952). *Notes and Records of the Royal Society of London, 30,* 45–63.

Sherrington, C. S. (1906/1989). *The integrative action of the nervous system.* Birmingham, AL: Classics of Medicine.

Shinn, M. R., Ramsey, E., Walker, H. M., Stieber, S., et al. (1987). Antisocial behavior in school settings: Initial differences in an at risk and normal population. *Journal of Special Education, 21,* 69–84.

Sidman, M. (1952). A note on functional relations obtained from group data. *Psychological Bulletin, 49,* 263–269.

Sidman, M. (1960a). Normal sources of pathological behavior. *Science, 132,* 61–68.

Sidman, M. (1960b). *Tactics of scientific research: Evaluating experimental data in psychology.* New York: Basic Books.

Sidman, M. (1989). *Coercion and its fallout.* Boston: Authors Cooperative.

Sidman, M. (1994). *Equivalence relations and behavior: A research story.* Boston: Authors Cooperative.

Skinner, B. F. (1938). *The behavior of organisms: An experimental analysis.* New York: Appleton-Century-Crofts.

Skinner, B. F. (1945). The operational analysis of psychological terms. *Psychological Review, 52,* 270–277.

Skinner, B. F. (1950). Are theories of learning necessary? *Psychological Review, 57,* 193–216.

Skinner, B. F. (1953). *Science and human behavior.* New York: Free Press.

Skinner, B. F. (1954). The science of learning and the art of teaching. *Harvard Educational Review, 24,* 86–97.

Skinner, B. F. (1961). Why we need teaching machines. *Harvard Educational Review, 31,* 377–398.

Skinner, B. F. (1981). Charles B. Ferster—a personal memoir. *Journal of the Experimental Analysis of Behavior, 35,* 259–261.

Skinner, B. F. (1983). *A matter of consequences: Part three of an autobiography.* New York: Knopf.

Skinner, B. F. (1985). Cognitive science and behaviorism. *British Journal of Psychology, 76,* 291–301.

Smith, L. D., Best, L. A., Stubbs, D. A., Archibald, A. B., & Roberson-Nay, R. (2002). Constructing knowledge: The role of graphs and tables in hard and soft psychology. *American Psychologist, 57,* 749–761.

Smith, R. G., & Churchill, R. M. (2002). Identification of environmental determinants of behavior disorders through functional analysis of precursor behaviors. *Journal of Applied Behavior Analysis, 35,* 125–136.

Smith, R. G., Iwata, B. A., Goh, H., & Shore, B. A. (1995). Analysis of establishing operations for self-injury maintained by escape. *Journal of Applied Behavior Analysis, 28,* 515–535.

Spradlin, J. E., Cotter, V. W., & Baxley, N. (1973). Establishing a conditional discrimination without direct training: A study of transfer with retarded adolescents. *American Journal of Mental Deficiency, 77,* 556–566.

Springer, B., Brown, T., & Duncan, P. K. (1981). Current measurement in applied behavior analysis. *The Behavior Analyst, 4,* 19–32.

Staats, C. K., Staats, A. W., & Schutz, R. E. (1962). The effects of discrimination pretraining on textual behavior. *Journal of Educational Psychology, 53,* 32–37.

Stokes, T. F., & Baer, D. M. (1977). An implicit technology of generalization. *Journal of Applied Behavior Analysis, 10,* 349–367.

Strain, P. S., & Timm, M. A. (1974). An experimental analysis of social interaction between a behaviorally disordered preschool child and her classroom peers. *Journal of Applied Behavior Analysis, 7,* 583–590.

Strain, P. S., Shores, R. E., & Kerr, M. M. (1976). An experimental analysis of spillover effects on the social interaction of behaviorally handicapped preschool children. *Journal of Applied Behavior Analysis, 9,* 31–40.

Sulzer, B., & Mayer, G. R. (1972). *Behavior modification procedures for school personnel.* Oxford, England: Dryden.

Sulzer-Azaroff, B., & Mayer, G. R. (1991). *Behavior analysis for lasting change.* New York: Harcourt Brace Jovanovich.

Symons, F. J., Davis, M. L., & Thompson, T. (2000). Self-injurious behavior and sleep disturbance in adults with developmental disabilities. *Research in Developmental Disabilities, 21,* 115–123.

Tang, J.-C., Patterson, T. G., & Kennedy, C. H. (2003). Identifying specific sensory modalities maintaining the stereotypy of students with multiple profound disabilities. *Research in Developmental Disabilities, 24,* 433–451.

Taubes, G. (1993). *Bad science: The short life and weird times of cold fusion.* New York: Random House.

Tawney, J. W., & Gast, D. L. (1984). *Single subject research in special education.* New York: Merrill.

Taylor, L. K., Alber, S. R., & Walker, D. W. (2002). The comparative effects of a modified self-questioning strategy and story mapping on the reading comprehension of elementary students with learning disabilities. *Journal of Behavioral Education, 11,* 69–87.

Thiemann, K. S., & Goldstein, H. (2001). Social stories, written text cues, and video feedback: Effects on social communication of children with autism. *Journal of Applied Behavior Analysis, 34,* 425–446.

Thompson, T. (1984). The examining magistrate for nature: A retrospective review of Claude Bernard's *An Introduction to the Study of Experimental Medicine. Journal of the Experimental Analysis of Behavior, 41,* 211–216.

Thompson, T., Felce, D., & Symons, F. (1999). *Behavioral observation: Technology and applications in developmental disabilities.* Baltimore: Brookes.

Thorndike, E. L. (1898). Animal intelligence: An experimental study of the associative processes in animals. *Psychological Review Monograph Supplement, 73,* 16–43.

Todd, J. T., & Morris, E. K. (1994). *Modern perspectives on John B. Watson and classical behaviorism.* Westport, CT: Greenwood.

Todd, J. T., & Morris, E. K. (1995). *Modern perspectives on B. F. Skinner and contemporary behaviorism.* Westport, CT: Greenwood.

Touchette, P. E. (1971). Transfer of stimulus control: Measuring the moment of transfer. *Journal of the Experimental Analysis of Behavior, 15,* 347–354.

Trent, J. W. (1994). *Inventing the feeble mind: A history of mental retardation in the United States.* Berkeley: University of California Press.

Trout, J. D. (1998). *Measuring the intentional world: Realism, naturalism, and quantitative methods in the behavioral sciences.* New York: Oxford University Press.

Tufte, E. R. (1983). *The visual display of quantitative information.* Cheshire, CT: Graphics Press.

Tufte, E. R. (1997). *Visual explanations: Images and quantities, evidence and narrative.* Cheshire, CT: Graphics Press.

Ulman, J. D., & Sulzer-Azaroff, B. (1975). Multielement baseline design in educational research. In E. Ramp & G. Semb (Eds.), *Behavior analysis: Areas of research and application* (pp. 377–391). Englewood Cliffs, NJ: Prentice Hall.

Underwood, B. J. (1957). *Psychological research.* Englewood Cliffs, NJ: Prentice Hall.

Van Houten, R. (1979). Social validation: The evolution of standards of competency for target behaviors. *Journal of Applied Behavior Analysis, 12,* 581–591.

Vargas, A. U., Grskovic, J. A., Belfiore, P. J., & Halbert-Ayala, J. (1997). Improving migrant students' spelling of English and Spanish words with error correction. *Journal of Behavioral Education, 7,* 13–24.

Vollmer, T. R., Ringdahl, J. E., Roane, H. S., & Marcus, B. A. (1997). Negative side effects of noncontingent reinforcement. *Journal of Applied Behavior Analysis, 30,* 161–164.

Von Neumann, J., & Morgenstern, O. (1947). *Theory of games and economic behavior* (2nd ed.). Princeton: Princeton University Press.

Wacker, D., Berg, W., Harding, J., & Cooper-Brown, L. (in press). Use of brief experimental analyses in outpatient clinic and home settings. *Journal of Behavioral Education.*

Wacker, D. P. (2000). Building a bridge between research in experimental and applied behavior analysis. In J. C. Leslie & D. Blackman (Eds.), *Experimental and applied analysis of human behavior* (pp. 205–234). Reno, NV: Context Press.

Wacker, D. P., Steege, M. W., Northup, J., Sasso, G., Berg, W., Reimers, T., et al. (1990). A component analysis of functional communication training across three topographies of severe behavior problems. *Journal of Applied Behavior Analysis, 23,* 417–430.

Walker, H. M., & Buckley, N. K. (1968). The use of positive reinforcement in conditioning attending behavior. *Journal of Applied Behavior Analysis, 1,* 245–250.

Walker, H. M., & Hops, H. (1976). Use of normative peer data as a standard for evaluating classroom treatment effects. *Journal of Applied Behavior Analysis, 9,* 159–168.

Wallace, A. R. (1875). *Contributions to the theory of natural selection.* London: Macmillan.

Wallace, M. D., & Iwata, B. A. (1999). Effects of session duration on functional analysis outcomes. *Journal of Applied Behavior Analysis, 32,* 175–183.

Ward, P., & Carnes, M. (2002). Effects of posting self-set goals on collegiate football players' skill execution during practice and games. *Journal of Applied Behavior Analysis, 35,* 1–12.

Ware, C. (2000). *Information visualization: Perception for design.* New York: Morgan Kaufmann.

Watson, J. B. (1924). *Behaviorism.* New York: Norton.

Watson, P. J., & Workman, E. A. (1981). The nonconcurrent multiple baseline across-individuals design: An extension of the traditional multiple baseline design. *Journal of Behavior Therapy and Experimental Psychiatry, 12,* 257–259.

Wehby, J. H., & Hollahan, M. S. (2000). Effects of high-probability requests on the latency to initiate academic tasks. *Journal of Applied Behavior Analysis, 33,* 259–262.

Werle, M. A., Murphy, T. B., & Budd, K. S. (1993). Treating chronic food refusal in young children: Home-based parent training. *Journal of Applied Behavior Analysis, 26,* 421–433.

Werts, M. G., Caldwell, N. K., & Wolery, M. (2003). Instructive feedback: Effects of a presentation variable. *Journal of Special Education, 37,* 124–133.

Whaley, D. L. (1973). *Psychological testing and the philosophy of measurement.* Kalamazoo, MI: Behaviordelia.

White, O. R. (1971). *A pragmatic approach to the description of progress in the single case.* Unpublished doctoral dissertation, University of Oregon, Eugene.

Whitehead, A. N., & Russell, B. (1925). *Principia mathematica* (2nd ed.). Cambridge, England: Cambridge University Press.

Wolery, M. (in press). Norris G. Haring: Biographical sketch. In G. M. Sugai & R. H. Horner (Eds.), *Encyclopedia of behavior modification and cognitive be-*

havior therapy (Vol. 3: *Educational applications*). Menlo Park, CA: Sage.

Wolery, M., Ault, M. J., & Doyle, P. M. (1992). *Teaching students with moderate to severe disabilities.* New York: Longman.

Wolf, M. M. (1978). Social validity: The case for subjective measurement, or how applied behavior analysis is finding its heart. *Journal of Applied Behavior Analysis, 11,* 203–214.

Wolf, M. M., Risley, T. R., & Mees, H. (1964). Application of operant conditioning procedures to the behavior problems of an autistic child. *Behaviour Research and Therapy, 1,* 305–312.

Index